NORTH OF MAIN

NORTH OF MAIN

Spartanburg's Historic Black Neighborhoods of North Dean Street, Gas Bottom, and Back of the College

BRENDA LEE PRYCE

JIM NEIGHBORS

BETSY WAKEFIELD TETER

HUB CITY PRESS | 2024

Cover design: Meg Reid
Interior design: Bonnie Campbell
Copy editor: Laura Corbin

The authors will donate 100 percent of their royalties annually to projects that preserve Black history or serve Black children.

FRONTIS:
Top photo: courtesy of Jeffrey Jackson.
Bottom photo: courtesy of the Willis Collection of the Spartanburg County Public Libraries.

Manufactured in the United States of America by Versa Press
Second Edition

HUB CITY PRESS
200 Ezell Street
Spartanburg, SC 29306
864.577.9349 | www.hubcity.org

DONORS

Hub City Press and the authors gratefully acknowledge our friends who made contributions in support of this book.

City of Spartanburg
John and Lisa Featherston
Spartanburg County Public Libraries
Horace & Ruth Littlejohn
Mount Moriah Baptist Church of Spartanburg
Lindsay Webster
Wofford College

C. Mack & Patty Amick
Marjorie Boafo & Kofi Appiah
Greg & Lisa Atkins
Andrew & Kitsy Babb
Balmer Foundation
Valerie & Bill Barnet
Susan Bridges
Bea Bruce
Lacy Chapman
Dave Clifton
Linda & Bill Cobb
Victoria T. Colebank
Stephen Colyer
Michele & Halsey Cook
Haidee B. & Gardner Courson
John & Kirsten Cribb
Magruder H. Dent
Jessica & Butler Derrick
ExxonMobil Foundation
Manning & John Fairey
Spartanburg County Foundation
Katherine & Charles Frazier
Marguerite McGee, Kathleen M. Cates & Elisabeth E. Hayes
Laura Beeson Henthorn
Jimmy & Ann Hunt
George Dean & Susu Johnson
Stewart & Ann Johnson
Frannie Jordan
Betsy Teter & John Lane
Sara & Paul H. Lehner
Rhett & Anne McCraw
Nancy Milliken
Weston Milliken
Carlin & Sander Morrison
Dwight Patterson
Rotary Club of Spartanburg
Alane & Rex Russell
Mary Ann Claud & Olin Sansbury
Betty Snow
Michel & Eliot Stone

Heather & Winthrop Allen
Paula & Stan Baker
John & Laura Bauknight
Charles & Christi Bebko
Sally & Jerry Cogan Jr.
Mary Crowley
Coleman Edmunds
Edwin Epps
Megan DeMoss
Barney & Elaine Gosnell
Lennetta Gray-Brewton
Susan Hamilton
Nancy Hearon
Nick & Silke Jager
Cynthia & Keith Kelly
Nancy Kenney
Kirkus Media LLC
Tom & Nan McDaniel
Boyce & Carole Miller
Laura & Scott Montgomery
Kam & Emily Neely
Cecile & Chris Nowatka
Erin Ouzts
Ron & Ann Rash
Ricky & Betsy Richardson
Pamela Smith
Mark & Meredith Van Geison
Susan Webb
William & Teresa Webster
Alanna & Don Wildman
Dennis & Ana Maria Wiseman
Diane Smock & Brad Wyche

Mo Abusaft
Heather Bell Adams
Mitch & Sarah Allen
Vic & Lynn Bailey
Susan Baker
Harold L. & Georgianna Ballenger
Tom & Joan Barnet
Glory Boozer
Jetta & Pascal Boyd
Lori Boyd
Erica Brown
Sheri Reynolds & Barbara Brown
William W. & Katherine K. Burns
Randall & Sally Chambers
Robert & Janeen Cochran
Rick & Sue Conner
Chris & Garrow Crowley
Mary Washington Deku
Jean Dunbar
Susan Duncan
Alice Eberhardt
Wendy King & Dan Ebin
Eugene Elrod
Lynn Ezell
Beth Cecil & Isabel Forbes
Delie Fort
Andrew Green
Susan C. Griswold
Jo Hackl
Kimberly & Chris Hall
Mary Halphen
Al & Anita Hammerbeck
Thomas & Tracy Hannah
Carolyn C. Harbison
Frances Hardy
Kathryn Harvey
Darryl Harmon
Hastie Psychiatry LLC
Attorney & Mrs. Calvin K. Hastie
Mark Hayes
James Hendrick
Stacey Hettes
Erin & Yogi Hiremath
Marilyn Hubbell
Jeffrey Jackson
Anne Chapman & Al Jeter
Geordy & Carter Johnson
Steve & Melissa Johnson
Wallace Eppes Johnson
Francie Little
George & Frances Loudon
Elizabeth Lowndes
Mary Speed Lynch
Julia Lyons
Joe & Keysie Maddox
Nancy Mandlove
Bill Cooper & Martin Meek
Stephen Michelman & Karen Goodchild
Larry E. Milan
Don & Mary Miles
Cabell Mitchell
Karen & Bob Mitchell
Tom & Marsha Moore
Susan Myers
Margaret Neighbors
Liz Newall
Aimee Nezhukumatathil
Pamela Nienhuis
Walter & Susan Novak
W. Keith & Louise Parris
Janice Piazza
Jan & Sara Postma
L. Perrin & Kay A. Powell

Mary Price
Terry Pruitt
Norman & Jo Pulliam Sr.
Philip N. & Frances M. Racine
Betsy & Charlie Jones
Cathryn Judice
Daniel & Vivian Kahrs
Lynn & James Karegeannes
Beverly Knight
Mark & Sharon Koenig
Lilly Kohler
Anne Lander
Barbara Latham
Jack & Kay Lawrence
Meg Reid & Matthew Lewis
Rose Mary Ritchie
Rev. Eugene Rivers III
Elisabeth & Regis Robe
Elena Pribyl Rush
Janie & Roland Salley
Kaye Savage
Susan Schneider
Garrett & Cathy Scott
Joy Shackelford
George Singleton
Danny & Becky Smith
Eugene & Rita Spiess
Brad Steinecke
Tammy & David Stokes
Phillip Stone
Chris & Jessalyn Story
Kay Stricklin
Merike Tamm
Nancy Taylor
Cathy Terrell
Reginald Thomas II
Landon Thorne
Nick Trainor
Malinda & Charles Tulloh
Thomas Vinh
Holly & Adair Watters
Cathy & Andy Westbrook
Richard Wheeler
Karen & John B. White Jr.
William & Floride Willard
Elizabeth "Libbo" Wise
Susan Wolfe
Bob & Carolyn Wynn
Steve & Charlotte Zides
Susan & Wayne Zurenda

Hub City Writers Project is a literary nonprofit organization located in Spartanburg, South Carolina. Comprised of an acclaimed book publisher, an independent bookshop, and a literary programmer focused on education and outreach, our mission is cultivating readers and nurturing writers in both the Spartanburg community and throughout the South to foster an inclusive literary arts culture.

Tax-deductible donations support: The publication of extraordinary new and unsung writers from the American South; book prizes that support early career writers; workshops, scholarships and conferences aimed at fostering literary community in Upstate South Carolina and beyond; residencies and internships that support creative writers from across the nation, as well as local students, enabling them to learn about the business of publishing without requiring the traditional outlay of their own resources; access initiatives such as Growing Great Readers, Books at the Bus Stop and Books as Mirrors.

CONTENTS

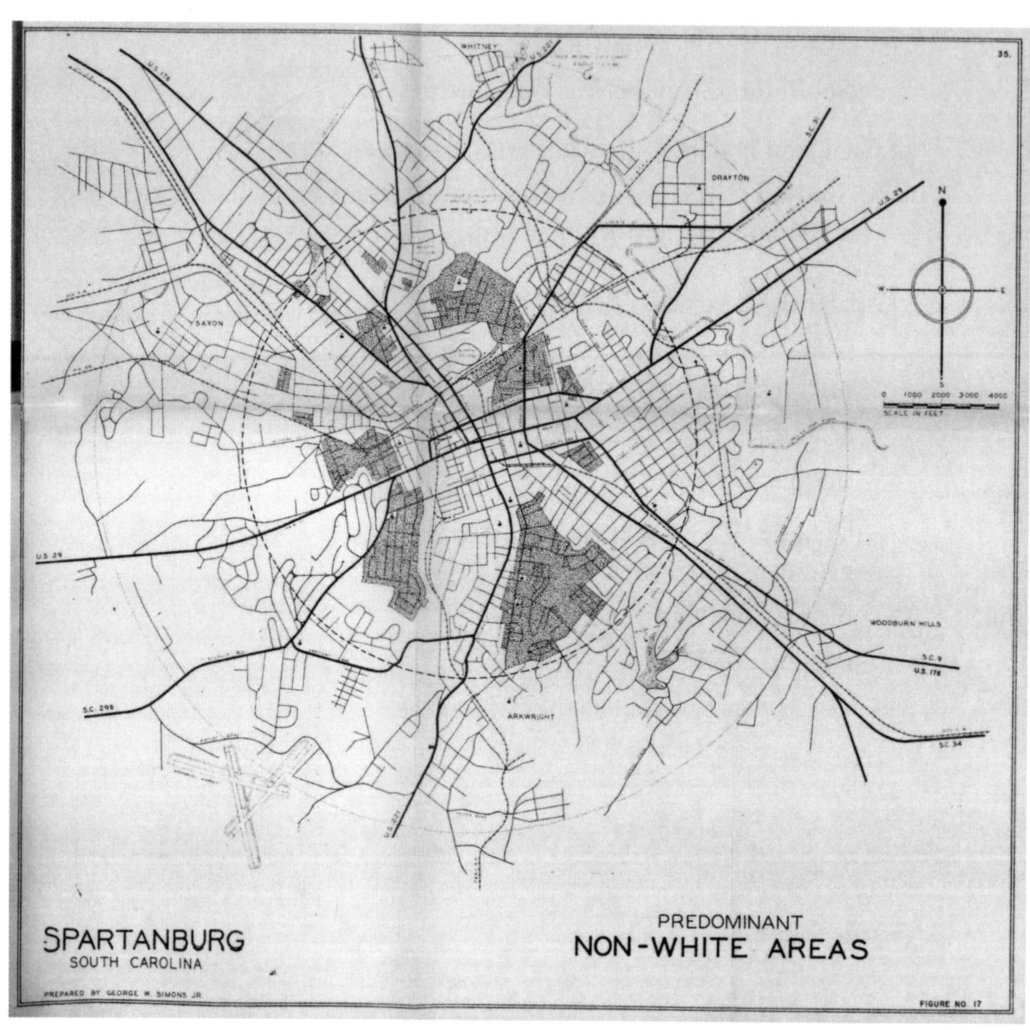

The large shaded area in the top right quadrant is the subject of this book. In 1954 this area was almost the same size as the Southside, which is located in the bottom right quadrant. The map was made after the Brown v. Board of Education *ruling.*

INTRODUCTION

NEW NEIGHBORHOODS BEGAN EMERGING north of Main Street in Spartanburg, South Carolina, in the 1870s as emancipated Black men and women spent their hard-won post-slavery wages to purchase lots and build homes. As the decades rolled by, they and their descendants established a string of neighborhoods stretching from modern-day Barnet Park and Converse University into a valley now occupied with car dealerships, through an area behind Wofford College, to the edge of what is now Spartanburg Medical Center. The settlement resembled a bowtie, with the center knot being an underpass at the Southern Railway and houses fanning out in both directions onto higher ground. Residents there raised children, often sent them to college, and served the needs of their neighbors. By the 1950s there were more than 600 dwellings in those 300 acres that housed at least 2,000 Black residents.

Today, about 25 of those homes remain. The hallways of two schoolhouses, including the first public elementary and high schools to serve Black children, are long empty of students. The church bells that rang on Sundays are gone or silent. The street corners where the Spartanburg soul-gospel sound emerged are no more. The neighborhood sports fields, playgrounds and recreation centers in the area have vanished.

The 2005 book *South of Main* described a similar Black district in Spartanburg dismantled in quick order by city-sponsored urban renewal in the early 1970s. The neighborhoods north of Main Street disappeared over a longer, 40-year period—through a combination of road building, urban renewal, redevelopment, and the expansion of Wofford College. The decisions to replace these neighborhoods usually took place, by design, in rooms without the input or the presence of Black homeowners. What was lost among these neighbors is their deep sense of place, the community they built together, the tangible history of their shared lives.

This was not an unusual story in 20th-century America. More than 1,500 Black neighborhoods rich in culture were bulldozed by governments, developers and institutions in the name of "progress." *North of Main* is another piece of the Spartanburg story. The history of this place is extraordinary in its demonstration of the heroism, courage, determination and pride of Black people in Spartanburg who built dynamic, thriving, historically significant neighborhoods in a society that frequently worked to undermine or limit their efforts. This book is an acknowledgement of the value of what they created. It is a story of both triumph and pain.

In their day these neighborhoods were known as "the northside" and, sometimes, as "Methodist-side," recognizing the importance of Silver Hill United Methodist Church and other churches of that denomination. The scope of this narrative generally does not include the area that today is known as Spartanburg's Northside—a rapidly redeveloping former cotton mill village west of Church Street. (That area, plus Highland and Hamburg, deserve their own in-depth study.) We also have used the term "Back of the College" to describe one side of this area, despite the fact that this moniker did not come into regular use until the 1960s. In places where the words "colored" or "negro" were used in primary source documents, we have left those to be true to their original use.

Research for this book began as a collaborative project that involved community members, organizations, students and faculty at Wofford College and is ongoing. Project members have collected oral histories from more than two dozen former residents and have created a database of Black residents who once lived behind the college. Wofford chemistry students have tested the soil behind their dorms to explore the long-term consequences of environmental hazards once imposed upon this community. They all may play a part in determining the future of the Cumming Street School building, one of the first historical centers of the neighborhood, now owned by Wofford College.

North of Main is dedicated to the people who once called these neighborhoods home. May their stories resound in future decisions about working-class neighborhoods in this city and others. May the memory of their lives, and the respect for their achievements, endure.

Brenda Lee Pryce
Jim Neighbors
Betsy Wakefield Teter
Spartanburg, South Carolina

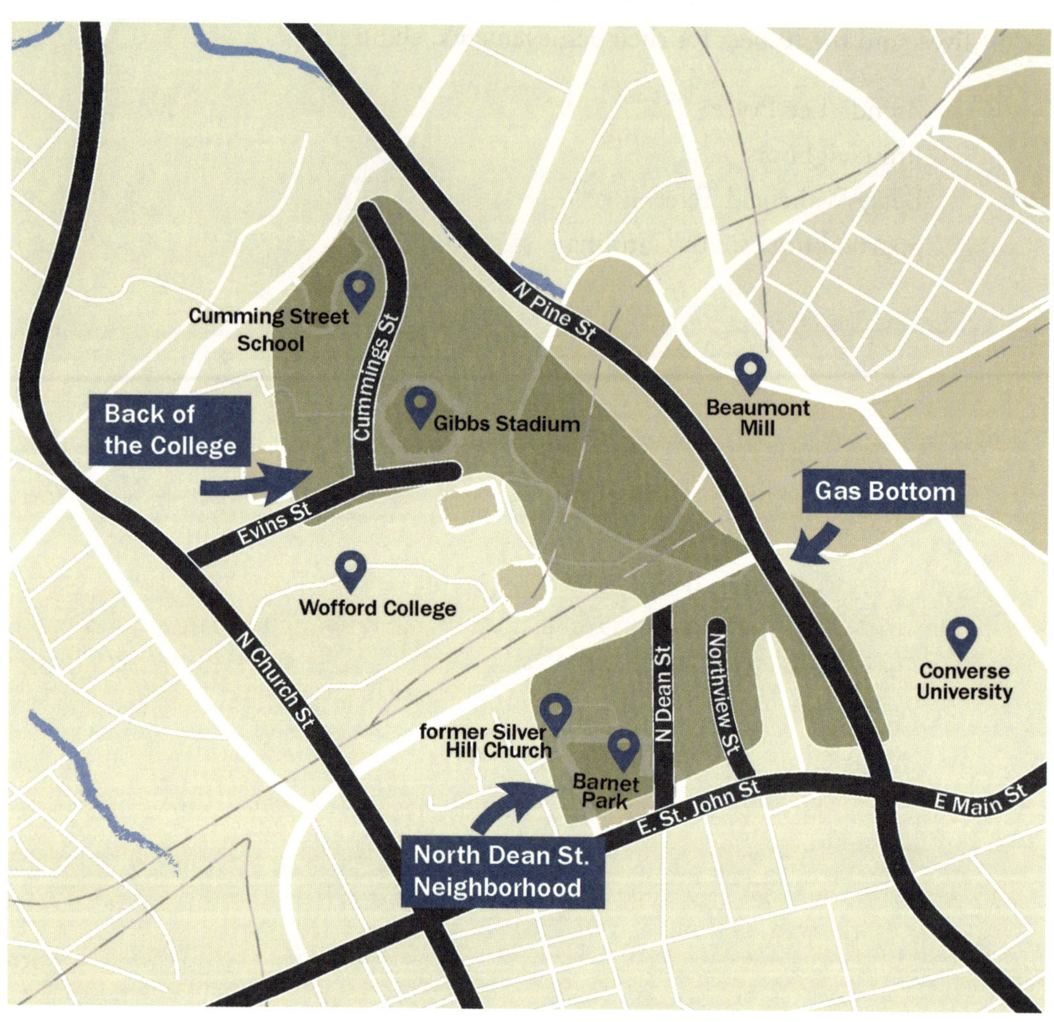

This shaded area shows the boundaries of the North of Main *area at its peak in the 1950s.*

ONE

FREEDOM

IN 1865 FREEDOM FINALLY ARRIVED for hundreds of enslaved people in the vicinity of Spartanburg's public square. Freedom came for Nelly Kirby and Ned Kirby, living on the grounds of a large, white-columned house on South Church Street, near the present-day site of Spartanburg's main post office. It arrived for Jimmy Johnson, a coachman in bondage to Dr. Lionel Kennedy, a white physician who lived on the square. It came for Lot Farrow, tending horses at a livery stable nearby. Freedom arrived for Hercules Huggins, a talented blacksmith living out of sight of white college students on the Wofford College campus.

And freedom finally arrived for a man named Toby Shipp, who had been in Spartanburg just six years, living near what is now the Wofford College baseball field. Within a year he would become Tobe Hartwell, one of Spartanburg's most respected Black men of the era. Over the next half century, Hartwell would become a powerful force in public education and race relations in a rapidly growing town where he was once held captive in slavery.

As the years went by, newly emancipated Black men and women in the village of Spartanburg came together with a strong desire to have their own churches, schools and neighborhoods. Neighborhoods were especially important. Neighborhoods ensured strength in numbers and a general sense of protection during the dangerous, post-war years. For Black people able to move to town from more rural areas of the upcountry, new Black neighborhoods provided proximity to employment, medical attention and churches, where community organization began to take place. Over the

TOP: *The slaveholding Kirby family lived at the current site of the U.S. Post Office. This photo is from 1874.*

BOTTOM: *The courthouse, where slave auctions were held, faced Spartanburg's public square.*

years, often against extraordinary odds and in the face of sometimes brutal oppression, the newly emancipated built the northside of Spartanburg into a dynamic and diverse community.

As the Civil War broke out in 1861, some 2,200 people lived in the commercial center of Spartanburg, with as many as 800 of them Black and held in slavery. About 30 were free people of color, including five Black shoemakers. The public square—known today as Morgan Square—was the hub of activity for the new town of Spartanburg. White-owned houses and businesses surrounded the square, along with a courthouse that resembled a Greek temple. On its wide, stone steps, Black men, women and children had been sold to the highest bidder throughout the previous decade. Nearby, residences stretched east and west on Main Street, down Magnolia, Church and Henry streets. Behind or alongside them stood as many as 150 simple cabins that housed the enslaved population of the village of Spartanburg.

Out in the countryside, thousands of enslaved people worked the antebellum farms and small plantations of the northern and southern reaches of the Spartanburg District. Their numbers increased from 866 in 1825 to 3,308 in 1850 to an estimated 9,000 at the brink of the Civil War. While it was not a major crop until after the war, cotton was being sown and picked in some fields of southern Spartanburg County, and its harvest was grueling work for the Black population. In most of Spartanburg County's northern rural areas, workers held in slavery grew food production crops such as corn, wheat and oats.

In the village of Spartanburg, many enslaved people performed domestic work for the emerging and often wealthy professional class of merchants, lawyers, doctors, professors and early textile company owners. Others provided them more manual labor: masonry, smithing, livestock-tending, digging or hauling. Yet even in the more urban and sophisticated part of the Spartanburg District, enslaved people could be subjected to brutality for not conforming to rules. In 1831—the year of Nat Turner's slave rebellion in Virginia—the town of Spartanburg instituted slave patrols, and they continued until the end of the Civil War. Every white man had to participate in a five-man patrol unit for one month out of the year. An updated law was passed by ordinance in September 1861: "It shall be the duty of the patrol to apprehend and whip all slaves, not exceeding twenty lashes, found without the premises of their master, or persons having charge of them between the ringing of the [night] bell and day-break, unless in company with some white person over the age of ten years who shall account for their absence, or shall have a ticket from their master." These tickets were passes that stipulated when and where Black people were allowed to travel. They were valid for no more than one month. The bell, located in the public square, would ring ten times, signaling that people of color must be inside.

In August 1863 the Spartanburg town council made it illegal for a slave or a free person of color to own a horse, mule or carriage, or to occupy a house in the town without a white person on the premises. It was also dangerous to be a free Black person in Spartanburg during the war. In December 1863 the town council ordered that "the girl Free Nancy" be required to leave the town and never return again—and if she did, the marshal was "to arrest the said girl and give her 25 lashes every day she remained." Even

This 1861 city ordinance references the curfew bell that dictated when enslaved people could be on the street.

6. It shall be the duty of the patrol to apprehend and whip all slaves, not exceeding twenty lashes, found without the premises of their master, or persons having charge of them, between the ringing of the bell and day-break, unless in company with some white person over the age of ten years, who shall account for their absence, or shall have a ticket, from their master, or person having charge of them, of leave of absence; also, all slaves, though having such ticket, who may have in their possession any gun, pistol, or other offensive weapon, also, all slaves not resident or employed in said town, who may be found therein at any time on Sunday, unless in company with some white person over the age of ten years, who shall account for their absence, or shall have a ticket from their master, or person having charge of them, giving them leave to visit the village; also, all slaves, though having such ticket, who may be found wandering about the streets or lots of said town, after eleven o'clock, P. M., unless peaceably returning to his home, after three o'clock, A. M.

the impending end of the war did not stop the town council from enforcing penalties on the enslaved. Five weeks after Gen. William T. Sherman burned the city of Columbia in mid-February 1865, the Spartanburg council convicted a slave named George of forging passes. He was sentenced to six weeks imprisonment, plus 50 lashes each week, "or until his master could cause said slave to leave town."

Major combat in the Civil War ended abruptly when Gen. Robert E. Lee surrendered his Army of Northern Virginia at Appomattox Courthouse on April 9, 1865. Confederate soldiers began straggling home to Spartanburg, but it took many weeks for freedom to truly arrive for the Black population in and around the public square. Those weeks were a time of great confusion in Spartanburg. The mayor of the town, John B. Cleveland, resigned from office just days after Lee's surrender, only to resume the job five months later. In the early days, Confederate dollars were still the currency in Spartanburg, but no one was sure how long that would last. Fights broke out on the street. Town minutes relate that 12 days after the end of the war, William H. Walker was fined $150 Confederate dollars for committing assault and battery on Capt. Hutson Wigg, a Confederate officer apparently on his way from the battlefront to Columbia where he later became a Reconstruction-era probate judge and was called a "carpet-bagger" by some locals. Three weeks after the Confederate surrender, a large group of federal cavalrymen camped at the Magnolia Street home of Simpson Bobo for two nights on their way south, purloining livestock and supplies and announcing that the U.S. government was now in charge.

That first summer of freedom was an uncertain and fearful time for the newly emancipated Black people of Spartanburg—freedom was not really assured until a second set of federal troops arrived on the public square from Charleston and Columbia on Aug. 21. Eventually, more than 100 Union soldiers, most from New York state, would occupy Spartanburg's imposing, columned courthouse. Their commanding officer, Capt. Norris Crossman, moved his headquarters from Union on Sept. 19 to keep the peace in Spartanburg and protect new Black citizens from vigilante whites. He arrived in time for an emancipation jubilee, held three days later at a spot southeast of the village reportedly owned by Elizabeth H. Fairchild, widow of a Charleston brick and lumber dealer.

The first year of freedom was a time of both jubilation and privation for Spartanburg's Black citizens. Some institutions that previously had welcomed them as enslaved people suddenly rejected them as freedmen. Several were excommunicated at Spartanburg's First Baptist Church, where Black attendance had been robust during the war. The rejection was particularly acute for an apparently hungry freedman known as "Brother John," formerly held in slavery by Wofford College professor David Duncan. Church minutes at First Baptist relate that John was brought to trial among church leaders in August 1866 for stealing corn from White's Mill. John "denied the charges of stealing the corn but acknowledged that he had gone into the house and taken out of the box some corn which he said he borrowed at the same time he acknowledged no one was in the mill at the time." The church sought to question a witness who could no longer be located. At the following meeting, they rescinded his church membership. "As there was not the slightest doubt of his guilt and as [John] had failed to attend in person and in fact had left the District: On motion he was excluded from the church by unanimous vote."

Freedpeople generally continued to attend Spartanburg's white churches—Baptist, Methodist, Episcopalian and Presbyterian—in the

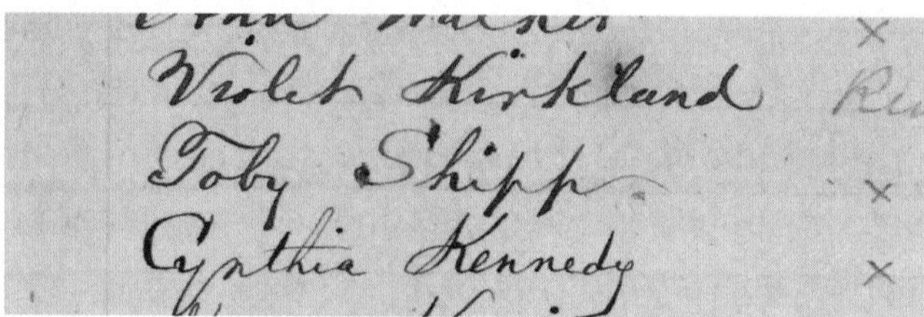
Violet Kirkland
Toby Shipp
Cynthia Kennedy

TOP: *An 1865 Sunday School roll lists an enslaved man named Toby Shipp.*

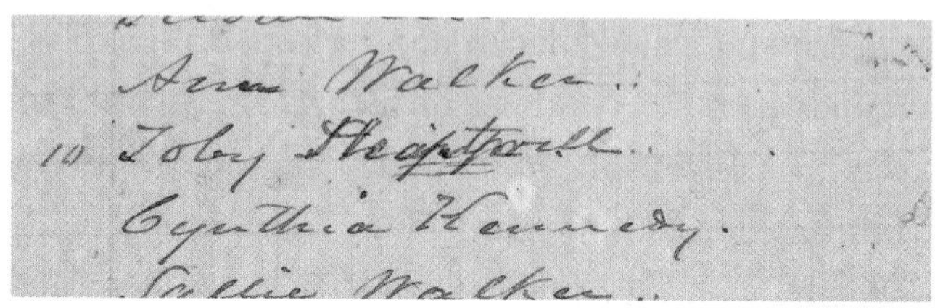
Ann Walker.
10 Toby Hartwell.
Cynthia Kennedy.

BOTTOM: *By 1866 he had changed his last name to Hartwell.*

year after slavery, but by 1866 began drifting away to hold their own services in brush arbors or houses. The white churches were having trouble keeping track of them anyway. A frustrated church secretary at Central Methodist wrote a note to the Rev. Whitefoord Smith in November 1865: "The colored people change their names so often that I find it impossible to furnish you with a correct list of the probationers remaining in Spartanburg."

Hercules DuPre became Hercules Huggins. Susan Shipp became Susan Burnett.

Some of the newly emancipated left Spartanburg, but others hunkered down in their cabins and negotiated new working relationships with their former enslavers. The historical record suggests a small number of enslaved persons lived on or immediately behind Wofford's campus. The 1860 U.S. Slave Schedule reports at least six slave cabins owned by faculty of Wofford College. Five Wofford professors were enslavers in 1860—President Albert M. Shipp (22 slaves), Warren DuPré (16 slaves), David Duncan (five slaves), Whitefoord Smith (five slaves) and James Carlisle (one slave). Some enslaved persons may have lived inside the campus homes of professors, performing domestic work. Black tradesmen, such as masons and blacksmiths, likely lived in cabins behind the campus. Still others worked farms outside the town. Adjacent to the college, off North Church Street, there were as many as four additional slave dwellings on the vast acreage behind what is now known as the Evins-Bivings home, housing up to 16 more enslaved people. Together, this group of Black people formed a nucleus of residents "Back of the College" in the early days after the Civil War. Within 15 years, there were at least 47 households and 181 Black people living in a place a census-taker called "Street behind College (no name)."

The typical slave cabin in the Carolinas in this era was a one- to two-room building made of wood or mud brick, often with dirt floors. Most had fireplaces for cooking and warmth. Often, enslaved people had built their own homes at the instruction of their owners. Census data shows that many of the Black persons living in this vicinity in 1870 were carpenters and masons.

Closer to town, Black people suddenly were living as freedpeople at the Magnolia Street homeplaces of attorney Simpson Bobo and former newspaperman John Earle Bomar. They were free at the homes of dry goods merchants Hiram Mitchell and Augustus Kirby, and at the homeplace of D.W. Moore, a dealer in saddles and leather goods. They were free at the homes of several white women who had lost their husbands: Emily Cleveland Choice on Main Street and Mary O. Dean, widow of state legislator Hosea J. Dean, also on Main Street. They were free at the home of Lizzie Fleming, whose surgeon-husband had just returned to town after being away at war for four years.

Longtime Spartanburg educator Hattie Bell Penland, who died in 2000, often related the journey of her great-grandmother, Sophie, who had been held in slavery on a farm in Rutherford County, North Carolina. At the time of emancipation, Sophie's enslaver—a man named McKinney—sent Sophie to Spartanburg atop a feather-tick bed in the back of a mule-drawn wagon. According to family lore, when the driver came to North Church Street, roughly the present-day site of the Spartanburg Marriott Hotel, he put Sophie out on the street. Left behind on the Rutherford County farm were Sophie's 16-year-old daughter, who had been impregnated by the farmer McKinney, and Sophie's mother. McKinney had refused to let the daughter travel because of her pregnancy, and the grandmother stayed behind too.

In her wanderings on the streets of Spartanburg, Sophie met another Black woman named Caroline. The two of them went in search of a job at the Female College, located near the present-day site of VCOM-Carolinas medical school. They were hired in the laundry and, after some period of

The late Hattie Bell Penland. Her family lived Back of the College for more than 120 years.

time, were able to save enough money with their families to buy lots on Twitty Street behind Wofford College and build small houses. One day, Sophie heard that a baby had been born in a cabin nearby on Chinquapin Creek. When she went to the cabin, she surprisingly encountered her own mother and her own daughter, who also had been sent in a wagon to Spartanburg. The teenaged daughter carried with her a baby. That baby was Millie Penland, who in 1902 gave birth to Hattie Penland.

THE EFFECTS OF THE CIVIL WAR were devastating to the local economy and fundamentally disruptive to conventional life as it existed to that point. Approximately 25 percent of the white male population in Spartanburg County was killed or wounded. In 1860 the combined personal and real wealth in the Spartanburg District was valued at $16 million, but by 1870 it had dropped to $4 million, with most of the loss seen in property or the ownership of enslaved persons. The deprivations of war left many farms depleted and farmers without capital to restock or buy seeds to sow. Since most of the county's significant institutions had invested in Confederate war bonds and lost everything, very little earning potential existed in the immediate aftermath. People faced starvation, the inability to earn an income, bad weather, and smashed railway systems.

While farming was hit especially hard, and significant poverty persisted for decades, much of the war machine that was built to sustain Confederate forces in their losing effort functioned to rebuild Spartanburg County's economy relatively quickly. Cotton production and the infrastructure necessary to distribute it became the engine to restore Spartanburg's economy. Cotton production had been increasing before the war, but after the war, a massive expansion of railways, factories and cotton production combined to generate a viable and increasingly productive economy. The Air-Line railway, which connected Charlotte to Atlanta, came through Spartanburg, and opened in 1873. It ultimately became the Southern Railway, connecting Spartanburg to the Midwest, the Northeast and the deeper South. Other railroads followed.

Any town on these lines was expected to boom, and entrepreneurs got busy. At least nine separate cotton factories sprung up or expanded in Spartanburg County, and by 1873, at least nine companies in Spartanburg town were engaged in the cotton business. The infrastructure necessary to get crops to depots followed suit. Carriage factories, sawmills and brickyards all developed in or near the village of Spartanburg to accommodate building needs. Spartanburg's streets and sidewalks were enlarged and improved to accommodate industrial and commercial traffic, and many new stores were built—often by paid Black labor—to capture and expand growth. At least a dozen Black men found work at Fowler, Robison & Co., a large carriage factory and smithing business located just off the public square on Magnolia Street. Several others worked for the carriage factory and lumberyard that Confederate veteran Isaac H. Cantrell opened in 1868 near the corner of Main and Liberty Streets.

Emancipated people unfortunately did not have the capital to buy significant tracts of property or the necessary goods to start their own farms. And many white planters did not have the capital to pay a labor force. The system of tenant farming or sharecropping, therefore, developed quickly out in the countryside, originated by the Union Army as an expedient solution to a shortage of cash and the impending spring planting season. White planters would divide their land into 35- or 40-acre sections and lease them out to families, most of whom were freedpeople. Sharecroppers would sign contracts to lease the land, equipment, stock, seed and provisions either from the landowner or from a merchant in town and hope the crop yield would be sufficient to pay their debt and provide a bit of extra capital. Rarely did it work out. Either the crops would be compromised for standard farming reasons, or the landowner or merchant would cheat them.

David Golightly Harris, for example, contracted with freedpeople to sharecrop his land in the southern part of the Spartanburg District. A crop lien was established in which it was stipulated that Harris would receive half of the total yield, a generous concession compared to that of other farms where planters received more. But midway through the growing season, Harris changed his percentage of the yield to two-thirds, attributing it to his own financial distress. The people sharecropping his land had no recourse to object. Such tenant farmers typically were indebted to landowners and forced to work on their farms the next season, which resulted in the same outcome. This never-ending cycle of debt—debt slavery, or peonage—was outlawed by Congress in 1867, but it was practiced nevertheless and affected hundreds of thousands of freedpeople in the Southern states for generations.

The Freedmen's Bureau sent agents to the Upstate to ensure Black civil rights as determined by congressional action in 1865. The closest office to Spartanburg was in Union, and officials there were spread thin, managing affairs affecting some 12,000 Black people. The staff of this government agency worked to make sure freedmen were paid wages, and they attended to issues of hunger, medical attention and transportation. It was the job of federal troops stationed at Spartanburg's courthouse to deter extralegal violence, but they could not be everywhere either. And even this protection was fleeting. A general draw-down of U.S. troops began quickly. From January to October of 1866, troop numbers in South Carolina dropped from 7,408 to 1,506. As troop numbers declined, freedpeople became more vulnerable. Crossman and his troops left Spartanburg in early October 1865 and relocated to Union, after state law had turned all criminal cases over to Spartanburg town council and the new courts.

In June 1865 U.S. President Andrew Johnson installed Benjamin Franklin Perry of Greenville as the provisional governor of South Carolina with the charge of developing a new state constitution to warrant the state being readmitted into the Union. Perry set up basic infrastructure within each county and held a convention to frame a new constitution. Delegates were sent from each county. Spartanburg County's were James Farrow, J.W. Carlisle, John Winsmith, M.C. Barnett and R.C. Poole—all white, but also pragmatic enough to join other state representatives in adopting federal requirements to allow South Carolina to join the Union. So while Spartanburg's delegates supported the state's ratification of the 13th amendment to the U.S. Constitution, they also helped develop a system of laws, called "Black Codes," that enforced severe restrictions against free Black movement and intercourse with the free trade market. Such laws were put in place across the South, drastically limiting employment opportunities. In South Carolina the codes quickly were suspended by the U.S. Department of the South in Hilton Head.

In 1866 the Spartanburg Court of General Pleas and the Court of General Sessions were convened. Magistrates were generally white planters, and their friends served on juries. Most of the crimes addressed by courts in Spartanburg County between March and November 1866 were larceny, assault, rape and various misdemeanors. Despite widespread documentation of white people committing crimes, all of those convicted and sentenced in 1867 were Black Americans. Sentences were severe. William Dawkins, convicted for burglary, was sentenced to be hanged in June 1867.

The Spartanburg Town Council functioned as a sort of "People's Court" for less serious crimes. Much of its business was taken up with prosecuting freedmen for "disturbing the peace and quiet of the town." For the guilty, fines ranged from $1 to $10. And for those who could not pay there was "road duty"—forced labor in the construction and repair of city streets.

THE STORY OF SPARTANBURG'S ALLEY BROTHERS—white men who created havoc in the Black community—illustrates what freedmen were up against in the four years after the conclusion of the war. The saga is an example of how town officials tolerated intimidation and violence against its new Black citizens, even allowing a convicted criminal to serve its own law enforcement.

Henry C. Alley, age 32 in 1865, was a brawler. He had a particularly troublesome older brother, James. Just days after Lee's surrender at Appomattox, both Alley brothers were involved in a melee in the village with three other white men. Henry was fined $25. Despite Henry Alley's criminal record and reputation, Spartanburg town council hired him as its chief law enforcement officer on Sept. 15, 1865. His first assignment as a town marshal was to keep an eye on a gathering of freedmen at a site southeast of the public square. He was to "overlook and keep order at the Pic Nic."

The Alley brothers had grown up in a building on the corner of Main and Church streets where their father ran a grocery and a liquor stand. Patrons could walk up, hand old Mr. Alley their pint bottle through the window and get a fill up. Henry Alley had gone off to fight for the Confederacy but returned home in the war's third year when he was shot in the face. Many years later, his obituary would describe him as "a terror to evil-doers." One prominent local citizen of the era recalled that Alley would "cuss on very short notice and beat the proverbial sailor."

In November 1865 the new marshal's brother, James Alley, was brought before council "for a general riot and endeavoring to raise a difficulty with part of the Yankee garrison." James apparently was tangling with federal officers who were there to protect the village's freedpeople. James pleaded "guilty—but drunk." Barely a month later, on Jan. 10, 1866, Henry Alley was charged with a misdemeanor "disturbance" in the town and chose to resign. This was but a prelude of the trouble the Alleys would cause with their true target: Spartanburg's freedmen.

Remarkably, two months later, Henry Alley was reappointed chief marshal and put in charge of Spartanburg's "road hands," many of whom were Black. Then, in July 1866, town minutes relate that his brother, James, "shot the Negro boy Dennis." No other public documents appear to shed light on this incident. As there was no inquest filed by federal troops, the victim may have survived. The clerk of the town court was sent "to make a report in full to the commander of the garrison in Union as to the affair." By mid-September, Henry Alley was no longer on the town payroll. Four months later Henry was charged with throwing rocks at a "freedman team," presumably a work crew. The town council minutes relate that he pleaded "guilty to the charge being drunk and not knowing what he did," and was given a $10 fine.

The real trouble began, though, when Spartanburg's September 1869 town election swept in a "dry ticket" of council members who intended to outlaw the sale of "spiritous liquors" by small dealers, including Henry and James Alley. *The Carolina Spartan* newspaper suggested that the Alley brothers violently took out their frustrations on two Black citizens. According to initial newspaper reports, Henry Alley shot Black carriage maker Monroe Burnett on Sept. 14, 1869, in retribution for his vote against the "wet ticket." Burnett, who resided behind Wofford College, was described as "an honest, industrious and peaceable man . . . favorably known by the citizens generally." He was employed by James A. Fowler, proprietor of Spartanburg's carriage and wagon factory. The bullet hit Burnett in the foot, with the wound described as serious. Henry Alley later was found and arrested in Columbia and held on bail of $1,000. But before that could happen, two assailants slipped up on Frank Burnett—Monroe's brother—killing him with a shot to the chest. Witnesses saw the shooters escape into the darkness of the night from a blacksmith shop off the public square. "It is with feelings of the deepest regret that we record the assassination which we remember to have disgraced the annals of our peaceful and quiet town," wrote a journalist for *The Carolina Spartan*.

Notorious town marshal Henry C. Alley is buried in Spartanburg's Magnolia Cemetery.

James Alley was arrested, with the local speculation that the murder of Frank Burnett also was motivated by a vote against liquor sales. A coroner's jury quickly concluded that James Alley was innocent. Instead, the shooting was blamed on two Black men in Spartanburg, and they were charged with murder. "From the evidence adduced, strong suspicion rests upon Henry Jones and Moses [Young]," *The Carolina Spartan* reported. "We forbear making public the evidence given at the inquest, as we do not wish to influence the minds of the community before an official examination of the matter can be had." Henry Jones, a 20-year-old railroad worker who lived Back of the College, was found not guilty at a jury trial in November 1869, and the prosecutor dropped the charges on his supposed accomplice, Moses Young. Monroe Burnett, the Black carriage maker, survived the gunshot to his foot, serving Spartanburg as a blacksmith for many years and living out his life on the northside. The casualty, Frank Burnett, presumably was buried in the city's Black cemetery off West Main Street. Little is known about the later years of the white ruffian James Alley. Henry Alley resurfaced in law enforcement in the late 1880s, when he became the city of Spartanburg's police chief. He died in 1896 and is buried in Magnolia Cemetery, along with his brother James. There is no indication that anyone was ever convicted in the shootings of the Burnett brothers.

THE 1867 CONGRESSIONAL RECONSTRUCTION ACT extended basic civil rights for freedpeople, including the enfranchisement of Black men, and addressed the "discrimination in the courts, extralegal violence, and a general refusal on the part of white people throughout the South to accept the basic rights of Black people." The act and amendments to the U.S. Constitution were largely written by abolitionist "Radical Republicans" in Congress and stipulated far greater reforms than U.S. President Andrew Johnson—or any white conservative in the South—wanted. Dramatic changes in its wake took place in Spartanburg County, the most significant perhaps being the right to vote. Among the freedmen who cast votes in that election were early leaders of the neighborhoods, churches and schools that would be built north of the town. Among the four Republicans elected to the constitutional convention in 1868 from Spartanburg County were two Black men: brick mason Rev. Rice Foster, formerly enslaved by the Bivings family, and farmer Coy Wingo.

With Black Republicans in the majority, the new legislature legalized the right for anyone, regardless of race, to serve on juries or be appointed a magistrate. Freedpeople were encouraged, at least initially, by these reforms. They could own guns, bring charges against white people in court, assemble where they pleased, seek an education, own property, be compensated for their labor, legally dispute contracts in a representative court system, and hold public office.

White conservatives, meanwhile, organized "Constitutional Clubs" in various counties across the state to fight against the implementation of the new constitution. Spartanburg's was called to order in February 1868 and was led by several white business and civic leaders, including Simpson Bobo, Dr. Lionel Kennedy, John B. Cleveland and John H. Evins. Opponents organized into the Union League. By July 1871 federal troops were back in Spartanburg. Persistent Ku Klux Klan attacks in the rural areas of the Piedmont forced the hand of President Ulysses S. Grant, and he sent the 7th Cavalry, led by Maj. Marcus Reno, to various hotspots in the upcountry to round up the perpetrators. A large group of federal soldiers camped in Twitty's Grove, located at the present-day intersection of West Henry Street and West Daniel Morgan Avenue. In mid-October Grant imposed martial law, meaning his soldiers could hold Klansmen in jail without trial for as long as they cared to. Roughly 230 of them ended up behind bars locally. The presence of the soldiers—and the long jail terms—served to greatly quell the violence in the Spartanburg District, even after they departed in 1873.

Meanwhile, amid the tumult, Black communities began taking shape on all sides of Spartanburg's commercial district. Spartanburg's new Black voters and many other freed people quietly began building lives for themselves and their families. The fact that they were able to gain a legitimate foothold in a society that only months earlier fought a war to prevent their license indicates both the massive rupture and transformation occurring at the time and freedpeople's drive to be citizens.

In the dangerous years after the war, Black families navigated white militias, white law enforcement, white elites and white people generally, all of which could have spelled disaster at any point. But navigate through it they did. They found their way to one another, organized themselves into an extraordinary group of activists for self- and collective improvement, and took action. Whatever possible divisions or differences between them, or whatever they might have carried with them from their experience of being enslaved, did not prevent their collaboration. They found common ground and worked to build a better life together, despite the persistent, intense and ubiquitous resistance they faced.

This montage depicts so-called "Radical Republicans" in the first S.C. Legislature during Reconstruction. Fifty were Black, though none were from Spartanburg because Blacks were in the minority in the district and could not get elected.

SPOTLIGHT

LOT FARROW AND THE FEDERAL CAVALRY

Perhaps the best account of the activities of federal troops in Spartanburg at the conclusion of the Civil War comes from northside pioneer Lot Farrow, who was enslaved to Milo A. Harvey, owner of a livery stable near the center of town. The Union cavalry troops stopped in Spartanburg April 30 through May 2, 1865, in their hunt for Jefferson Davis, president of the Confederacy. As a free man seven years later, Farrow gave testimony to the Southern Claims Commission as it sought to determine whether the Harvey family was entitled to compensation for the seizure of horses by the federal troops. Farrow's testimony has been condensed here and likely paraphrased by the interviewer.

Oct. 16, 1872

I was born a slave in the state of South Carolina and am 47 years of age. I belonged to Mr. Milo A. Harvey. After the war ended I was hired by him until the time of his death. He kept a livery stable at Spartanburg while I was employed. I also drove the mail coach during the war between Shelton and Blackstock. After the death of my master, I bought some of the horses and carriages formerly owned by him.

I saw the horses taken from [Mr. Harvey's] livery stable just about the time peace was declared by U.S. soldiers. There was a raid of Yankees under the command of General Palmer. I saw about 20 of the Yankee soldiers come in the stable asking for horses. I had seen both the officers at the stable before. During a month before the taking, the two officers were at Spartanburg in disguise as Confederate officers, and they put up their horses at [Mr. Harvey's] stables. They knew me and spoke to me about their having made believe that they were rebel soldiers from Tennessee.

I saw the soldiers take the saddles from their own horses and put them on [Harvey's] horses. I saw the soldiers take away with them all the horses they brought here. They were badly used up and all [of Harvey's] horses were in fine order. I saw 11 horses and two mules taken from the stable by the Yankee soldiers. There were three stallions among the horses. One of them was an imported horse and very valuable.

The provisions were taken by some of the same soldiers and by many other Yankee soldiers who came and went from the stable. I saw the 10 barrels of flour opened and taken away in sacks and bags by the Yankee soldiers until all of it was gone. I also saw the soldiers take away large quantities of bacon and saw them give large pieces of it to the colored people about the street. I heard them ask the colored people if they didn't want some bacon and saw them throw large pieces to them. The salt was taken away in sacks by soldiers and some was given in small quantities to the colored people. I helped the soldiers haul away two or three horse wagon loads of the corn from the stable to the place where the soldiers fed their horses—about 1/4 mile from the stable. Some of the fodder was carried away by soldiers but most of it was taken away by colored boys who toted it for the soldiers.

I sent word to [Mr. Harvey] as soon as the soldiers began taking his property but he sent back reply that he could not help it. [He] lived less than 1/4 of a mile distance from his stable. The Yankee soldiers remained at the stable from about 2 o'clock p.m. and remained there until about 10 o'clock on the same night. I went to the courthouse about 300 yards from the stable and told the officers that the soldiers were taking all the provisions from the stable. They told me that the soldiers needed it much more than I did.

The $4,735 claim from the Harveys ultimately was denied on the grounds that Harvey had been a Confederate sympathizer. A native of Pennsylvania, Harvey apparently was initially opposed to secession yet he delivered mail for the Confederacy and did not denounce the Southern war effort.

SPOTLIGHT

POST-SLAVERY LABOR CONTRACTS

The first step out of slavery for many Black men and women in Spartanburg was to sign a labor contract with an employer. These hand-written contracts, required by the "Black Codes," were overseen and held at the small Freedmen's Bureau office in Union County. Many times, the working conditions in the contracts were hardly better than slavery itself. The pay was typically paltry. Henry C. Alley, for instance, paid his new employees just $3 a month. Often these jobs provided the only way for freedpeople to get a roof over their heads or have regular access to food. They also locked freedmen into a year's worth of labor with no ability to bargain for something better.

Several of the first settlers of Spartanburg's northside neighborhoods signed such contracts. Hundreds more freedmen in the countryside signed them too. Some freedmen found themselves working under contract for the same people who had held them in slavery. Others had a succession of contracts with different employers. "The control of blacks by white employers was about as great as that which slaveholders had exercised," wrote pioneering Black historian John Hope Franklin.

The northside's Lydia Hardy, for instance, signed a one-year contract with Dr. James. J. Boyd, a physician who lived on East Main Street in Spartanburg and was a prominent member of First Baptist Church. She was paid $5 a month for housekeeping and childcare in exchange for room, board, firewood and two suits of clothing a year. She also was required to make and to repair clothing for the Boyd children. For his part, the doctor agreed to give her free medical and obstetrical attention. The contract was signed not by Lydia Hardy, but by her husband, George Hardy, with an X for a signature. A decade later, the Hardys would build a house off North Converse Street.

Boyd also employed Joseph Hardy, a young man who formerly had been enslaved by the family of Dr. Charles E. Fleming. For $5 a month in 1866, Joseph Hardy "was to at all times to be ready to perform whatever Dr. Boyd may require him to do." He was not to be "absent from the yard" except on Sundays, or when feeding the horses and cows, or when sent on an errand. Boyd also hired him for a second job: Joseph Hardy was to be the sexton of the First Baptist Church, ringing the bell for all the services on Sunday and prayer meetings during the week. He also was to sweep and dust the church every Saturday, to keep the lamps in order, and "to suffer no one to enter the church who may steal, mutilate or do any damage whatsoever." He was to be paid $25 a year for those services.

A formerly enslaved man named Jack Thompson, who later raised a large family Back of the College, was hired by Spartanburg attorney William Choice. In his one-year contract in 1866, Thompson was to work and live on the "John Gossett place," about six miles from Spartanburg Courthouse, presumably to farm it for himself. He was to repair and keep fencing and houses in order, "to ditch, tend, and otherwise improve the bottoms." The contract stipulated that Jack Thompson was not to "clear up or wastefully use any wood or woodland without permission." He also was to keep "any dishonest or disorderly or idle persons to come loiter or frequent about said premises." Thompson agreed to lease the premises at the expiration of the contract, and if he didn't, he would have to refund Choice "two hundred dollars in good money."

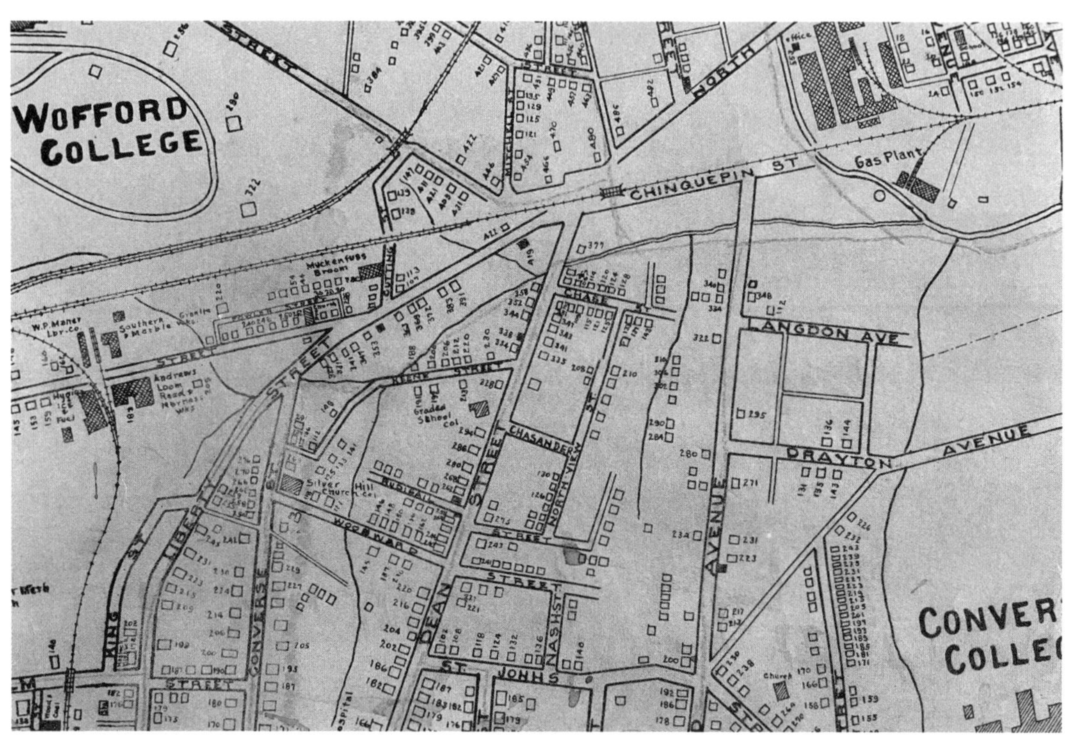

A 1910 map of the North Dean Street and North Converse Street areas. Included are Silver Hill Church and Dean Street School.

TWO

BIRTH OF THE NORTH DEAN STREET NEIGHBORHOOD

THE SPARTANBURG MEN who gathered to build a wood-frame Methodist Episcopal church at a place then known as Academy Street already were stalwarts in their community. Prior to emancipation, some had risen to positions of confidence and responsibility in the households of Spartanburg's tight, slave-holding elite. Resourceful, focused and savvy, these Black men had endured the human degradation of slavery while moving among the parlor society of Main and Magnolia streets.

From the spot where they cut pine trees and began construction on a gently sloping hillside about 1870, the founders and their families could see the twin towers of Wofford College's Old Main building, built with slave labor, to the north. Behind them to the south—a five-minute saunter away—were the large homes of the people who had held them in captivity most of their lives. The builders of Silver Hill Church had entered freedom with decades-long relationships with the leading white citizens of the village. In fact, for the year prior to construction, Silver Hill members had met in a rented union hall on Wall Street, just off the public square, amid the homes of the town's wealthiest citizens.

Ironically, the land they stood upon had belonged in the previous year to a former Confederate officer, Lt. Col. George Washington Hamilton Legg. An antebellum Spartanburg mayor, Legg had come home from the war to assume a job as a magistrate and assistant provost judge in charge of trying cases "wherein freedmen were concerned or implicated." Legg soon ran into financial trouble and was forced into bankruptcy in October 1869, losing control of most everything he owned, including the wide field off Academy Street (later known as North Converse Street) where he once had overseen military drills. A local man named James C. Wilson grabbed the property out of bankruptcy court and flipped a one-acre lot to the trustees of Silver Hill Methodist Episcopal Church in February 1870 for $100.

The published history of Silver Hill Methodist Episcopal Church lists Tobe Hartwell among several others who would have been present on the celebrated day that silver dollars were placed under each corner of the future sanctuary. Property deeds and newspaper articles list even more founders.

Thomas Pickenpack was there in the beginning. Then roughly 50 years old, he had been enslaved by a blind German immigrant named John Pickenpack, who owned a large farm off East Main Street. When the elderly German died in the 1850s, Thomas was then enslaved by another resident of East Main Street: Col. Henry Hopson Thomson, a South Carolina state senator and the second mayor of the antebellum village of Spartanburg. Thomas and his ultimate enslaver apparently had a solid bond: on his deathbed in 1858, the colonel deeded a tract of land to him in a trust. He empowered local attorney Jefferson Choice "to make good, sufficient, and lawful title" to the land for Thomas at an unspecified later date. The parcel that Thomas Pickenpack ultimately received was located on what became South Liberty Street, a few blocks off Main. Pickenpack became a barber after the war, married a woman named Winnie and later became a pastor. They had at least eight children. And unlike most formerly enslaved people, Pickenpack could read and write.

Richard Rivers was there at the beginning too. The official history of Silver Hill, penned by educator MacArthur Goodwin in 1970, reports that Rivers, then about 32 years old, walked 200 miles from Charleston to Spartanburg after the Civil War and joined the group founding the church, possibly bringing others with him. The trek took him through swamp, snakes, militias, and a lot of hard country. It remains unknown why Rivers set out for the upcountry, but he made good time. He arrived in Spartanburg before 1865 was out—his name is penciled in at the bottom of the roll of a Black Sunday School class at Central Methodist Church that year. Rivers bought his home and a one-acre lot in 1877 on the east end of Evins Street,

Back of the College, and made his living as a house carpenter. He and his wife, Sophy, had at least eight children. In 1887 he would be elected to Spartanburg Town Council, one of four Black men in that era to serve as aldermen for the local government. The Rivers family continued to live on Evins Street for four generations, and their descendants distinguished themselves both in Spartanburg and beyond.

Among the other founders of Silver Hill was Thornton Williams, a skilled stone mason and one of the earliest Black landowners in Spartanburg. On Nov. 28, 1868, Williams purchased 3.75 acres west of the public square, in what was known as "the Trimmier lands," roughly where Austin and Baltimore streets are today. Williams lived there with his wife, Charity, and a family of at least four children. This was a small Black enclave in an area known in the 19th century as Hamburg. Another Silver Hill founder, carpenter Abram Smalls, bought a small tract of land from Williams and moved his family there.

Other Black Spartanburg residents present at the beginning of Silver Hill were Paul Simmons, Hercules Huggins, the Rev. "Ranse" McKinney, Jack Thompson and Lot Farrow. Almost all of them lived out their lives in the shadow of Wofford College.

GEORGE HARDY WAS THERE in the beginning too. In 1875, a few years after the church groundbreaking, he bought the two acres directly across from Silver Hill Church for his own homestead. He and his Virginia-born wife, Lydia, a nurse, raised four children on their plot of land, large enough for a sizable vegetable garden. George worked at the local railroad shop and was a white-washer, which meant he likely worked painting and cleaning buildings in the commercial district of a downtown that was beginning to grow rapidly. Some accounts describe him as brother to livery stable operator Lot Farrow, making him the uncle of noted Spartanburg educator Mary H. Wright. In the years right after the war, his opinion was valued by the white community. When Black magistrate Anthony Johnson was brutally murdered by the Ku Klux Klan at his home in Pacolet in December 1870, George Hardy was named to a committee made up of prominent white businessmen and lawyers who drafted a "peace resolution" calling for the arrest of the perpetrators.

There were other Black people named Hardy scattered throughout Spar-

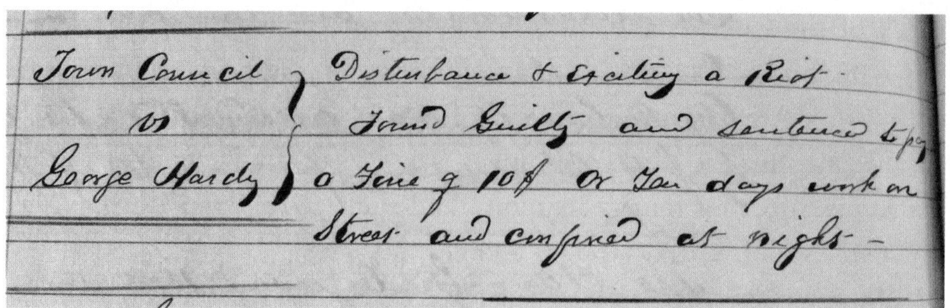

Town Council vs George Hardy } Disturbance & Exciting a Riot. Found Guilty and sentenced to pay a Fine of 10$ Or Ten days work on Street and confined at night –

Town Council minutes reference George Hardy's fine for "inciting a riot."

tanburg County in the 1800s—and a significant number of them had been free before the Civil War. In fact, as early as the 1820s, a Black man named William "Free Bill" Hardy owned an 82-acre parcel of land between Pacolet and Glenn Springs. And Spartanburg District court records contain the names of 31 Black people named Hardy who were granted freedom between 1823 and 1863 with a court-appointed white guardian, as was the law.

George's connection to them is not clear. What is clear, though, is that George Hardy was a man with a strong sense of justice and was quick to come to the aid of victims of racial violence. On Christmas Day 1877 Hardy was with a group of men in the village. According to an account in the white-owned newspaper *The Carolina Spartan*, a Black drayman named Peter Grant "attempted to crowd" a law enforcement officer, Marshal W.P. Campbell, who then proceeded to shoot Grant at close range with a pistol. The newspaper called it "a centre-shot" that hit Grant "square in the forehead." Amazingly, the report said, the shot did not kill him, with the bullet flattening and producing a fracture of Grant's skull. At that point, "some of Peter Grant's friends became rather turbulent and riotous, and tried to get up a sensation over the matter, which was speedily squelched without further trouble and several parties heavily fined by Mayor [Joseph] Walker putting a quietus to the affair."

The man with the biggest fine from the incident was George Hardy. At the town council meeting the next day, he was fined $10—a not-insignificant sum in those days—with the option instead of performing 10 days' labor on the streets and being confined at night.

THE FIRST, WOODEN SILVER HILL CHURCH stood until about 1875, when a sturdier building replaced it, likely constructed by the many brick masons who were members of the congregation. The area around the church and the Hardy home filled in quickly with Black neighbors. Benjamin Cash, Willis Clawson and Simpson Wiggins purchased lots in 1875 next to the Hardys. In 1880 North Converse Street also was home to David Montague, a 26-year-old railroad worker. Montague was one of at least four men in the neighborhood employed by the Atlanta & Richmond Air-Line Railroad, which passed through town between his home and Wofford College. Montague would go on to have a 32-year-career with city government, overseeing the construction of downtown's cobblestone and brick streets. He also provided lodging in his home to Black visitors traveling to Spartanburg.

Fifteen years after the war, North Converse Street was a neighborhood of single, young, working men and some families. Twenty-five-year-old James Hamilton told the census-taker in 1880 that he was a baker. Ralph Morgan, 27, was a carriage driver. Julius Haynes was a "huckster," a peddler of fruit and vegetables. Charles Edwards, 24, was a street cleaner. Most of the residents in this area were service workers, as opposed to the tradesmen—blacksmiths, brickmakers and carpenters—who settled Back of the College.

One block over on North Dean Street, Joseph Williams, 20, was a porter in a store. Willis Campbell, 23, worked in B.L. Potter's shoe shop on Church Street. James Jackson, 19, was a hotel waiter. This was the up-and-coming generation of Black Spartanburg residents in the 1880s. John P. Boyden, a 32-year-old porter in a store, would be the second Black man elected to Spartanburg Town Council as an alderman in 1883, succeeding the more elder Charles C. Bomar, who was the first. Boyden, who was born in North Carolina, lived on North Dean Street with his wife, Laura, a nurse. He became chairman of the Spartanburg County Republican Party and attended the 1888 national Republican convention in Chicago as a delegate. Boyden left Spartanburg in 1889 for a federal appointment in a printing office in Washington, where he died of a fever a year later at age 42.

Many of these young Black Spartans wanted their futures to be focused on the commerce taking place on Main Street, Church Street and Magnolia streets. But for the women, both there and Back of the College, there was very little opportunity. Most of them worked as domestic servants, seam-

Phyllis Goins with one of the white children she cared for.

stresses, cooks and laundresses. The rare 19th-century success was independent nurse Phyllis Goins, who moved into the neighborhood sometime by 1900. She and her husband, Robert, lived on nearby Keene Street with her mother, Winnie Pickenpack, who moved over from Liberty Street.

For many, the foundation and the magnet for the budding neighborhood was Silver Hill Methodist Church, which in its early days served not only as a place of worship, but as a school, a community center, a law office and a refuge. Spartanburg's northside became known as "Methodist-side," as opposed to the Southside, which was replete with Baptist churches and known as "Baptist-side." Silver Hill's first pastor was the extraordinary Rev. James Robert Rosemond, who was enticed to Spartanburg in 1870 from Greenville, where he had established a church also named Silver Hill Methodist three years earlier. Rosemond's name is on the deed for the Spartanburg church property, along with Tobe Hartwell, Hercules Huggins and four others. His early leadership made sure that Spartanburg's Silver Hill would be the spiritual and community cornerstone of the northside neigh-

The Rev. James R. Rosemond served Silver Hill Church from 1869 to 1874.

borhoods—a foundation built by people whose lives were not their own just a few years before.

Formerly enslaved in the households of Greenville aristocrats Waddy Thompson Jr. and Vardy McBee, Rosemond (1820-1902) was the most important leader in the 19th-century Black Methodist Church in South Carolina. Called "the little Negro Jim" as a boy in Greenville, Rosemond felt the call to preach early in his life, but his enslavers refused to grant him permission to seek ordination in the Methodist conference, although they did encourage his religious fervor. When Rosemond turned 16, he was able to apply for the "privilege to exhort," which he received and exercised as much as possible. In 1864 Rosemond launched his own ministry with all the duties and privileges of a "colored preacher," which included ministering to mixed audiences. Rosemond preached in Greenville County, mostly in houses, fields and groves, and once delivered a sermon in Anderson County to a mixed congregation of 300 people. The congregation was so impressed they offered to buy his freedom but could not raise all of the $800 McBee demanded. The war was nearing its end, and Rosemond had to await emancipation instead.

Rosemond's stint in Spartanburg (1869-1874) was an incredibly dangerous time for circuit-riding Black ministers—as well as anyone else of their race. The Ku Klux Klan was rampaging through the countryside. Rosemond reported to Methodist Church officials that it had been too dangerous during the entire winter of 1870-71 for him to visit the rural congregations of Spartanburg County in his circuit. A number of his people "were most brutally whipped," he reported. Just south of Spartanburg, in the Union County hamlet of Goshen Hill, a colleague of his, the Rev. Lewis Thompson, was accosted by 20 Ku-Kluxers on June 16, 1871. They tied him up, dragged him behind a horse, "mutilated him in a way that cannot be with propriety described; hung him, and threw his body in the Tyger River, leaving a notice forbidding anyone to bury him."

Rosemond survived that treacherous year, and in the summer of 1871 the U.S. Army cavalry arrived in the upcountry to curb the violence and keep the peace. Later, in his 60s, he married Spartanburg's Adaline Farrow—the widow of Lot Farrow, who died in 1885—and became the stepfather of educator Mary H. Wright, then an adult. By the time of his death, Rosemond was credited with establishing 50 Black churches across South Carolina. A monument to his life stands on Rutherford Road in Greenville and lists Spartanburg's Silver Hill as one of the many churches he served in the upcountry.

Silver Hill grew quickly in the era between 1895 and 1905 with the Revs. C.C. Scott and I.E. Lowery at the helm. Adroit fundraisers, they were able to raise money from the community to greatly expand the red-brick building. It featured Gothic lancet windows with colored glass, a belfry with a church bell that could be heard throughout the area, and a sanctuary that could seat as many as 800. Wide, stone steps led to a double-door entranceway, with a porch on the right-hand side. When Spartanburg's Opera House was torn down in 1907, Silver Hill purchased and repurposed much of the seating from the theater, which had hosted white audiences on West Main Street for 26 years. The church later was painted a cream color, and stood for at least six decades, when it was replaced with a new edifice in 1968.

Across the street from Silver Hill, the Hardy family anchored the neighborhood for more than three decades, raising their children and actively supporting their church. Lydia Hardy had a special role in early Spartan-

Silver Hill Methodist Church as it appeared in the late 1890s. This photograph was made just prior to a major expansion of the sanctuary.

burg history. For decades she had in her possession one of the town's most important and iconic artifacts—a cowbell worn by a cow that, according to tradition, helped lay out the property lines for the first lots to surround Spartanburg's courthouse and public square. Prior to emancipation, Lydia Hardy had been enslaved to the family of Richard Thomson (1771-1844), an enormously wealthy man who owned much of what is now recognized as downtown Spartanburg. Thomson—and his cow—apparently somehow helped survey the earliest Morgan Square in 1809, creating a map that showed 24 lots for development. Lydia Hardy, born in 1835, came into the Thomson household at some point, likely as an enslaved child. She was given the bell, either by Thomson or one of his heirs. When she died at her home on North Converse Street about 1910, the bell passed to a white woman who lived nearby, Mary Elizabeth Fleming Trimmier. Mrs. Trimmier displayed the bell at the Spartanburg County Fair in 1913 but died eight years later. Her surviving husband moved to North Carolina. When the bell passed from Lydia Hardy's hands, it ultimately disappeared.

So did the Hardy family homestead. It was seized for back debt and sold at auction at the Spartanburg courthouse in May 1911. The acreage the Hardys occupied for 35 years was subdivided into 14 lots for the construction of tiny, wooden rental houses.

THE YEARS 1880 TO 1929 are sometimes called Spartanburg's "Golden Period." The newly incorporated city became the economic and cultural center of the county. Cotton production and sharecropping increasingly turned the county's economic engine away from rural planters and toward merchants and entrepreneurs who were living in the city of Spartanburg. Cotton mills began going up all over the county, including one near the front entrance of Wofford College and another on the campus's back side. Freedpeople and white laborers sought better paying jobs in town if they could extricate themselves from onerous crop liens and labor contracts that tied them to farms. Cotton mills in Spartanburg, however, did not hire Black laborers, and in 1915, state law officially blocked Black and white textile operatives from working beside each other on the manufacturing floors. With the success of the textile economy, the white elite saw their bank accounts grow and enjoyed many of the new comforts and cultural attractions Spartanburg city life provided. Converse College hosted musical and theater productions, including the inaugural South Atlantic States Music Festival in 1895, Wofford became increasingly more prominent to the state's professional affairs as graduates entered medicine, law and business, and the city's hotels and meeting spaces filled with entrepreneurs, piedmont adventurers and festival attendees.

Black Spartanburg experienced growth as well. The southside and northside neighborhoods expanded rapidly. On the southside, more than 125 homes emerged by 1896 around South Liberty Street, housing several hundred people. Multiple streets branched from South Liberty Street, including Cudd Street, Young Street, Cemetery Street and East Valley, followed by Carrier, Rigby and East Hampton. Founders Joseph and Priscilla Young encouraged growth, entrepreneurship and home ownership in the

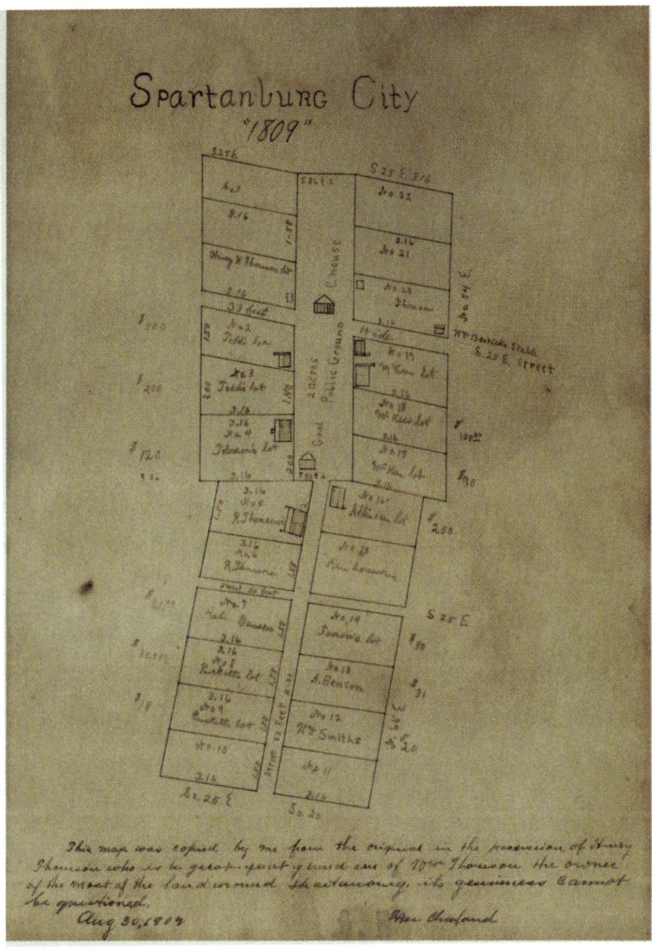

Lydia Hardy was enslaved to the Thomson family, which once owned the Morgan Square area. According to lore, she was given a cowbell from a cow that assisted in the original survey.

area. Black-owned businesses opened regularly, with particular growth in the early part of the 20th century on or near South Liberty Street, and later on Short Wofford Street, just off Morgan Square. Another small Black neighborhood began taking shape just north of the front entrance of Wofford College, on Vernon, Aden, Fulton and Howard streets.

Black population swelled in the North Dean Street area and Back of the College, as people trickled in from the countryside. By 1912 more than 250 homes stood there, with a population of perhaps 1,000. Life in town for Black people was better than life in the country. So-called "Black Code" laws made it easy for county law enforcement officers to arrest Black laborers who walked out on their tenant-farming contracts with white farmers. Once convicted and imprisoned, Black laborers could be leased out for work

Nathaniel, Seawright, and Clyde Campbell of Northview Street about 1930. They were raised by their sister, Charlie Mae Campbell, after the death of their mother.

at other sites. County and municipal courts and sheriff's offices would see their budgets increase every time they secured another person whose labor could be leased. The convict leasing system placed people into brutal conditions regardless of where they came from. Those fortunate enough not to be conscripted into forced labor saw their basic civil rights erode.

For a period beginning in 1868, Black residents of Spartanburg could vote, and 254 Black men in the town of Spartanburg registered that year. Among them: Tobe Hartwell, Richard Rivers, Thornton Williams, Jack Thompson, Frank and Monroe Burnett, Lot Farrow, Hercules Huggins, George Hardy, Squire Mintz, Paul Simmons, Abram Smalls, Joseph Young Sr. and Thomas Pickenpack. But by 1895, their vote officially was taken away as part of Gov. Ben "Pitchfork" Tillman's new constitution—and most likely earlier, as campaigns of white terror kept Black citizens from the polls in South Carolina for fear of being hurt or killed. News from Wilmington, North Carolina, was chilling. In 1898 a mob of 1,500 heavily armed white people looted and destroyed Wilmington's Black business district in a fury over election results, killing as many as 300 people.

Those who could move to the growing city of Spartanburg, from such farming-intensive places as Laurens, Woodruff and Union, did. Spartanburg's post-war recovery and rapid growth from cotton production and textile manufacturing required equally rapid carpentry and construction

LEFT: *This is believed to be Frances Campbell (1885-1924), mother of educator Charlie Mae Campbell. This photo dates to about 1905.*
RIGHT: *Isaac Miller, resident of Northview Street. He was employed by Beaumont Mills and was father to neighborhood advocate Harold Miller.*

efforts to sustain it, which opened doors for some Black artisans. White entrepreneurs needed good, reliable workers and sometimes were willing to look past race to move their projects along. Thomas M. Bomar (1861-1905) became one of the pre-eminent brick masons of the era, employing teams of Black laborers to build Pacolet Mills in 1883 and Spartan Mills in 1890. A Charlotte newspaper in 1898 noted that "one of the biggest contractors in all the southland is a colored man, Thomas M. Bomar," adding, "a building that costs no more than $10,000 or $20,000 he will rarely accept, because he cannot put his hands to work on an edifice so small."

An older relative, Charles C. Bomar (1847-1912), had multiple ventures that catapulted him into the upper class of Black Spartanburg, where he became the first Black man elected as alderman to the town council in 1879.

T. M. BOMAR,
CONTRACTOR OF
BRICK WORK,
Cotton Mills a Specialty.
All work intrusted to me will receive prompt and careful attention.
A share of your patronage solicited.
20 N. CHURCH STREET, SPARTANBURG, S. C.

Among the local mills Bomar built were Spartan, Arkwright, Pacolet, Union, and Tucapau as well as Columbia's Richland and Granby mills and Enterprise in Orangeburg.

He founded the first Black-owned grocery store on Church Street in the mid-1880s, opened the first Black mortuary, and erected two brick stores at the corner of South Liberty and Cemetery streets in 1910. Bomar's first home was located near the modern-day corner of South Church and Broad Streets. When he died at Johns Hopkins Hospital in 1912, the local newspaper estimated his assets at $25,000, an extraordinary amount for a Black man in a small Southern town at that time. Thomas Bomar, who died young, served as Spartanburg's fourth Black alderman in 1889. The owner of 23 acres near downtown, Thomas Bomar built and lived in a home at 595 Howard Street, the present-day site of the John W. Woodward Funeral Home.

Black carpenters and brick masons also were hired by Black landowners to help build their homes, and the neighborhoods developed into centers of mutual care and support that nurtured and stimulated professionals. One of the most successful early Black carpentry contractors was Henry Lewis. Born into slavery about 1835, Lewis was one of the first residents of North Dean Street in the 1870s. When he died in 1913 at the age of 75, *The Carolina Spartan* noted that "his real estate is quite valuable, being worth $5,000 to $6,000." During his life, Lewis accumulated a 40-acre farm on Howard Gap Road, property on Evins Street near Wofford College, and his large landholdings on North Dean Street were subdivided into lots for eight family members when he died. An early street in the North Dean neighborhood was named after him: Lewis Street.

LOCAL.

Municipal Election.

The election for Town Council came off, last Monday. The bar-rooms were all closed consequently there were very few intoxicated men seen on the streets. The so called Bolters' ticket was elected with the exception of J. A. Henneman. S. T. Poineer from the Regular Ticket was elected in his stead. The following is a result of the election, the first six Wardens being elected. Those marked with a star are Republicans, and one of them is a colored man.

INTENDANT:

Joseph Walker, 377; W. K. Blake, 274;

WARDENS:

Dr. Joseph Hill, 394; F. M. Trimmier, 363; Dr. Jesse F. Cleaveland, 369; W. L. Parker, 370; S. T. Poineer, * 334; C. C. Bomar, * 315.

Charles Thomson, 294; R. L. Bowden,

TOP: *The first Black man elected to Spartanburg Town Council was Charles C. Bomar in 1879. This is the* Carolina Spartan *announcement.*

BOTTOM: *A sketch of Charles Caesar Bomar from the December 7, 1889, edition of* The Indianapolis Freeman.

Another successful early builder was Jesse Carter (1874-1928), who lived at 244 North Dean Street, along with his wife, Louisa, and young daughters. In 1911 Carter was hired by Nicholas S. Trakas as contractor for the first Greek Orthodox Church in Spartanburg. With the confidence of one of Spartanburg's first immigrant communities, Carter built the tiny church serving 50 Upstate Greeks in Trakas's backyard on Pierpont Avenue on the northside. Jesse and Louisa Carter raised a family of schoolteachers, including the influential Ellen C. Watson, a Columbia University graduate and longtime guidance counselor at Carver and Spartanburg high schools.

Black laborers and service workers supported Black merchants, blacksmiths and grocery owners. Industrial education for freedpeople was encouraged to help produce a larger pool of skilled workers to fuel the growth. The Colored Industrial Training School opened around 1891 on the Southside—near the original site of Mary H. Wright Elementary School—to funnel more young Black people into trades. Between realizing economic and educational opportunities as well as pursuing community-building and religious life activities, Black people in Spartanburg improved their situation in many ways.

Health care emerged as an important occupation. Phyllis Goins, daughter of Thomas and Winnie Pickenpack, stepped into the role of midwife and nurse for the Black community as early as the 1880s. A resident of Keene Street and a congregant at nearby Silver Hill, Goins tended to both Black and white babies and mothers. At her death in 1945, an appreciative newspaper columnist estimated that Goins had tended 400 babies in her lifetime, including such white notables as textile executive Victor Montgomery Jr. and state Sen. Howard McCravy. "She knew when to minister and when to call the doctor," columnist Mary Phifer wrote. Goins' remarkable career helped set the conditions for Dr. W.C. Rhodes, Spartanburg's first Black physician, to open his practice at the age of 30 on the Southside in 1895 and to work alongside Dr. G.W. Harry, who began the first statewide Black physicians organization. Ptolemy C. White opened a pharmacy on Kennedy Street in 1896, and in 1903 the city got its first Black dentist—indeed, the state did—in Dr. George K. Adams, originally from Laurens County. Later, Dr. T.K. Gregg, a much-respected physician and community leader, moved into a large house on North Dean Street where he lived until his death in 1939.

The early crown jewel of the northside was the John-Nina Hospital, which opened in 1913 on North Dean Street and was the only licensed Black hospital of the era. Led by the indefatigable Nina Littlejohn, the

The state's first Black dentist, Dr. George K. Adams, lived in the North Dean Street neighborhood and served patients from his practice on North Church.

facility had eight patient rooms, accommodating two patients each, two wards, an operating room and a kitchen. In its early days it was served by Spartanburg's two Black physicians, Dr. H.C. Hardy and Dr. J.W. Sexton, and a staff of nurses. But it was Nina Littlejohn (1879-1963)—its determined, focused and unstoppable superintendent—who was responsible for the hospital's success. Born near Gaffney, she married Worth Littlejohn, a Black barber serving the white trade from a shop at 107 Magnolia Street, in 1895. They had one daughter who moved away to Texas, at which point Nina Littlejohn plunged into her life's work. Seeing the need for medical service on the north side of town, she and Worth built a two-story hospital next to their home. Prior to its opening, most Black hospital patients had been shunted into a small basement in the City Hospital, located just off Main Street in what is now known as the Georgia Cleveland Home or were treated at the financially struggling People's Hospital on South Liberty Street.

In August 1920 the John-Nina Hospital was nearly destroyed by a highly publicized fire in a case later determined to be arson caused by two former employees. The 12 patients in the hospital were removed to the Littlejohns' home. Nina and Worth made sure they were cared for continuously through-

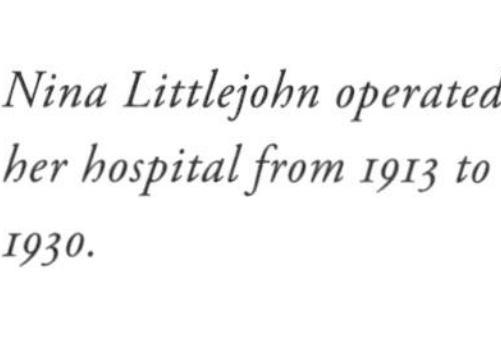

Nina Littlejohn operated her hospital from 1913 to 1930.

out the ordeal while their hospital was repaired. In 1923, after repeated appeals from the Littlejohns and the larger Black medical community, the hospital was merged into the government-run county hospital system, though Nina remained owner and director and continued to serve patients through its closing in 1930. That year, the "negro wing" of the Spartanburg General Hospital opened, thanks to a $40,000 gift from the Julius Rosenwald Foundation. Nina Littlejohn's home later became home to Callaham-Hicks Funeral Home but was ravaged by fire in 2008. A mostly new building still houses the Black-owned funeral home on the site. The John-Nina Hospital and its owners are remembered by the presence of a tiny street on the east side of Barnet Park called Littlejohn Circle.

JUST AFTER THE TURN OF THE CENTURY, the expansion of Spartanburg's Black community drew the interest of a white developer. John W. Alexander moved to town in 1898 and began eyeing a 12-acre estate that bordered North Dean Street and straddled what later became North-

SPARTANBURG COUNTY COLORED HOSPITAL

—and—

NURSES' TRAINING SCHOOL

Young women desiring to take nurse-training may enter at any time. Patients may be accommodated as they wish — Private, Semi-Private or Ward. For further information, apply to—

Mrs. Nina E. Littlejohn, Superintendent, Phone 261

or Miss Arrie Bell Smith, Head Nurse, Phone 469

226 N. Dean Street Spartanburg, S. C.

TOP: *The John-Nina Hospital ultimately became the M.S. Callaham Funeral Home in 1933.*

MIDDLE: *Littlejohn also trained nurses at her hospital.*

BOTTOM: *After much controversy about its location, the so-called Negro Wing of the General Hospital opened in 1930.*

view Street. Originally from Charlotte, and more recently of St. Louis and Texas, Alexander convinced a prominent female philanthropist in Spartanburg, 81-year-old Eliza "Lizzie" Attleton Judd, to buy the property.

Lizzie Judd, the childless widow of a leading white merchant and bank president, was left with significant stockholdings after her husband's death. And she was a Yankee, hailing from Springfield, Massachusetts. Together in 1908 she and Alexander created a new subdivision with 52 lots "for colored people exclusively." They called it Chasander Hill—"Chas" for the popular Southern Railway conductor Capt. Eugene "Boney" Chase, and "ander" for its male developer. An ad in the Sunday *Herald* announced the names of nine Black citizens who already had purchased lots. Among the first owners were: the Rev. James W. Eichelberger, owner of a grocery store; Will Glen, a head waiter at a downtown hotel; Francis S. Burnett, a young blacksmithing business owner; Albert Brown, a laborer at Spartan Grain Mill; Oscar Clark, a road worker; and C.B. Morrison, a railroad porter. Another early buyer was Dr. George K. Adams (1881-1954), who practiced dentistry in the city for many years and was active in Republican politics locally and statewide. Adams lived on Chasander Street for many years with his wife, Maggie, and other family members.

The name of the development, Chasander Hill, did not stick. Two years later, there were still 23 lots, and they were sold at auction in 1910 for $5 down and $10 a month to buyers of any race. The slow pace of sales was an indicator of the general economic plight of Spartanburg's Black citizenry, struggling through the marks of slavery and the impact of Jim Crow policies imposed by the town's whites.

Meanwhile, just a few blocks away from Chasander Hill, a massive new subdivision that catered to the upper class of Spartanburg was under construction. "A big force of laborers and 25 mules" began grading 80-foot-wide avenues in an area that would forever be known as Converse Heights. There were granolithic sidewalks, water lines, sewer lines and shade trees planted in front of each lot. A full-page newspaper ad made the restrictions clear—one race of people were not welcome: "Property not to be sold, rented or otherwise disposed of to negroes."

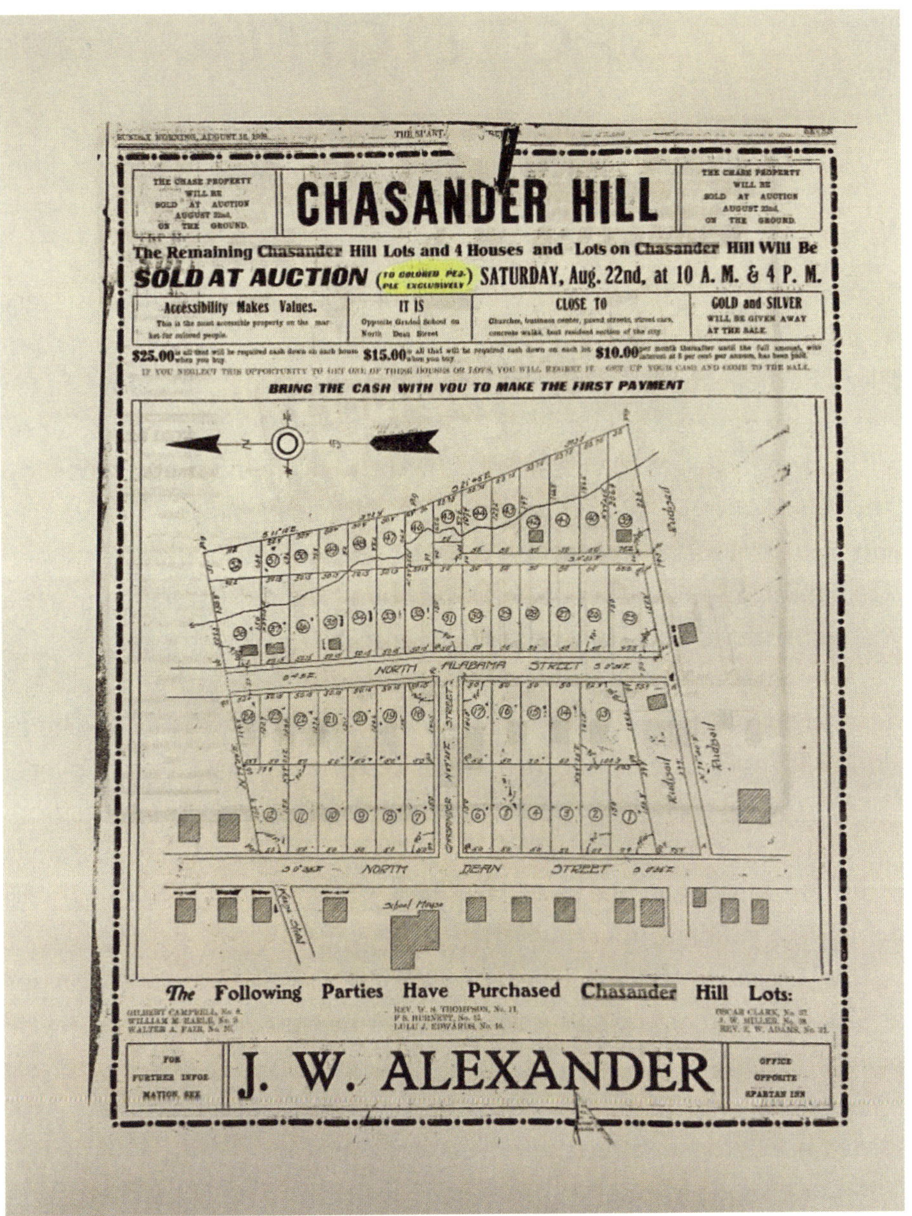

The original ad for the Chasander Hill development in 1908. Lots were sold "to colored people exclusively."

SPOTLIGHT

MARY H. WRIGHT'S EARLY YEARS

Spartanburg's most legendary Black educator was born into slavery Aug. 11, 1862, at a place called Kirby Hill, roughly the location of Spartanburg's Bethel United Methodist Church, at the corner of South Church and Henry streets. As a toddler, Mary Honor Farrow likely lived in one of the two primitive slave cabins behind the home of prosperous local merchant James H. Wilson and his wife, Alta Kirby Wilson. Mary's parents were Lot Farrow, a native of South Carolina born about 1825, and Adaline Farrow, born about 1840. Mary had an older sister, Ellen, and a younger sister, Clara. The family attended Silver Hill Methodist Church.

Five years after the end of the Civil War, Mary's father purchased for $130 a small piece of property from white attorney William Choice along Magnolia Street, not far from the entrance to Wofford College. Lot Farrow, who made his early living selling fruits and vegetables from a cart and later ran a livery stable near Morgan Square, moved his family there. He was one of the first Black men of the post-war era to own his own home in Spartanburg.

By her 10th birthday in 1872, Mary was leading Sunday school classes at Silver Hill, according to family lore. She earned degrees at Asheville Normal School, Scotia Seminary and Claflin College. During her formal schooling, she continued to teach at Silver Hill Church when she returned home for summer and holiday breaks.

In her late teen years a man named Foster offered Mary the opportunity to teach at a new school in Inman. Her father was dubious. "Why, Mary, honey, you'd be scared to death away from home," she recalled him saying. "You'd be coming home the next day." Undeterred, she found a boarding house north of town in 1879 and rode an ox cart to the school site each day. She taught under a brush arbor while workers cut pines to build a 12-by-14-foot schoolhouse, which became known as the Ben Bomar School. At the Inman school she received just $30 a year for her labor, "and sometimes she didn't get anything," recalled her granddaughter Farrow Bell Foster in a 1991 interview. Lot Farrow died just six years after Mary Farrow began work, when she was in her early 20s. ***The Carolina Spartan*** called him "the most industrious colored citizen we had."

Mary married William Corbert Wright. Together they had 10 children, including a set of twins. Over the course of her lifetime, she would teach more than 3,200 Black children at schools across Spartanburg County. Those schools included a rustic one at Factory Hill, Stephens Grove, Carrier Street and Highland School. Sixty years into her teaching career, in 1940, she was making less than $15 a week. She died Aug. 25, 1946.

TOP: *Mary H. Wright, right, with sisters Clara, left, and Ellen*

BOTTOM LEFT: *Their mother, Adaline Farrow*

BOTTOM RIGHT: *Mary H. Wright in her later years*

SPOTLIGHT

THE NORTHSIDE'S FIRST BLACK CHURCH

While Silver Hill Methodist is recognized as the first substantial Black church built on the northside of Spartanburg, it may not have been the first Black church organized there. Now-defunct Saint John AME Zion Church was meeting as early as 1866, according to records collected during the Great Depression by the federal Works Progress Administration.

Records are sketchy about its early days. Members initially may have met in a house on Evins Street. After that, they met in "a frame building erected on North Church Street," according to the WPA's Survey of State and Local Historical Records conducted in 1938. That church "blew down, date unknown," according to the report. A lot was purchased on Charles Street (now known as East Daniel Morgan Avenue) and a second frame church was built about 1900. "Used until 1918 when it also blew down." The record collector wrote: "Owing to lack of records unable to determine just who organized this church, but according to the oldest living member the first trustees were J.R. Heath, W.M. Ray, A.M. Shelton, Geo. Coleman, Oscar Clark, Will Dorrah, Jno. Alexander, Mose Durham, Dave Johnson and M.H. Holland." The church's first settled clergyman was the Rev. N.B. Stelley, who served from 1900 to 1901.

At the time of the survey, the church had split into two, with most members moving to the rechristened Metropolitan AME Zion Church built in 1921 on North Dean Street, just across from the Dean Street School. Other members stayed behind at the smaller Saint John AME Zion, which appears to have met into the late 1930s, in its latter days in a building on East Cleveland Street.

Metropolitan AME Zion was a flourishing church in the 1930s with 300 members, led by the Rev. A.H. Hatwood, a resident of Chasander

Street. The church's edifice during this era was a rectangular brick structure with a square bell tower, pointed arch windows with opaque glass, and seating for up to 400. Over the door was the word WELCOME.

In the 1940s and 1950s its pastor was H.C. Young, who was called "the community walking preacher." He also sometimes used his son's bicycle for transportation. Active in civil rights issues as co-founder of the Peoples Citizens Committee, Young led the church when its mortgage was burned in a 1945 celebration, and when new pews and an organ were installed. Charlie Mae Campbell, former principal at Mary H. Wright, served as organist there for 40 years until her death at age 93 in 2002. A new church was built in 1981 and still stands on North Dean Street. Its congregation has dwindled to a tiny handful of regular attendees.

The story of Metropolitan AME Church on North Dean Street dates back to 1866. This photo was taken shortly after the current church opened in the 1980s.

Children from Back of the College, sometime in the early 20th century. Wilma Barnhardt was their school teacher. Image courtesy of Concordia Historical Institute, Saint Louis, Missouri.

THREE

BIRTH OF BACK OF THE COLLEGE

THE NEIGHBORHOOD THAT ROSE behind Wofford College owes much of its existence to two men keenly interested in social justice—one white and one Black—who ensured that landless Black families in Spartanburg had a place to build homes after emancipation and the end of the Civil War.

The first of these was a quixotic New York-born white educator named the Rev. Anson Cummings, who arrived in Spartanburg in April 1866 as a one-time slaveowner and supporter of the Confederacy and departed five years later as a Radical Republican newspaperman focused on exposing the Ku Klux Klan and protecting the lives of the community's Black citizens. Before leaving town for the city of Columbia in 1873—ultimately to become the leader of the University of South Carolina—he bought property and laid out a small subdivision behind Wofford College. It is his name that adorns the historic school building that educated Black children for four decades and is still standing behind the college.

The second was a brilliant Black pastor named Cornelius Chapman Scott, who, long after his death, was compared to the Rev. Martin Luther King Jr. A former student of Cummings's, Scott was a subsequent developer in the new neighborhood, offering an even larger number of lots for sale. While Scott, too, lived in Spartanburg only a short time, his imprint on the local Black community lasted more than a century. Together, this unlikely tag-team helped to create a safe and stable place on the northside for Black working people to live and raise their children in an often dangerous city.

This sketch of Anson Cummings appeared in the 1879 book, History of Allegany County, New York.

This story begins in upstate New York in 1815, when Anson Watson Cummings was born to white Canadian parents. He attended the prestigious Wesleyan University in Connecticut, receiving degrees in law and divinity. His road to Spartanburg took him to cities in New York, Illinois and east Tennessee, where he served as a teacher of mathematics, clergyman and president of small colleges. In 1855 he was hired by a fledgling Methodist-run college for women in Asheville, North Carolina, called the Holston Conference Female College. That college closed during the Civil War—as did many in the South—so Cummings tried his hand as a newspaperman, serving as associate editor of *the Asheville News.*

Meanwhile, down in Spartanburg, local businessmen began looking for a new president for the Spartanburg Female College. This small college, which opened in 1855 on College Street, served the daughters of planters and aristocrats across South Carolina. It too had shuttered during the war.

The Spartanburg Female College, which hired Anson Cummings in the 1860s, was located behind modern-day VCOM Medical School.

The board of trustees, most of whom had been enslavers, reached out to 51-year-old Anson Cummings. He took the job and moved to Spartanburg along with his wife, Isabella, and six children.

But Cummings's noteworthy past obscured a more complicated person. He was once described by a regional Methodist publication as a man who "loved money too well." And a church committee in Buncombe County found him guilty in 1866 of "an attempt to defraud the trustees of Holston Conference Female College by erasing from one of their account books entries of money received from him at sundry times to the amount of several hundred dollars." As punishment he was suspended from the Methodist Episcopal ministry for 12 months. Nevertheless, the Spartanburg Female College trustees deemed Cummings "a great success" at Holston and welcomed him enthusiastically.

For two years, Cummings presided over a college where young white women took classes in such subjects as Latin and moral philosophy—as the men did at nearby Wofford—but they also received training in music, embroidery and painting. Spartanburg Female College was not financially sustainable, and in 1868, it went into bankruptcy, ultimately transitioning into an orphanage, then a prep school for Wofford. Cummings, a lifelong educator, was out of a job again. Despite that, he elected to stay in Spartanburg, purchasing a large house that year at the corner of Henry and Spring streets. He picked up work as a property assessor and tax collector for the local Spartanburg government.

When the 1868 election rolled around in November, Cummings voted straight-ticket Democrat, choosing a New York-born Democratic candidate over Republican President Ulysses S. Grant. He had been an enslaver himself before coming to Spartanburg: the 1860 Buncombe County census indicates he had two Black women and five Black children in bondage. But within a few years of coming to Spartanburg, he underwent a transformation, turning into one of the most vocal white advocates in the town for the safety and well-being of Black families—so much so that his zealous empathy for Spartanburg's newly freed Black citizens would sometimes cross over into a know-it-all, white paternalism that put him at odds with the people he sought to help.

As the next election of 1870 dawned, Cummings witnessed the rise of the Ku Klux Klan and was horrified. From various people in town, he heard tales of beatings, whippings and even murder of Black citizens in the countryside. Masked riders were harassing Black citizens to keep them away from the voting booth and bringing terror to such communities as Glenn Springs, Pacolet, Woodruff, Cross Anchor and the area known as Limestone. Prominent Black members of the Republican Party were targeted for violence. That winter, many Black men were sleeping in the forests and fields to avoid being found. Anthony Johnson, Spartanburg's first Black magistrate, was murdered near Pacolet while his mother watched in horror.

Cummings joined a weekly newspaper in Spartanburg called the *Carolina New Era*, one of the few Republican-leaning newspapers in South Carolina, serving as its business manager and associate editor. This publication was founded by Dr. Javan Bryant, a Spartanburg educator and Reconstruction-era legislator. It folded in fall 1874, and no issues of the newspaper seem to have survived. But a publication that supported the Reconstruction-era "radical" Republican government in South Carolina hardly would have been welcomed in the white-majority town of Spartanburg.

By this time, Cummings had become interested in local land speculation, picking up various large tracts outside the village. In the 1870 census, he estimated that his personal property and the value of his real estate in St. Louis, North Carolina, Wisconsin, Iowa, Illinois, Asheville and Spartanburg topped $34,000, a figure that meant his holdings were greater than that of Glendale Mill owners Edgar Converse and Albert Twichell combined. On Feb. 6, 1871, he attended an auction and sheriff's land sale for a key tract of land north of downtown. As "the last and highest bidder" he purchased a 99-acre parcel for $1,089 located behind Wofford College and the Evins-Bivings estate on North Church Street. This property had gone on the market when John B. Cleveland died without a will. The tract was larger by 10 acres than the entire Wofford campus in 1870. Little did anyone know—perhaps not even Cummings himself—that he was setting the stage for the first Black subdivision in Spartanburg County.

But first, Cummings was intent on bringing the Ku-Klux horror around him to a national audience. He and a white associate, county treasurer Peter Quinn Camp, began compiling a list of names of Black people who had been injured or killed by Klansmen and other whites. They wrote letters to Republican South Carolina Gov. Robert Scott and to Spartanburg's Republican congressman, Alexander S. Wallace, recounting the terrorism. In July 1871 an investigating committee of three U.S. congressmen came to Spartanburg to take testimony from Blacks and whites, and rich and poor, about the violence occurring in the county. Thirty-six Black citizens, most of them from the countryside, gathered at the post office, awaiting their turn to tell their stories. Cummings made sure he was on the docket to testify too. He brought with him a list of 227 victimized Black people, most of them in the north and south of the county. Three names on his list were murder victims. The Congressional panel was incredulous, grilling him repeatedly about his methods of compiling the list. Cummings answered that he had begun making the list ten months earlier and had added names up until the very day of his testimony.

"I have been desirous to secure safety to the people of this county—these poor people I have found so distressed and ruined," Cummings told the panel, "and I made the list with the view and with no other object than to seek protections for them."

Wofford College's Main Building in 1854, the year its professors brought enslaved people to the new campus.

Under questioning, he disclosed that he was a member of the Loyal League, a mostly Black organization with a chapter in Spartanburg. Members of the League took an oath to support the Republican-led national and state governments, but Cummings was hesitant to reveal anything else about the group, as its policy was to keep its actions secret. He related how he had turned away from his earlier views as the Klan began to take hold. "I did not believe in the existence of any such people until last October or November," he said of the Klan. "I discarded it. I believed it to be a hoax, a phantom." Before he left the stand he said with regret: "The colored people are despised because they are colored, and strangely blamed for being free. They are blamed for it in a rather mysterious way."

In an account of his testimony, *The State* newspaper later wrote that Cummings "had degraded his calling by engaging in the work of a spy." Yet Cummings was risking his life by testifying. He told the panel that he slept away from his house some nights when he perceived threats from local residents.

Sometime after the federal inquiry, Cummings began to get a vision for what to do with his property behind Wofford. Few white people in Spartanburg—and across the South, for that matter—were interested in selling land to freedmen. The 1870 census shows a tiny handful of Black people in the village of Spartanburg owning real estate. After the war, the State Legislature had created the South Carolina Land Commission as a kind of middleman to give away tracts of land to Black families—land that previously had been sold to the agency by destitute post-war white families who declined to sell directly to Black people. But the commission was not particularly active in the Upstate. Cummings began drawing out a subdivision on his land behind Wofford College. The neighborhood is referred to in deeds from the 1870s as "the Cummings addition to the town of Spartanburg." He named the first street after himself—Cummings Street—and he named a second street after his wife, Belle Street.

He also secured an $800 contract with the U.S. government to open a school for freedmen. Not realizing that the Air-Line Railroad would need the property for its tracks north of the public square, he soon had to abandon the project. In seeking a financial settlement from the railroad, Cummings managed to get into a major tussle with the school's Black trustees, who resented his heavy hand. The trustees wanted self-determination; the wealthy, well-educated Cummings sought a better financial arrangement and pushed for control.

Despite Black leaders rejecting his attempts to oversee them, Cummings decided to ramp up his publicity campaign against the Ku Kluxers who were terrorizing the countryside with their midnight raids. In February 1872 Cummings traveled to New England for a lecture tour about the outrages of the terrorist organization. At a speech in Boston, he charged attendees 25 cents, which he said would be donated to a building campaign for a Methodist meetinghouse in Spartanburg. He even brought a black Klan robe and mask, donned by an assistant, to illustrate what the raiders looked like. *The Daily Phoenix*, a newspaper in Columbia, caught wind of his visit and ridiculed his reported contention that there were 2,810 Klansmen in Spartanburg County. The newspaper accused him of sensationalism and "adding fuel to minds already inflamed to the highest pitch against us."

By this time, Cummings was likely a pariah in white Spartanburg. He had sold off half his land behind the college to a colleague, the Rev. True Whittier, a fellow Methodist minister originally from Maine who was living in Greenville. Whittier then sold it to the Simpson Bobo family, which had close Wofford ties. Eventually, Bobo's grandson and other heirs also would sell lots to Black families and white landlords in the Twitty, Jones and Evins street area, greatly expanding the neighborhood.

Three months after his trip to Boston, Cummings received a job offer to be chair of the mathematics and engineering department at the University of South Carolina, which in 1873 became the only integrated university in the South. Faculty members opposed to integration had been fired or left, creating positions for those willing to work in an integrated setting. White enrollment at the university dropped precipitously when South Carolina's Reconstruction-era Legislature had opened the doors to Black men. Down to fewer than 100 students, the college promoted him in 1875 to be chairman of the faculty, its de facto president. But by 1877 the tide had quickly turned against the Republicans in South Carolina, and Reconstruction was over. With four years' service under his belt, Cummings left his position, moved to a small town in New York, never to live in the South again. He purchased the Riverside Seminary in Wellsville, New York, served as principal there for many years and wrote a deeply researched 432-page book titled *The Early Schools of Methodism*. A son, Edward, stayed behind in Spartanburg, married a woman from the Trimmier family, and died relatively young.

Relocating to New York did not mean the end of Anson Cummings's vision of a Black neighborhood in Spartanburg, however. Stories handed down by residents of Back of the College indicate that Cummings may have donated land to some Black families. That cannot be verified by property transaction records. What does show up in records is a series of sales of one-acre lots along Cummings and Belle streets to Black men and women of Spartanburg during a 25-year period.

On Jan. 4, 1875, brick mason George Mason, husband of Harriet and father of two sons, became the first buyer. He paid $70 for a one-acre lot on

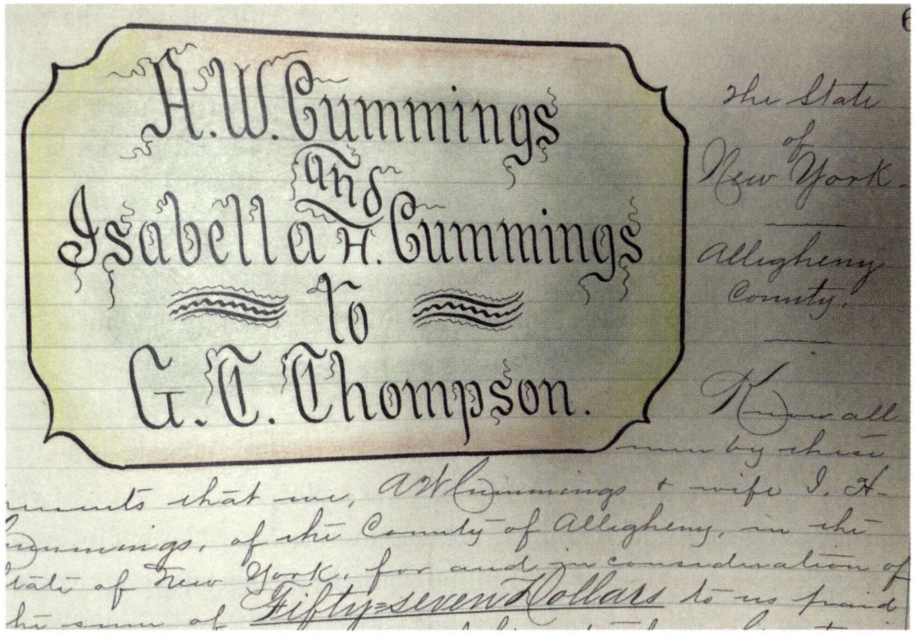
A.W. Cummings
and
Isabella H. Cummings
To
G.T. Thompson.

The State
of
New York.
Allegheny
County.

Know all
men by these
...nts that we, A.W. Cummings & wife I. H.
...mmings, of the County of Allegheny, in the
...tate of New York, for and in consideration of
...he sum of Fifty-seven Dollars to us paid

The deed from the Cummings family to G.T. Thompson for a lot behind the college.

the corner of Cleveland and Cummings streets, a spot not far from where Wofford College's Sandor Teszler Library now stands. The deed refers to the property as Lot 2. Ten days later, Cummings sold a half-acre lot, Lot 1, to Harriet Black for $30. This lot is described as being next to Dinah Harvey's lot, of which there is no sales record.

On Dec. 7, 1876, Cummings sold another one-acre lot to 27-year-old Henry Jones, a truckman at the Air-Line depot and father of four children. This deed mentions the adjacent Lot 3, owned by Hercules Huggins, a 47-year-old blacksmith originally from Virginia, married to Minda and father of eight children. There is no sales record of his purchase. Other lots went to James Brown, an 80-year-old Black farmer and grocery worker, and to Lewis J. Thompson, son of Silver Hill founder Jack Thompson. Other buyers over the next several years include George W. Nichols, Andrew Moore, G.T. Thompson and Thomas Thomson.

Then in 1890 Cummings sold the bulk of his remaining land holdings behind the college—37.5 acres—for $1,200 to someone he had known for 17 years: the dynamic orator and beloved Black pastor Rev. Cornelius C.

Scott, who then was serving Spartanburg's Silver Hill Church. The two had overlapped as teacher and student at South Carolina College all four years (1873-1877) and apparently had not lost touch. With Cummings in his twilight years some 700 miles away in New York, the work of building Back of the College could continue with Scott now at the helm.

CORNELIUS CHAPMAN SCOTT was born in September 1855 on James Island near Charleston at a time when almost all Black people in South Carolina were held in slavery, yet his parents were free persons of color. His artist-father, Tobias Scott, was a maker of fancy fans crafted from peacock feathers and sold to aristocrats. His mother, Christiana, kept house. Known as C.C., the young man—one of 11 children in his family—was educated in the Freedmen's Bureau Schools and the Avery Normal Institute in Charleston, then studied at Claflin College in Orangeburg and the college preparatory department of Howard University, the historically Black college in Washington, D.C. In January 1874 Scott chose to continue his education in his home state of South Carolina, enrolling at the state college in the waning years of Reconstruction when the college was predominantly Black and very small. Ten professors were on faculty that year, and one of them—Anson Cummings—had just arrived from Spartanburg, where he had fought for Black causes.

With four years to get to know each other, there likely was plenty of wisdom exchanged between Cummings and Scott. Two of Cummings's sons were among Scott's white classmates at the university. In a newspaper column late in his life, Scott called his former professor "painstakingly exact, thorough, evidently a born mathematician." The two men also shared a deep commitment to the temperance movement, each joining various local organizations of the Order of Good Templars throughout their lives. Scott's biography in the 1919 *History of the American Negro* book notes that he was a "lifelong teetotaler."

Scott graduated from the University of South Carolina with a bachelor of arts degree in 1877, the last year that Black students were allowed to attend the institution. He studied mathematics, natural history, rhetoric, modern languages, chemistry, geology, history, political science and economics. His diploma ironically bore the signature of Gov. Wade Hampton,

The Rev. C.C. Scott, from History of the American Negro, South Carolina Edition, *1919*

a former Confederate general and notorious politician who had been one of the largest enslavers in South Carolina. It was Hampton who brought white rule back to South Carolina when he was elected governor in 1876. Various accounts of Scott's life reference both bitterness and humor he felt seeing Hampton's name on his diploma.

After graduation from college, Scott moved to Greenville and for 10 years served as a principal of Black schools there. In 1886 he was called to the ministry. He joined the South Carolina Conference of the Methodist Episcopal Church and began his career as a pastor, moving from one church to another as was the practice of the denomination. One of his early stops was Spartanburg in the late 1880s, where he took on the leadership of Silver Hill Methodist Church for an unusually long five-year stretch.

Scott made a big impact at Silver Hill. When he arrived, the church was "in a very ordinary style, with a school room on the first floor and the church auditorium above," according to a book penned in 1911 by the Rev. Irving E. Lowery, who followed Scott as pastor at Silver Hill. Soon after Scott arrived, he undertook "the tremendous job" of remodeling the church, Lowery said, using donations from Black and white Spartans alike. Congregants of the church contributed at least $1,600, and white citizens, at least $500. Among the white contributors were the men who built the industrial base of Spartanburg: John B. Cleveland, Capt. John Montgomery, Edgar Converse and Albert Twichell. During construction, Scott's church met in the Spartanburg Courthouse, a public building that opened its doors to gatherings by Black citizens during Scott's tenure. When church construction was complete, congregants were able to meet in a much larger, brick building with a basement. An early Black school operated there, and Scott was the principal.

It's not clear exactly where Scott and his wife, Rosa, lived while they were in Spartanburg, but most pastors in that day lived in parsonages near their churches, which would place them in the North Converse Street area. They began raising a family, which ultimately grew to eight children.

With his reputation growing around the state, Scott was invited in 1889 to be one of three South Carolina delegates to a mixed-race, international Sunday School conference in London. When he returned to Spartanburg, the *Charleston News and Courier* took note of his two-month journey with a long article and interview that was carried in other newspapers around the country, including the *Hartford Courant*. The newspaper referred to Scott "as a rather young man, with chin clean shaved, and sort of 'English, you know' appearance about his side whiskers." It continued: "His dialogue and pronunciation are still Southern, such as our best educated men, both black and white, use." In the article, Scott related a story about being on the British steamship SS Bothnia when a white man from North Carolina refused to sit beside him. But in London, "I had access to any hotel or public institution without question. . . . London is one place that I was not reminded on every corner that I was a negro." He visited Paris as well as states in the northeastern U.S. before returning to Spartanburg.

Upon his return, he closed a deal with his old college professor to become the owner of most of Cummings's remaining land behind Wofford College, 37.5 acres. Cummings had sold about 15 lots by 1890 but there was room for a whole lot more. Together with his father, Tobias, in Charleston, Scott purchased the remaining acreage, much of which now lies under the Jerry Richardson Indoor Stadium, Wofford's football practice fields and lacrosse field. The $1,200 sales price was an enormous amount of money for a Black family in the 19th century to pull together. But Scott's father was one of the most successful Black businessmen in the Lowcountry. His fan-making business, located on Charleston's Eastside, shipped its products all over the East Coast.

Soon after his land purchase, Scott began advocating for the city to build a new road to connect the North Dean Street neighborhood with Back of the College. The Air-Line Railroad had severed one side from the other years earlier. In June 1891 he appeared before Spartanburg town council to lobby for the new route. At the next meeting, Mayor John A. Henneman and the four council members—Thomas Bomar among them—voted to extend North Liberty Street to Cleveland Street and to build a new street connecting Dean and Converse Streets.

Meanwhile, C.C. Scott's years in Spartanburg coincided with another wave of grave danger to Black citizens: lynching. While the KKK campaign of nighttime terror had subsided, mob violence in broad daylight emerged as the next threat. At midnight on July 16, 1892, under a downtown streetlight near the Merchants Hotel, a verbal altercation between a white Spartan Mills factory worker named William Atkins and Black resident Andy Jeffries, 23, turned deadly. Jeffries pulled out a knife and slit the mill worker's throat. The next day, a "howling, demonical" white mob of at least 100 people found Jeffries hiding out in a swampy spot in the Back of the College area, behind the Evins house and above Chinquapin Creek—coincidently, either on or near the property Scott recently had purchased. The armed throng beat Jeffries, stoned him, stabbed him and then put a chain around his neck in preparation for lifting him into a tree. The sheriff and "prominent conservative citizens" led by young attorney Andrew E. Moore arrived to plead for his life and were able to stop the hanging.

In response to this gruesome episode, Scott and Charles C. Bomar, a Silver Hill congregant and successful businessman, immediately called a meeting of Black residents at the new Spartanburg Courthouse on Magnolia Street. About 50 people who worked in the vicinity left their places of work at lunch hour to attend. The attendees passed resolutions condemning the murder of Atkins and expressing sympathy to his family, even taking up a collection for them. But they also put on the record a long statement that condemned lynching "because it is mob law and contrary to the law of God and our country and in many instances is brutal and cowardly as the crime for which the party lynched is put to death, and sometimes an innocent party is lynched instead of the guilty one." With Scott and Bomar leading the way, the Black community stood its ground on the immorality of lynching.

Jeffries was hanged for murder in the Spartanburg jail yard alongside a second young Black convict on Sept. 9, 1892. Scott baptized both of them before their execution. "Nothing sensational occurred," wrote a blasé reporter on the scene.

Two weeks later, Scott was again present on a somber day in Spartanburg history. On a Sunday in late September, there was a second double hanging at the local jail of two other Black convicted murderers. John Williams was executed for the murder of Spartanburg Mayor J.A. Henneman, who had tried to stop an act of spousal abuse, and 14-year-old Milbry Brown for killing a white infant in her care by pouring acid down the baby's throat. The crimes made headlines all over the nation, as did the hangings. Large numbers of Spartanburg residents, white and Black, petitioned Gov. Ben Tillman to spare young Milbry's life, alluding to a diminished mental capacity—to no avail. Scott served as spiritual adviser to the condemned. He held religious services in their cells, securing late-hour conversions, and handled their funeral services after their bodies were dropped from the scaffold.

Scott departed Spartanburg in February 1894, moving on to churches in Anderson, Sumter and Yorkville. In his parting message, he told his congregation, "Here I spent the best and most eventful years of my life." The property that he bought behind the college sat idle for about 13 years. But in 1907 he hired a surveyor who drew a plat and laid out 52 new lots on the property, as well as new streets: Scott Street, which T-boned Cummings Street at the future site of Cumming Street School, and Peachtree Street.

A flurry of land sales then ensued. C.H. Barber was the first, paying $100 for Lot 1. Walter L. Kellett paid $50 for his. Fred Talley, a laborer at a cotton mill, paid $39 for his. Ella Whitmire, a widowed cook with a house full of children who would later distinguish themselves, bought a lot on the back row, fronting Twitty Street. The Scott property went quickly to other buyers: James Wiggins, Butler Rookard, J.D. Hamilton, Jennie Scott, J.M. Newton, T.H. Jennings, A.T. Sherard and many others. By 1913, Scott was selling lots for far higher prices, $366 in one case, $750 in another. At some point, the lots were gone, and the neighborhood was full of new homes.

Meanwhile, adjacent to Scott's development, a sprawling new neighborhood of white-owned houses was going up simultaneously. It was situated on a parcel of more than 100 acres formerly owned by the Evins family, with lots along Pearl Street, Serpentine Drive and Wood streets—now home to Spartanburg Medical Center. According to a 1910 advertisement in the *Spartanburg Herald*, each lot came "with a negro clause in each deed thus assuring you of protection as to neighborhood."

Scott went on to great acclaim in the Methodist Church. At the end of his career, he went back into the field of education, serving as superintendent of the Black schools in Bennettsville, South Carolina. He bought a home in Darlington. In the fall of 1922, Scott died in a hospital in Florence at the age of 67 and was buried in Camden. He was not, however, forgotten. On Feb. 28, 1963, *Jet* magazine ran a six-page spread on him, noting that "with power and eloquence he espoused the cause of justice and equality for the Negro with the same dedication common to the Rev. Martin

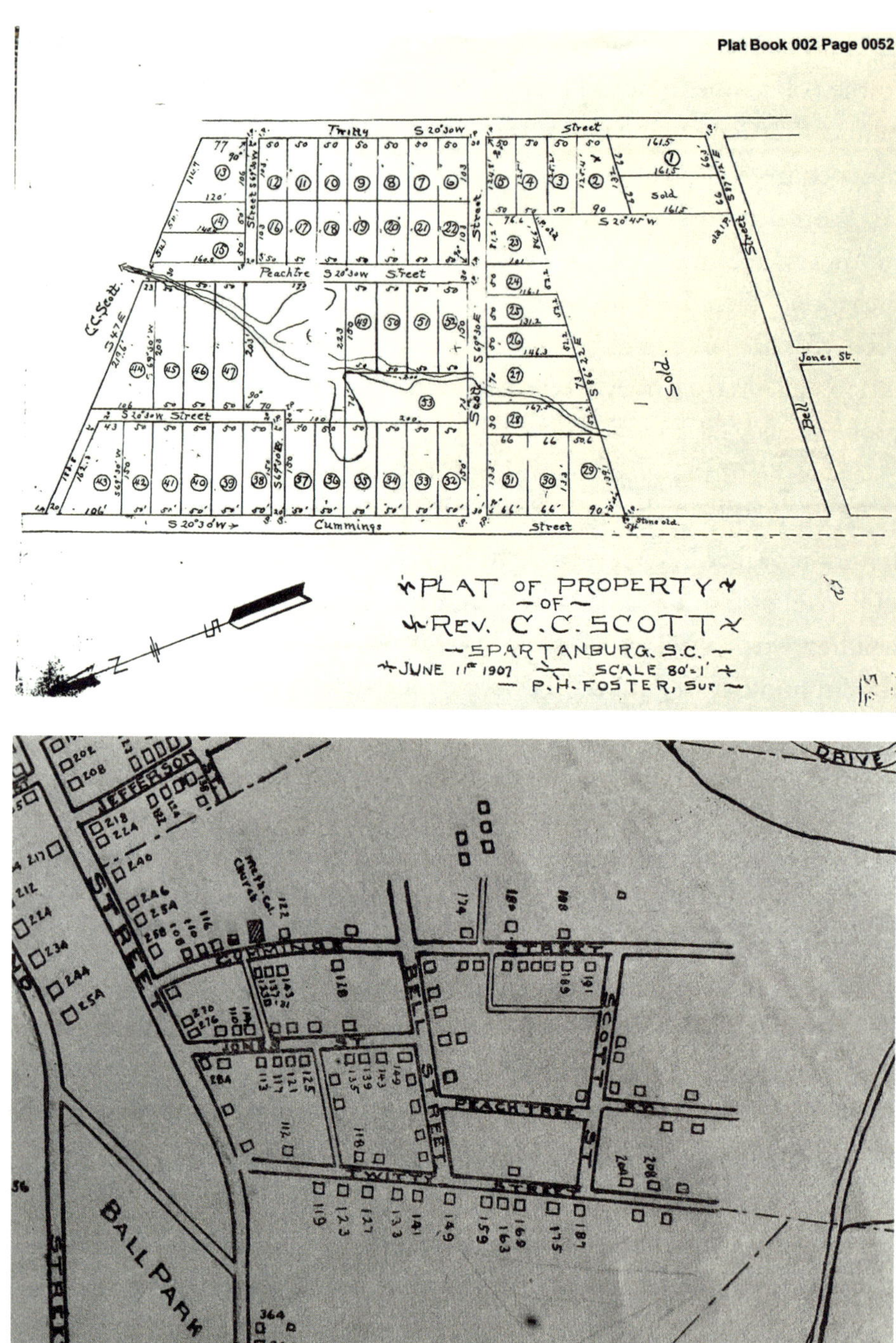

TOP: *Scott laid out 52 lots behind Wofford College.*

BOTTOM: *A 1910 map showing early homes built Back of the College. Wofford is located to the left of this area.*

Ella Whitmire, born about 1861, was the matriarch of a distinguished Back of the College family.

Luther King Jr., Roy Wilkins, or the student freedom riders of today." Calling him a "fiery and outspoken pastor," *Jet* wrote, "Scott was a member of a bold band of pioneers who, long before current integration efforts began, stood up for their rights in a frightfully hostile South."

Nowhere in the articles or book passages written about his life is Back of the College mentioned. Its development apparently was but a small piece of Scott's good work throughout South Carolina. Three years before his death, the South Carolina edition of *The History of American Negro* may have come close to acknowledging that Scott was making a tidy profit on his land deal with Anson Cummings in Spartanburg: "Dr. Scott, while not seeking primarily to make money, so handled his affairs as to have placed himself in a position far beyond that of the average minister of the Gospel." He died with a net worth of about $25,000.

Neither Scott nor Cummings—both fine educators—lived to see the beautiful, two-story school building serving Black children open in the neighborhood they created. When Cumming Street School opened in 1926—35 years after its namesake was buried in a cemetery in tiny Wellsville, New York—the neighborhood was full of children and adults. The story of the lives of Anson Cummings and C.C. Scott disappeared in Spartanburg as surely as the Back of the College neighborhood eventually did.

A NEGRO ABROAD.

His Own Story of His First Visit to Europe.

(Rev. C. C. Scott of Spartanburg, S. C., in a Charleston News and Courier "Interview.")

The Rev. C. C. Scott reached his little parsonage near Silver Hill Church last Wednesday afternoon, after an absence of two months. He is rather a young man, with chin clean shaved, and a sort of "English, you know," appearance about his side whiskers. He makes no effort to drop his "haitches" in conversation, nor does he say "Paree." His dialect and pronounciation are still Southern, such as our best educated men, both white and black, use. He was born in Charleston, was educated in Avery Institute, then went to Claflin and then to Howard University at Washington. He went through the preparatory department there and returned, and graduated at the State University in 1876. His diploma contains the signature of Wade Hampton. After graduation he went to Greenville, and was principal of the colored schools of that city a number of years. He was a local preacher, and in 1885 he joined the conference, and has been preaching regularly ever since that time. His education has raised him considerably above his race in point of intelligence and attainments. He is a Good Templar and Odd Fellow, and is thorougly interested in the progress and development of his race. Such is the Spartanburg's delegate to the great Sunday-school convention.

An interview with the Rev. C.C. Scott appeared in The Hartford Courant *in 1899.*

SPOTLIGHT

THE BARKSDALE BOOK

The most valuable document recording early life Back of the College is Louvenia Barksdale's small book *Historically and Statistically Yours: Back of the College 1887-1981*, published in November 1981. There she lists numerous notable people who called the neighborhood home, including government employees, teachers, ministers, doctors, musicians, law enforcement officers and many others. Few copies survive.

According to Barksdale's book, among the last names of the earliest settlers of the neighborhood were: Auskew, Bates, Bearden, Benson, Blake, Boozer, Byrd, Cantrell, Chambers, Charles, Clemens, Donaldson, Edwards, Ferguson, Floyd, Foster, Gist, Gray, Greene, Hamilton, Hicks, Holcombe, Jackson, Jeter, Johnson, Letmon, Level, Lindsey, Littlejohn, Mack, Mayfield, McCullough, Means, Miller, Montgomery, Peak, Penland, Quarles, Robinson, Scott, Simmons, Shelton, Spears, Talley, Tinsley, Wardlaw, West, Wertz, Whitmire, Wiggins and Young.

"The community consisted of undeveloped land except for cottonfields, mulberry trees, walnut, figs, chinaberry and later two hundred pecan trees," she wrote. "Geese, horses, cows, goats were in large numbers." Among the historical places listed was the Cleveland Street Spring, located on the corner of Cleveland and Cutting streets, on the Wofford side of the railroad underpass on present-day North Liberty Street.

Barksdale's book was produced with the help of Ida Foster Adams, Otis Hill, Earline Thompson and John Mintz. On Nov. 29, 1981, there was a huge celebration at Cummings Street Baptist Church for the release of the Barksdale book. The theme of the event was "A Community Looks at its Past, Present and Future." Among the speakers were U.S. Rep. Liz Patterson; state Rep. Hudson Barksdale Sr.; City Councilwoman-elect Ellen Hines Smith; Georgia T. Anderson of Washington, D.C., the first basketball coach at Cumming Street School; Dr. Joab Lesesne, president of Wofford College; the Rev. Harold Cox, president of Greater Spartanburg Ministries; Cheryl Harleston, representing the staff of the city of Spartanburg; and others.

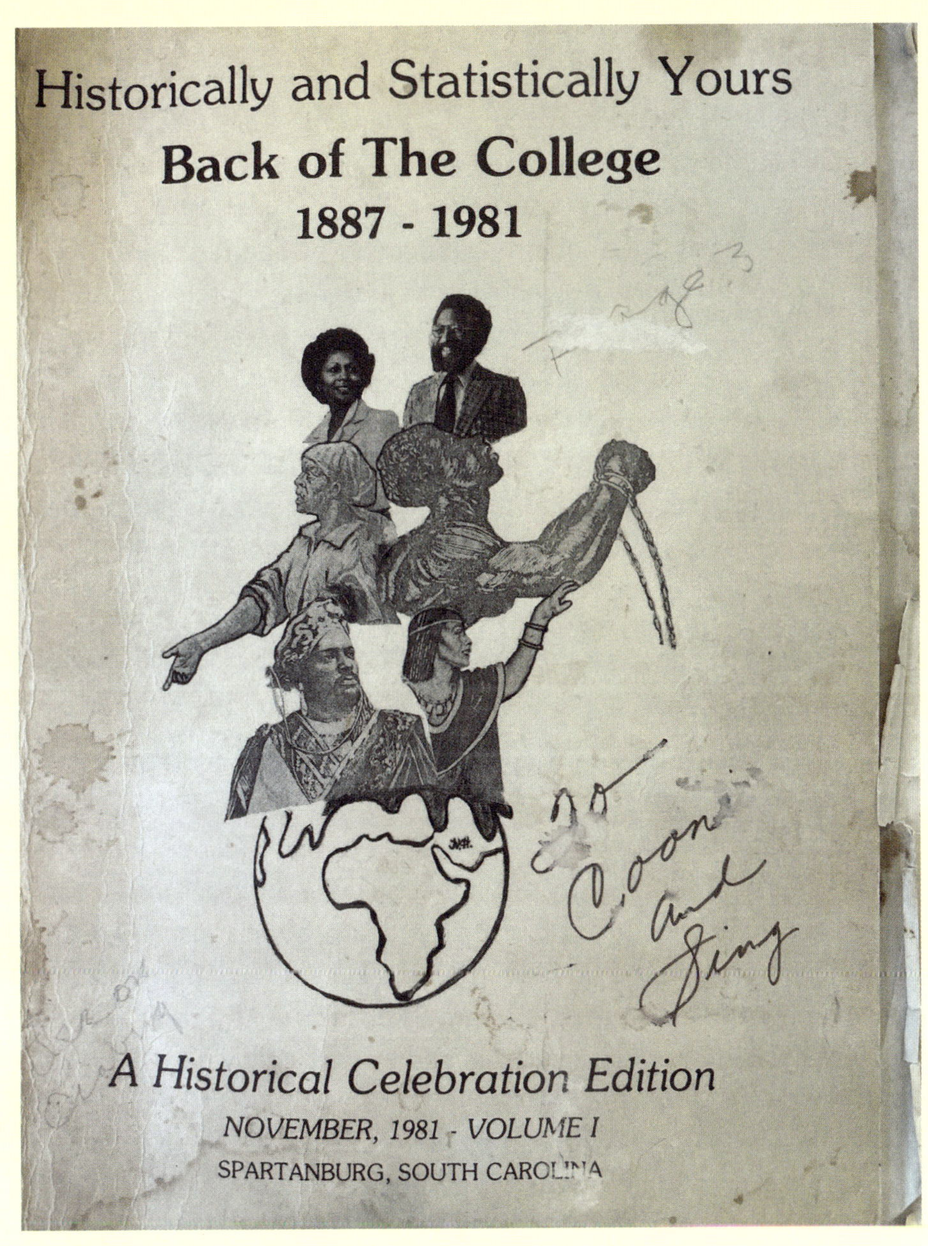

A copy of Louvenia Barksdale's 1981 book, signed to members of the Whitmire family..

SPOTLIGHT

THE OTHER NORTHSIDE

Across Church Street from Wofford College, another Black neighborhood arose in the 1870s. By the end of the decade, there were about 40 dwellings that housed formerly enslaved people along College Street, Howard Street and an area the census-taker called "the extremity of Magnolia Street"—roughly the modern-day location of Spartanburg's Chapel Street Park. Many of the residents in this area were renters, and several lived in boarding houses. They were laborers, domestics and tradesmen.

The early focus of the community was a small wooden church, Trinity AME, which opened in 1872 on the corner of Howard and College streets. It was led by the Rev. McKnight for its first two years. Church members built a second wood-frame building at 457 Magnolia Street in 1889. With strong growth, Trinity AME began construction in 1922 on a $50,000 brick church on the same site, which held up to 800 people in its sanctuary. That church, with its two square towers, stained glass windows and bell, was demolished in recent years as membership dwindled away.

In its early days the neighborhood was anchored by three prominent families: the Bomars, the Farrows and the Adens. The Bomars—Elias and Matilda; Thomas M. and Carrie Bomar; Charles and Annie Bomar; and Thomas H. Bomar—ultimately owned more than 20 acres along Howard Street. In 1920, after the death of her husband, Carrie Bomar Perry opened the Provident Hospital in her large home, located at the corner of newly paved Howard Street and Arch Street. The 20-bed hospital cared for Black patients and was served by both white and Black physicians until 1930. Since then, this structure has housed the J.W. Woodward Funeral Home, a thriving business with more than 100 years of service in Spartanburg. Other notable early residents included the Adens—Nathaniel "Nat" Aden, a brick mason born in 1823, and his wife, Duskey, who purchased land there in 1875 and farmed it thereafter; a street in this area still bears their name. The family of Lot and Adaline Farrow, parents who raised educator Mary H. Wright, lived on

Carrie Bomar Perry's Provident Hospital operated on Howard Street during the 1920s. The J.W. Woodward Funeral Home is in this building today.

Magnolia Street from 1870 until after the turn of the century.

When Capt. John H. Montgomery moved into the neighborhood and built Spartan Mills on his northside property in 1890, several Black families relocated from the College Street area to accommodate "Montgomeryville," the large mill village that served the factory's white workers. Eventually, a robust Black neighborhood came together farther north along Vernon, Fulton, Aden and Howard streets, adjacent to Fremont School. Among this neighborhood's early 20th-century residents was Arthur Herndon (1873-1938), owner of the Southern Candy Co., which shipped its Dixie Dandy candy throughout the South. Herndon, whose factory was on Wofford Street, employed about a dozen workers and a corps of white and Black salesmen. By 1927 he was doing $40,000 a year in sales.

The Chapel Street Park area remains a viable neighborhood, populated mostly by Black families.

Tobe Hartwell, pictured in his bank courier's uniform about 1930

FOUR

TOBE HARTWELL'S STORY

IN LATE NOVEMBER 1874 there was a horrible tragedy at the tenant house of Tobe Hartwell. Hartwell and his wife, Catherine, lived behind Wofford College on East Cleveland Street, just up the hill from present-day Beaumont Mill and North Pine Street. Somehow, as Catherine Hartwell was ironing, her clothes caught fire. The 30-year-old mother of five died from the burns. *The Carolina Spartan*, which rarely covered news from Spartanburg's Black community, took note of her death, calling her "a very respectable, industrious, hard-working woman." Tobe Hartwell was left to raise a house full of children, ranging from 3 months to 7 years in age.

Over the course of his lifetime, Hartwell would overcome the calamity and become the most recognized Black man in Spartanburg. He would serve as a constable, one of the town's first Black seekers of public office, a courier, a vital member of Silver Hill Church, and an advocate for education of Black children.

Hartwell, in his 30s at the time of the fire, had experienced a long road to Spartanburg. According to a short biography published in the *Spartanburg Journal* in 1932, he grew up in Chapel Hill, North Carolina, where he was enslaved by the prosperous shopkeeper and future mayor John Wesley Carr. Chapel Hill was a tiny college town then, with just a few hundred residents. As a boy circulating in the Carr household, Hartwell would have been raised on Chapel Hill's Franklin Street alongside a white child named Julian "Jule" Shakespeare Carr, who ultimately became owner and president of the Bull Durham Tobacco Co., the best-selling tobacco in the world. The city of Carrboro is named after this family.

At some point in the 1850s, Hartwell apparently changed households. In his teens, he was enslaved by Dr. Albert Shipp, who had moved to Chapel Hill from Greensboro. Shipp was then a 30-year-old history professor at the new—and quite small—University of North Carolina, located across the street from the Carr home. Shipp also was a religious man who helped found the first Methodist church in Chapel Hill, now called University Methodist Church. This church encouraged Black membership, and in the 1850s, there were some 40 Black congregants. Names of those congregants have been lost to history, but there is little doubt that Hartwell was among them as he joined Central Methodist Church after he arrived in Spartanburg. The little church where Hartwell would have become a Methodist still stands at the corner of Henderson and Rosemary streets in Chapel Hill.

Then in 1859 Shipp was hired as president of Wofford College. On what was then a three-day carriage ride from Chapel Hill, Shipp brought with him a group of about 20 enslaved men, women and children, among them Toby, Susan, Sarah, Catie and George. All of these enslaved people appear on the "colored Sunday School" rolls of Spartanburg's Central Methodist Church during the Civil War, with the last name Shipp. They were among more than 100 Black people at the church bearing the last names of Spartanburg slave-holding families, including Trimmier, Kennedy, Durant, Kirby, Bobo and others. Another enslaved woman in the Shipp household, Nina Scott, was Hartwell's sister, according to her obituary many years later. This obituary indicated their mother also came to Spartanburg with Shipp.

After emancipation, Hartwell stayed put in a cabin, roughly 200 yards behind the large home of Wofford President Shipp, who lived near the present-day site of the Wofford baseball stadium. When the census-taker came by his home in August 1870, Hartwell reported his occupation as "keeping house." His post-slavery work could have included carpentry projects, personal service to Shipp, including driving him to destinations in town and the county, limited subsistence farming on campus, and campus maintenance.

Soon Hartwell was active in local politics, associating with white Republican diehards in town—a small group that apparently did not include his employer or other Wofford personnel. In September 1872 he attended the Spartanburg County Convention of the Union Republican Party held

Albert M. Shipp, the first president of Wofford College

at the local courthouse and was one of four men nominated to run for Spartanburg's four seats in the state House of Representatives. The local Republican ticket, which advocated for more rights for Black citizens, was crushed in 1872, receiving about half the number of votes that Spartanburg's conservative Democratic ticket did. Hartwell notched 1,079 votes, presumably many from new Black voters. The other Black man on the ticket, Hiram Hobby of Woodruff, South Carolina, received 1,125. A Spartanburg correspondent for the white-owned *Charleston Daily* News crowed, "We have routed the Radicals, horse, foot and dragoon, electing our entire county and legislative ticket."

That was Hartwell's last foray into politics. In 1880, after his employer had moved on to assume a professorship at Vanderbilt University, Hartwell gave his occupation as a carpenter.

By that time, Hartwell also was a homeowner. Two weeks after the accident that had killed his wife, Hartwell purchased his house on East Cleveland Street, along with 2.3 acres of property, for $158. Also purchasing a cabin and a lot that day for $93.25 was Kitty Mitchell, wife of William Mitchell, fellow members of Silver Hill. These purchases predate the Anson Cummings transactions and would appear to be the earliest land sales to Black buyers in the place that would mushroom into the neighborhood known as Back of the College. About a month later, another Black neighbor, Lorenzo McKinney, bought his home on East Cleveland Street for $87.50. This is likely the man known as the Rev. "Ranse" McKinney, who served Silver Hill Church. Each of these three families had members originally from North Carolina—a strong piece of evidence that suggests they were among those who came to Spartanburg with Wofford College President Shipp.

The seller of the land in these three transactions was Dr. Robert Easley Cleveland, a wealthy physician living near the town square. It would have been highly unusual in the tight community of Spartanburg in 1874 for a white man to sell land to Black buyers. If accounts from Spartanburg's Black Bomar family are true, Cleveland was the father of at least two mixed-race children, including one—Thomas Bomar—who grew up to be a town councilman in Spartanburg and a successful businessman. Allegations about Cleveland's paternity are included in three biographies of Chester Bomar Himes, a nephew of Thomas Bomar and a prolific author considered one the most important Black novelists of the 20th century. The accounts of Himes' life in his biographies include allegations from his family members that Cleveland likely impregnated Chester's grandmother, Malinda Bomar, an enslaved woman who grew up in two Cleveland homes.

Regardless of the reason for the property sales, it is clear that just seven years after the end of the Civil War, Cleveland knew Hartwell well enough to sell him and his neighbors a bit of property. The site was alongside the new Air-Line (Southern) Railway and just steps from Chinquapin Creek.

During the post-war years of Reconstruction, Hartwell was chosen to serve as Spartanburg constable to Black trial justice Alexander Jones. During the 1880s he served the town council as a contract police officer, along with Dennis Porter and Wallace Gaither. The Black officers were not

OPPOSITE: *A city publication listing Hartwell as assistant to police chief Henry C. Alley. The Town Council they served included John P. Boyden, a Black resident of North Dean Street.*

MAYOR AND ALDERMEN

Elected October 19th, 1885, for two years.

MAYOR:

JOSEPH WALKER.

ALDERMEN:

T. A. IRWIN.
L. A. MILLS.
H. A. LIGON.
G. A. LETHCO.
F. M. TRIMMIER.
JOHN BOYDEN.
L. A. MILLS, deceased, and
STANYARNE WILSON, elected,
as declared December, 31st, 1885.

STANDING COMMITTES

For Term of Two Years, Commencing October 20, 1885,

Ways and Means—F. M. Trimmier, H. A. Ligon, John Boyden.

Streets, Public Grounds and Cemetery—T. A. Irwin, S. Wilson, G. A. Lethco.

Lights and Water Works—John Boyden, T. A. Irwin, F. M. Trimmier.

License, Guard House and Police—S. Wilson, H. A. Ligon, G. A. Lethco

Public Buildings and Fire Department—G. A. Lethco, S. Wilson, F. M. Trimmier.

Accounts—H. A. Ligon, T. A. Irwin, John Boyden.

OFFICERS OF COUNCIL.

CLERK AND TREASURER:

J. M ELFORD.

POLICE:

H. C. ALLEY, Chief.
JOHN MILLER, Assistant
TOBE HARTWELL, Ass't and Night Watchman.

Hartwell in his later years in front of the bank on Morgan Square where he was employed.

allowed to arrest white people and served in a kind of unofficial capacity. One account of Hartwell's life relates that in the days before the invention of the alarm clock, he often "gave the morning alarm or 'get up' signal, going about the streets of the hamlet tossing pebbles against the window panes." In the days before electricity came to Spartanburg, Hartwell also was in charge of lighting the town's kerosene lamps in the late afternoon, assisted by his sons Tobe Jr., Jacob and James. They were often seen walking dirt streets where light from the flickering lamps illuminated shop windows. In the mornings the Hartwells would come back to extinguish them. Some residents considered Hartwell the town's night watchman.

In the 1870s and 1880s Hartwell was an important supporter of an early Black school at Silver Hill Church and another on the Southside, Lincoln School. When the city's white school trustees determined it was time to start the first government-supported school for Black students on North Dean Street, they enlisted Hartwell as an adviser.

From his home behind Wofford, Tobe Hartwell was witness to the birth of a flourishing Black neighborhood, which by 1903, included roughly 100 homes, some owned and some rented. He had seen new houses replace slave cabins, new churches organized, and four decades of white college students come and go. At the turn of the century, Hartwell was hired as janitor at the First National Bank of Spartanburg on Morgan Square, prompting him to move closer to town. In 1908 he and his second wife, Sallie, bought a lot near the corner of Northview and Woodward streets, just off present-day St. John Street, in Lizzie Judd's Chasander Hill development.

Soon the Hartwells were joined in Chasander Hill by two other important families in Spartanburg's Black history: the Carters and the Campbells. In 1910 Black building contractor Jesse Carter bought a lot in the next block and constructed a house for $300 for his wife and daughters. His youngest, Ellen, grew up on Northview Street and went on to have a long, remarkable career as guidance counselor at Carver and Spartanburg high schools. She married Robert C. Watson, longtime principal of Highland School, and they lived on Northview Street into the 1950s. Just a few doors down, elevator operator Charles Campbell and his large family moved into a house at 274 Northview Street in 1914. His oldest daughter, Charlie Mae Campbell, graduated from South Carolina State and then had a 45-year teaching career in Spartanburg, including two decades as principal at Mary H. Wright Elementary School. Charlie Mae Campbell, who helped raise her seven siblings after her mother died early, lived in the family home on Northview Street until she died in 2002 at the age of 93.

The Carters, the Campbells, the Hartwells and many others built a thriving community in Chasander Hill. Several residents held jobs in the downtown area. During his 33 years of service at Spartanburg's largest bank, Hartwell was entrusted with carrying money between the city's financial institutions and from the post office—an amount estimated at $1 million, according to an account in The *Spartanburg Journal*. Locals always recognized Hartwell in his blue uniform and cap. Some stopped him as he came through the streets "just to hear his quick 'comeback' or good-natured thrusts or words of raillery," wrote a white journalist in a 1925 newspaper

LEFT: *Charlie Mae Campbell, principal at Mary H. Wright Elementary School*
RIGHT: *Ellen C. Watson, guidance counselor at Carver High School*

account, "for Tobe is likewise good at repartee, though entirely respectful always, with a courtesy all his own. Nothing pleases the old fellow more than to escort some acquaintance of his race to the window and identify him, which he does with impressive gravity, and stately dignity, courteously inclining his white head now to the teller, then to the customer, as he performs the serious ceremony, punctuating his clauses with graceful, sweeping gestures worthy of Henry Clay for Tobe's arms and hands are more eloquent than a traffic cop."

Hartwell was one of the few men of his race who was universally recognized by Spartanburg's white business leaders. But even in their respect, they casually attached a name to him that is now commonly considered racist: he was "Uncle Tobe" to them. The term "uncle" was typically used to denote a Black man who acted subservient to whites to curry their favor. They saluted him for voting in the mid-1870s for Democratic candidates, including Gov. Wade Hampton. This decision was made and regretted by significant numbers of Black voters of the era. Hampton had promised to improve the lives of Black citizens; instead there was increased racial segregation and erosion of civil rights.

In 1930 Hartwell was still on the job and may have been as old as 92. He and his wife, Sallie, returned to the Back of the College neighborhood, moving in with their son on property Hartwell had bought after his enslavement.

Sallie Hartwell passed away in the summer of 1932. Tobe Hartwell fell ill that same month. In August the *Spartanburg Journal* noted that he lay "sick and helpless and destitute at the Spartanburg negro hospital." The newspaper made a plea for charity for Hartwell, noting that "friends who were accustomed to greet the white-haired negro on the streets have forgotten Uncle Tobe whose last days will probably be spent alone."

Tobe Hartwell—resident of Back of the College, resident of the North Dean Street neighborhood, giant in his community—died on Oct. 4, 1932. Services were conducted at Silver Hill Methodist Church. He was buried at the Old City Cemetery on Spartanburg's Southside. His sister, Nina Scott, died in December 1938 at the age of 90.

IN 1940, as federal dollars arrived to support new public housing in Spartanburg, white business leaders suggested that the first Black housing project be named in his honor: Tobe Hartwell Courts. At a City Council meeting they described him as "courteous," "loyal" and "friendly," qualities that Hartwell likely adopted to fit into a white world. This was an example of how white people willfully confused good manners and pragmatism with acquiescence and agreement with an unjust system. Historian Marko Maunula notes there was "widespread white conviction [in Spartanburg] that local African Americans were content with the racial system that prevailed in the region." Eight years after his death, Hartwell was remembered fondly for what business leaders saw as a faithful regard of white conservative values, which had garnered him white Spartanburg's admiration and trust since the days of Reconstruction.

In September 1940 a group of more than a dozen white men posed with shovels for a newspaper photo as they broke ground for the 150-unit Tobe Hartwell Courts on the Southside. Nineteen Black homes had been demolished in an early slum clearance action to make way for the new project. Built on a grassy, terraced site, the $500,000 complex included 20 one-story buildings and 19 two-story buildings. Rent was about $11 a month. When it

September 10, 1940

Ground Broken For Slum Clearance Project Here

Groundbreaking for the 150-unit Tobe Hartwell Courts development

opened in the summer of 1941, Tobe Hartwell Courts was considered one of the finest addresses in Black Spartanburg, a family-oriented complex with a croquet field outside, a resident gospel choir and regular bingo and whist games inside for the adults. A large portrait of Hartwell was unveiled in the common area as Hartwell's former bank employer, A.M. Chreitzberg, made a speech about his life. Among the notable people who grew up at what residents fondly called "Tobe" was South Carolina Supreme Court Chief Justice Donald J. Beatty.

These Tobe Hartwell Courts lasted until 1998, when the complex was torn down to make room for the newer Tobe Booker Hartwell Campus of Learners complex, currently located between Hudson Barksdale Drive and Hartwell Street.

Meanwhile, Tobe Hartwell's original, three-room house behind Wofford stood for many years. His son, Tobias Jr., a house painter born in 1870,

Affectionately called "Tobe," the original housing complex included 39 buildings.

lived in a house on the property in 1920 with his wife, Celia, and his three sons and four daughters. A third-generation Tobe Hartwell, born in 1905, attended college, served in World War II and lived there for most of his life, dying in 1966. A fourth and fifth generation of Hartwell family members lived there for the next three decades. The family's 137-year history in the area ended when the property was sold to Wofford College, which tore down the dwellings.

SPOTLIGHT

THE BLACK POET LAUREATE

A musician, teacher and prolific writer, Jimmy Johnson (1849-1939) claimed to have written more than 1,300 poems in his lifetime in Spartanburg. Because of his many talents, he was known all over town by residents white and Black. His Back of the College neighbors called him "poet laureate."

Born into slavery east of Richmond, Virginia, Johnson was sold along with his mother and older sister to Dr. Lionel C. Kennedy of Spartanburg. The Johnson family—Jimmy; mother, Mary Frances; and sister, Margaret Marie—lived on the grounds of the doctor's home, located on the site of the present-day One Morgan Square building. Both before and after emancipation, Johnson served as the doctor's coachman and would drive the horse and buggy for him as he visited patients. He would use those opportunities to study. "He let me take my Webster's blue back speller and my history with me when I would drive with him," Johnson said years later when he was interviewed by a representative of the Federal Writers Project.

As he reached adulthood, Johnson taught at Grant Academy, the Presbyterian-affiliated Black school that opened on Wofford Street in the 1880s. Among his students was Carrie Bomar Perry, who grew up to be superintendent of the Provident Hospital on Howard Street. A longtime resident of Jefferson Street next to Wofford College, Johnson adopted four children and made sure they were educated. He taught music lessons on the reed organ and melodeon—which he learned to play at the Kennedy home—and later on the piano.

For at least 35 years Johnson also worked in the Wofford College campus home of Dr. Arthur Gaillard Rembert, professor of Bible and ancient languages. While working there, Johnson studied the languages of Latin and Greek. He also may have been employed for a time at the

Kennedy Free Library—Louvenia Barksdale's history of the neighborhood said he had the nickname "Kennedy" because he had a job there. At age 80 he was still offering piano lessons and had 12 pupils. Johnson was a deeply religious man who knew dozens of hymns. His poetry often reflected his Christian faith. One of his poems was published in *The Christian Advocate*, a weekly Methodist newspaper in New York City. While most of his poetry is not publicly available, this was one of his favorites:

The Eternal Gate

Yonder stands the eternal gate.
Where the angels gladly wait,
Over on that golden strand,
In that bright and happy land.

Yonder stands the eternal king,
Where the angels gladly sing
In the beautiful world above
Where remains eternal love.

Jimmy Johnson, from a 1927 newspaper article

SPOTLIGHT

THE MUCKENFUSS BROOM FACTORY

During an era when Black laborers were blocked by law from working inside Spartanburg County's numerous cotton mills, Muckenfuss Broom Works welcomed them for 50 years as employees on its shop floor. The factory, located along what is now known as East Daniel Morgan Avenue, grew to be the most significant broom manufacturer in the South, and many of its 20-plus jobs were filled by local Black men.

There was one other unusual feature of the Muckenfuss factory: its owner was completely blind.

Owner Wesley George Muckenfuss came from a prominent Charleston family with German roots. As a teenager without sight, he was sent to Spartanburg to attend Cedar Springs Institute, now known as the South Carolina School for the Deaf and the Blind. There, broom making was one of the traditional "blind trades" taught. At the age of 22, after attending Wofford College and graduating from the University of South Carolina, Muckenfuss opened his broom-making factory in a small wooden building near the Wofford campus, adjacent to the Southern Railway underpass—in the center of the emerging 300-acre Black neighborhood. Among his earliest employees were five young Black men: Laban Brown, Andrew Williams, Alex Smith, William Cooper and Columbus Holtsy. They and scores of other Black laborers over the years crafted "the brooms with the blue label," some of the most coveted brooms on the East Coast and the Midwest.

Early laborers at Muckenfuss turned out nearly 50,000 brooms a year, along with a variety of brushes. "They make as good brooms as can be made anywhere in this country," wrote *The Atlanta Constitution* in 1902, "and sell them to the trade direct from the factory through their own traveling salesmen." On the night of Nov. 17, 1909, a fire of unknown origin burned the factory to the ground and consumed six cottages, all occupied by Black families. "For a time it seemed if the whole section was threatened, including Fowler's Row and the Silver Hill church neighborhood," one journalist wrote. Residents "wild with fright" dragged possessions from the homes, but fortunately no one was killed. While the ruins still smoked, Muckenfuss proclaimed, "We are all young. The factory will be rebuilt."

He was good to his word. In 1920 the new broom factory was producing three times the previous volume. By that time, though, Wesley Muckenfuss was gone. He died suddenly of heart failure at his home at 167 North Dean Street in 1914. His obituary described him as an expert typist who kept the books "neatly and accurately by a method of his own origination." His wife, Rida, ran the factory in his place for many years. She continued to provide comparatively good jobs for Black laborers: Census data shows that Hughes Green, a resident of Cummings Street, made $780 a year at the factory in 1940—about twice what Black teachers of the period were paid.

The Muckenfuss era ended around 1945 when the company was merged with an out-of-town manufacturer. A Subaru dealership sits on the site today.

Originally named the Piedmont Broom Factory, this is the original Muckenfuss plant as it appeared in January 1900. It made 750 brooms a day at this time.

Students from St. Luke's Lutheran Day School pictured in front of a row of houses on Evins Street.
Image courtesy of Concordia Historical Institute, Saint Louis, Missouri.

FIVE

EARLY EDUCATION

EMANCIPATION BROUGHT A SCRAMBLE to educate the children. Idealistic educators and concerned citizens—Black and white, one after the other—launched new schools to serve the hundreds of newly freed children in the village of Spartanburg. The schools that opened in the two post-war decades generally were short-lived, underfunded, crowded and sometimes targets of white hostility. Support from state government and national institutions—and from those with money in Spartanburg—was meager and spotty. It would be nearly two decades before consistent public education could take hold. But that did not stop Black families in Spartanburg from rushing to enroll their children.

The first to open the doors of a Black schoolhouse in Spartanburg appears to have been Charleston minister Rev. Edward J. Snetter, who received permission from the South Carolina Freedmen's Bureau to start a school in 1866. Snetter, a Black circuit preacher in the Methodist Episcopal Church, once was described as a man who "found it necessary to carry with him to the pulpit his six-shooter and sometimes a Winchester rifle." Four months in, he still had received no paycheck from the Freedmen's Bureau. It's unclear how long this federally funded school operated—perhaps as short as one season—or exactly where it was located. Snetter ultimately moved back to Charleston.

On the heels of Snetter's school, a young white couple succeeded in providing a classroom for the town's Black children from 1867 to 1870 in a house near the southwest end of the public square. Twenty-six-year-old Eva Poole and her bookkeeper husband, Louis N. Poole, were among the

Teacher's Report

To be filled out and to accompany Teacher's Account for services rendered during the Fiscal year, commencing November 1st, A. D. 1868, and ending October 31st, A. D. 1869.

Report of Eva M. Poole Teacher of a Public School in Spartanburg C.H. County of Spartanburg State of South Carolina.

Eva M. Poole TEACHER.

1. Name of school? Colored Free School
2. Location of school? Spartanburg Village
3. When did your term or school commence? January 11th 1869
4. When did your term or school close? ~~May 14th~~ September 24th 1869
5. Give the length of your school or term in months (20 days to a month)? 9 Months
6. Has your school received aid from any source or sources other than the State, and if so, how much? None
7. How many teachers? ~~Three~~ 3 Male? 0 Female? 3
8. Name of principal teacher? Eva M. Poole
9. Names of assistant teachers? Estelle Morgan — Mrs [illegible] Mathew
10. How many Northern white teachers? — 0 Male? 0 Female? 0
11. How many Southern white teachers? One 1 Male? 0 Female? 1
12. How many Northern colored teachers? 0 Male? 0 Female? 0
13. How many Southern colored teachers? Two 2 Male? 0 Female? 2
14. Does the account accompanying this report include the salaries or amount due to all the teachers of your school? It does.
15. What number of scholars under 6 years of age? None
16. What number of scholars over 16 years of age? [illegible]
17. What number of scholars between 6 and 16 years of age? 179
18. Average attendance?* 25
19. Was your school for white or colored children? Colored

*To find the average attendance, divide the total number of days' attendance by the number of days of the school or term.

Eva Poole filed this report in 1869 about the Colored Free School in the village of Spartanburg. She had 179 students at the time.

town's few white Republicans, known as "scalawags" because of their sympathy to the Black cause. In a 1936 interview Mary H. Wright described them as "Yankees but not carpetbaggers," perhaps meaning that the political views of the local couple were more aligned with Northerners. The Pooles opened their state-funded school in a small, frame building lent to them by a representative of the John Bomar estate, and they initially named it the Hamilton School. Eva Poole complained it was a building "with many disadvantages and in a place I do not admire."

The Pooles previously had attempted to run a similar school in north Georgia right after the war, but low pay had forced them to close. Undaunted, the Pooles had come back to Spartanburg, their hometown, to try again. Within two years Eva Poole's school served 179 Black students between the ages of 6 and 16. Among them were the children of many of the founding Black families of the northside. The roll in 1869 included a 7-year-old Mary Honor Farrow (later to become Mary H. Wright), as well the children of the Bomar, Burnett, Choice, Hamilton, Hardy, Hartwell, Huggins, Thompson, Williams and Young families, among others. For these parents, it was critical that their children read and write, so they would not be left in the circumstances that many Black adults found themselves in—unable to read their own labor contracts or property deeds. Two Black teachers worked at this school: Estelle Morgan, 23, and a Mrs. Matthews. Many years later, Mary H. Wright described Hamilton School as "a rude log structure that grew into a building of some proportion."

The going was not easy for the staff. When asked to describe the public sentiment toward colored schools on her June 1869 Teacher's Report, an exhausted Eva Poole wrote, "Hostile. Hostile." The school desperately needed money for repairs and materials. Again, paychecks were sporadic. The state education department was supposed to pay her 2 1/2 cents per day, per student, but if she did not file paperwork on time, she was not paid. In January 1869 she filed an affidavit to the State Legislature saying she was "in necessitous circumstances" and needed payment of her [$181.50] account to provide food and clothing for her family."

By spring 1870 attendance had dropped to 70 students, and she and her husband apparently were the only teachers left. Not long after, their Hamilton School—by then renamed "Spartanburg Colored Free School"—

closed for good. Louis Poole stayed active in local Republican politics, serving along with Tobe Hartwell as a delegate to the Spartanburg Convention of the Union Republican Party in 1872. He briefly became Spartanburg coroner. But both he and Eva disappear from Spartanburg census records by 1880, apparently moving back to North Georgia.

As Eva Poole's school struggled through its final months, a mixed-race group of Spartanburg citizens began developing plans for a different schoolhouse on North Dean Street through the Freedmen's Bureau. They were led by John T. Hamilton, a 38-year-old Black businessman who is listed in the 1870 census as a commission merchant, with $550 in real estate and personal holdings—more wealth than any other Black man of that era in Spartanburg. In July 1869 Hamilton wrote a letter to the commissioner of the Freedmen's Bureau in Washington, D.C., seeking $800 toward construction of a $1,500 school. "The County Commissioner of Schools, a Democrat, is openly opposed to the education of colored people," Hamilton wrote, "nor has the Legislature done anything yet toward the building of Schoolhouses." He vowed to raise the rest of the funding through private subscriptions.

Soon after, Hamilton sold for $50 a one-acre lot on North Dean Street to the "Trustees of the Spartanburg Colored Schools," a group that included himself as chairman, Southside pioneer Joseph Young Sr., a 42-year-old Black shoemaker named Elias James, and three white men: the city's young postmaster Enoch Cannon, hotelier Alfred Tolleson and county auditor Frank Camp, all of whom were considered Republican scalawags. Not only were these white men controversial figures in the heavily Democratic village of Spartanburg, working alongside Black men was a bold move. Cannon later "ran away" from Spartanburg, according to an account of his short tenure as postmaster. John T. Hamilton disappeared from the Spartanburg census by 1880. The fate of his school is lost to history.

Simultaneously, another group of Black citizens affiliated with the AME Zion Church (which eventually became Trinity AME of Magnolia Street) were working to start a second Freedmen's Bureau school nearby. Their site was roughly the modern-day location of Spartanburg's train depot on a piece of land deeded to the church by the Cleveland, Evins and Choice families. Working with the Rev. Anson Cummings, who had an

REPORT—Continued.

NUMBER.	NAMES OF PUPILS.	BOYS.	GIRLS.	DATE OF ENTERING SCHOOL.	DATE OF LEAVING SCHOOL.	TOTAL DAYS' ATTENDANCE.	
1	Bula McClure	1		Jany 11th 1869	May 14 1870	83	
2	Miles Weaver	1		" " "	" " "	74	
3	Lige Preston	1		" " "	" " "	78	
4	Thos Bomar	1		" " "	" " "	83	
5	Jas Heyden	1		" " "	" " "	82	
6	Robt Hamilton	1		" " "	" " "	80	
7	John Hamilton	1		" " "	" " "	79	
8	John Miller	1		" " "	" " "	84	
9	Mag Bomar		1	" " "	" " "	87	
10	Hannah Vernon		1	" " "	" " "	81	
11	Lou Young		1	" " "	" " "	80	
12	Mamie Hartwell		1	" " "	" " "	82	
13	Fanny Carter		1	" " "	" " "	74	
14	Charty William		1	" " "	" " "	76	
15	Harriett Boyd		1	" " "	April 23 "	65	
16	Picken Louis	1		" " "	May 14 "	80	
17	Joseph Bogan	1		" " "	" " "	80	
18	Arkansas Benson		1	Feby 1st 1869	May " "	64	1
19	John Mozom	1		" " "	" " "	64	
20	Hattie Mozom		1	" " "	" " "	64	
21	Jane Mozom		1	" " "	" " "	65	
22	Flora Mozom		1	" " "	" 12 "	62	
23	Lizzie Cleaveland		1	" " "	" 12 "	60	
24	William Bomar	1		" 9 "	" 6 "	57	
25	Hattie Montgomery		1	" " "	" 14 "	62	
26	Henry Montgomery	1		" " "	" " "	60	
27	Dyme Perrin	1		" " "	" 10 "	54	
28	Susan Perrin		1	" " "	" " "	58	
29	Lizzie Hawkins		1	March 1st 1869	" 14	49	
30	York Hawkins	1		" " "	" "	49	
31	Pettus Hawkins	1		" " "	3	41	
	Continued of the Colored School					2318	Days
1	Picken Louis	1		June 7th 1869	Sept 24th 1869	78	
2	Joe Bogan	1		" " "	Aug 27	58	
3	Thos Bomar	1		" " "	Sept 24 1869	78	
4	Maggie Bomar		1	" " "	July 2 "	19	
5	Rose Ellison		1	" " "	S. 30 "	39	
6	Louis Forney	1		" " "	" 30 "	78	
7	York Hawkins	1		" " "	" " "	58	
8	E. P. Hawkins	1		" " "	July 3 "	18	
9	Robt Head	1		" " "	Sept 24 "	78	
10	Nancy Lancaster		1	" " "	Sept 24 1869	67	
11	Mary Lancaster		1	" " "	" " "	67	
12	Lou Young		1	" " "	Sept 24 1869	78	
13	Laura Evans		1	" " "		[illegible]	

Number and Amount carried forward.

A page from the attendance record of Eva Poole's school. Eight-year-old Thomas Bomar, who became a builder of cotton mills, was among her students.

$800 contract with the U.S. government to build the schoolhouse, they constructed a 30x40-foot wooden building. Among the school's organizers was 25-year-old Samuel Norris, a Black man who boarded with Eva and Louis Poole; Nathaniel "Nat" Aden, namesake of Spartanburg's Aden Street; and Alfred White, a laborer who lived Back of the College. Conflict flared when church members resisted Cummings's heavy hand with school affairs. In 1871 Oliver O. Howard, head of the Freedmen's Bureau office in Washington, D.C., stepped into the fray and deeded the schoolhouse to the AME group. His stipulation: "that pupils shall never be excluded from the benefits arising from the rental or sale thereof on the account of race or previous servitude."

This was all for naught, though. Shortly thereafter, the school was torn down to make way for the Air-Line Railroad and Spartanburg's first train depot.

THE PROBLEM WITH MANY of the early educational efforts was a lack of financial support by white residents, both in Spartanburg and in state government. Newly freed Black families could barely feed their families and keep roofs over their heads, much less pay teachers, build schoolhouses and purchase books. For most white Southerners, public education meant enforcing separation of the races and maintaining white control of society. The debate about how to establish public schooling at the 1868 South Carolina Convention to establish a new state constitution was "rancorous." White Democrats and some white Republicans opposed publicly funding Black schooling, and they fought against any form of integrated schooling. For conservatives, public education served two purposes: to educate white students and to maintain white control. Despite assurances of the kind heard from Spartanburg County School Commissioner Rev. R.H. Reid that school segregation "grows out of no prejudice or unkindness in the bosom of the whites toward the blacks," the possibility of an educated Black citizenry was harrowing to white people. The possibility of integrated education was intolerable.

Spartanburg's John Evins led conservative opposition to mixed-race schooling during the convention. His coalition of conservatives argued that no one—white or Black—wanted "to send their children to the same school" and that the Radicals were forcing the issue "to produce discord between the races." Evins argued that Black children would cost too much to educate and that integration was dangerous to society. Rancor notwithstanding, the state constitution established a uniform structure for public schools with a system of local districts governed by a superintendent. Schools would be funded by a state and local poll tax. The law technically allowed for integration, but it also allowed for public funding to support racially separate schools, which satisfied conservatives.

Funding for Spartanburg County's post-war Black schools continued to prove inadequate. The state budget for schools in 1869 was half of what it was in 1860, effectively ignoring the 100,000 new Black students seeking to be enrolled statewide. The Spartanburg County poll tax only yielded $2,400 in 1870, which combined with $1,600 from the state tax, was sufficient only to open half of the required number of schools in the county. A vote to raise taxes for education in Spartanburg County in 1874 failed in every single school district, primarily because of perceived "freeloading" on the part of Black families, according to historian Bruce Eelman.

When conservative Democrats regained control of the state in 1877, the prospects for publicly funded Black education worsened. After Reconstruction white conservative legislators would only agree to support public education for Black students under two conditions. First, Black educational curriculum must be limited to industrial training, not pre-professional training. Black students could learn to become better brick masons, carpenters, farmers and teachers—with teacher training being the highest aspiration—but Black students could not earn medical, law or business degrees. Second, the system of public education would be based upon the fundamental concept that white society would act as the civilizers of Black people. Black students would learn white history, white literature, white religion; they would learn white standards of discipline and hygiene. A representative passage from the editorial pages of *The Carolina Spartan* illustrates the point: "Now that the government of the State is in the hands of the white people, and the colored people dependent upon them for all educational advantages, (being poor and unable to help themselves to any degree)—we hope that a liberal policy will prevail. The colored man is dependent upon the white for education, moral and mental—in short, for civilization, and we hope it will not be denied him."

AFTER THE CHAOS of the early federally and state-supported Black schools in Spartanburg, Silver Hill Methodist Episcopal Church stepped into the education gap as early as 1874 with the opening of a substantial common school. This was just four years after the completion of the church's first wooden sanctuary. In its earliest days, the Silver Hill school served Black students during the months of July, August and September. Organized by prominent local merchant Charles C. Bomar, this school initially was staffed by local teachers Estelle and Julia Morgan and was led by an ambitious graduate of Charlotte's Biddle University, Walter I. Lewis, then about 20 years old. Lewis, who would go on to have a notable career as a writer and journalist, boarded with Charles and Annie Bomar on South Church Street during his time in Spartanburg. For six years Lewis dedicated himself to improving the Silver Hill school, growing the student body to as many as 134 students by September 1876. Soon after he arrived, he was joined at Silver Hill school by two other young Black educators: Kenneth M. Young (1849-1929), scion of the Southside's founding family; and Young's classmate at the University of South Carolina, 23-year-old John L. Dart, who had grown up in a free Black household in Charleston.

Lewis, Dart, Young and other teachers at Silver Hill were paid with funds granted by the white trustees of the Spartanburg township school district. Lewis typically was paid $35 a month. Female teachers received $20 a month. The trustees also paid for some furniture for the school—spending $20 in 1878—and, at least once, reimbursed Charles C. Bomar $10.50 for rent.

Lewis and Dart dreamed of having more than a grammar school at Silver Hill—they wanted a high school. They spent much of their time in Spartanburg in a desperate pursuit of funding for their vision. At one point Lewis wrote to former abolitionist Mary Anna Longstreth of Philadelphia seeking money for school operations. Her 1885 memoir mentions that she once received a solicitation letter from "the earnest principal of Spartanburg (colored) high school." In 1877 Lewis and Dart organized a commu-

Professor Walter I. Lewis, from the book Twentieth Century Negro Literature, *1902*

nity meeting to enlist the white community in providing more support for Black education. "White children of other towns of the state have enjoyed the blessings of Graded and High Schools during nine months of the year, and ours have received little more than the two or three months' public teaching every summer," according to a circular from that gathering. Eventually, Lewis sought and received a small grant from the Peabody Fund, a philanthropy that provided assistance to existing schools. The grant allowed the school to extend its school year to nine months. Principal Lewis, in fact, was ahead of the curve. A white reader of *Speight's Spartanburg Daily* newspaper lamented that Lewis had figured out how to get Peabody money even before the white schools did. "The trouble is, that our people have made no effort," the white reader lamented in his letter to the editor.

After six years in Spartanburg, Lewis moved on to Tennessee, Georgia and Florida, where he became a newspaper editor. Dart and his Spartanburg colleague, Kenneth M. Young, went on to Atlanta University. Dart then moved to Charleston, where he became the editor of *The Southern Reporter*, founded an industrial training school and served as the longtime pastor of Morris Street Baptist Church. Young wrote a novel, Selene, in 1896 and rejoined his family in Spartanburg, where he became an employee of the U.S. Postal Service.

After the trio's departure, the Silver Hill school was led by Mrs. N.F. Young, with Sallie Hartwell as her assistant. In 1880 it remained the largest and most important Black school in Spartanburg among seven other tiny common schools certified to teach Black students. Among them: Friendship School, Mount Moriah Baptist Church school, Howard Gap school and Daniel Academy.

WHEN THE STATE finally established the graded public school system in Spartanburg in 1884, white students received the majority of public funds. Spartanburg city officials did not issue bonds, raise taxes or allocate funds to build a new Black elementary school. Instead, the first Board of Education invited Tobe Hartwell and Charles Bomar to planning meetings to determine the best course of action for Black students in Spartanburg. They met in August 1884 and set up the Lincoln School, the city's first, fully publicly funded Black primary school, to be housed in the basement of Mount Moriah Baptist Church on the Southside. They hired four teachers—Phyllis Bomar, Mary Hartwell, Clara Farrow and L.B. Lord—and appointed the Rev. R.W. Baylor principal and teacher. Some repairs were needed to bring the basement up to speed, and 75 double desks, chairs, maps and blackboards were acquired. The initial outlay for the facility and supplies, as well as first month's salaries for the five employees, was a paltry $500. The school opened Oct. 13, 1884, with grades one through seven.

Church-related schools for Black children continued to flourish in this era. In 1889 a parochial school for Black children and teens opened on the grounds of Westminster Presbyterian, a Black mission church located on Wofford Street at a site behind the present-day Spartanburg County Courthouse. In its first year, the school—ultimately named Grant Academy—served 139 students and was led by P.G. Hammett, an alumnus of Charlotte's Biddle University. The academy's early teachers included "poet laureate" Jimmy Johnson and a teenaged Phyllis Bomar, daughter of the formerly enslaved couple Elias and Malinda Bomar. Among its key supporters were the Frank Thompson family, who lived on Evins Street behind Wofford College, and the Black Bomar family of Howard Street. With more than 200 students in attendance, there were 500 books in its library in 1895. Two years later, the school moved out of the church into an adjacent building. Hammett died suddenly of a stroke on the streets of Spartanburg in November 1898.

In a retrospective article written in 1901, Spartanburg letter carrier Frank Thompson wrote that the school prepared Black students for entry into such colleges as Biddle University (which later became Johnson C. Smith University) and Barber-Scotia College in Concord, North Carolina, a Presbyterian college for Black teachers. "The students are admitted to the higher institutions with a very high standing. The school has been of incalculable benefit to the race in which it was established." He lamented, though, that the school could not handle more students; in 1901 principal Rev. Hyder M. Stinson "has had to refuse admittance to a large number of ambitious youths on account of a lack of accommodations," he wrote. The school, later renamed Westminster High School, was supported by the national Presbyterian Church as well as local donations and tuition. Westminster High School ultimately moved to North Dean Street in the 1920s, and there were as many as 125 day students in 1933. That year, the school and church were severely damaged in a fire. The school's last year was 1940, and the church eventually moved to Saxon and still meets. The Dean Street edifice was torn down.

The original Dean Street School, 1928

AS ATTENDANCE at the earliest Black schools mushroomed—led by a rapidly growing Black population in Spartanburg—it was clear to many that public education had to come out of the basements and into a real school building. In 1891 the Spartanburg city school district opened the first consolidated school for Black students, calling it Dean Street School and locating it a couple blocks away from Silver Hill Church. The two-story, white, wooden schoolhouse served grades one through seven and added an eighth grade in 1898.

Among the earliest students at Dean Street was legendary journalist William Nesbitt Jones (1882-1940), the son of a Converse College cook who lived on South Church Street. Jones, who graduated from Dean Street about 1895 and briefly taught school in Spartanburg, later received a journalism degree from Columbia University. He ultimately rose to become managing editor, war correspondent and editorial writer of the Baltimore *Afro-American* newspaper, the most important Black newspaper of its day.

William N. Jones, as pictured in the Baltimore Afro-American *newspaper*

On one of several overseas assignments, Jones was in the press box in Berlin in 1936 when Adolph Hitler snubbed Olympic runner Jesse Owens. Jones also toured Russia, which contributed to his Communist Party leanings. He became a huge presence in Baltimore, serving numerous organizations until his death in 1940. When he died, he was called "one of the most renowned weekly newspapermen of the age."

The opening of Dean Street School served to solidify the neighborhood and set off a wave of land sales up and down Northview, Nash, Chase, Humber, Cherry and Golding streets. Roughly 100 houses were added there between 1903 and 1920 in the earliest days of the Gas Bottom neighborhood, so named for a coal-burning electric plant at the low end of a creek valley. The school's first principal was the Rev. C.C. Scott, pastor at Silver Hill. When the Methodist Church sent Scott to his next church appointment outside Spartanburg, his shoes were filled in 1893 by Robert Milton Alexander, a man born into slavery who would guide the school on North Dean Street for the next 37 years, training new generations of teachers and launching hundreds of Black citizens into their careers.

Upon arriving in Spartanburg, Alexander already had traveled na-

The 5th grade class at Dean Street School, late 1890s. Principal Robert Alexander is in the center. The woman to the right of him may be his wife, Elvira, who later served as principal. Carrie Clark, standing far right, was a teacher before her marriage to Thomas Bomar.

tionally—from Buffalo, New York, to Portland, Oregon—while serving the Presbyterian Church. A graduate of Biddle University, Alexander had begun his educational career with teaching stints in Columbia and Greenville. He also had embarked on a three-year, valiant—but ultimately unsuccessful—attempt to establish an institution similar to Alabama's Tuskegee Institute in Wellford. For many years he was not only a constant presence at the schoolhouse on North Dean Street, but he was a vital community member Back of the College, making his home on Evins Street. His wife, Elvira, also taught at Dean Street. They had one son, Robert Smith. Alexander also was an author, penning a biography of 18th century Black mathematician/astronomer Benjamin Banneker, and at least two other books.

Among the many who were educated at Dean Street and went on to become teachers were Hattie Bell Penland, Rosa Mae Rivers and Ada B. Foster, a future principal at Dean Street. Other early teachers included Hattie and Estelle Bomar. Estelle later gave birth to a son, Chester Bomar

Another Dean Street class, around 1919. Principal Alexander is at top.

Himes, who became one of the most important Black novelists of the 20th century. The *Spartanburg Herald* reported in August 1916 that "illiteracy among colored children is disappearing with remarkable rapidity."

What's impressive about the longtime principal and teaching staff at Dean Street are their accomplishments in the face of inadequate public funding and support. Early blueprints of Dean Street School show bathroom facilities consisting of outhouses near the main building, and indoor plumbing was not added for nearly 50 years. The school did not have a lunchroom or even an auditorium. School programs were held on the front porch. The principal's office doubled as a library. Students shared books and supplies, and communities stepped up to provide lacking essentials when they could. By 1901 Dean Street School served nearly 900 Black students.

In more practical terms, the white approach to public Black education in Spartanburg was to limit it to one school for a population of hundreds, limit the resources and amount of funding the school received, and limit the curriculum to what was acceptable for white society.

After a fire that consumed the second story, Dean Street School was clad in brick and renamed Alexander Elementary. This school closed in 1970.

That meant advocating for an industrial training curriculum espoused by Booker T. Washington, who argued that Black people should seek to improve their situation by becoming economically self-sufficient, not by seeking full civil rights. Valuing hard work, thriftiness, industriousness and self-discipline, Washington believed that Black people should accept and excel at labor-driven jobs with which they could improve their material prosperity and demonstrate their social value to white society. Washington was invited to Spartanburg in 1901 and spoke to a capacity crowd at the city's 700-seat Opera House. Six years later he hopped off the train in Spartanburg and made a quick visit to Dean Street School "where he spoke in highly complimentary terms of what he saw in the carpentry shop."

In 1905 Dean Street won a $500 grant from the John F. Slater Fund for the Education of Freedmen and used the money to implement further industrial curriculum for boys and girls—woodworking and sewing. Patrick H. Foster, a graduate of the Tuskegee Normal and Industrial Institute, founded by Booker T. Washington in 1881, was hired to teach woodworking. School superintendent Frank Evans visited Dean Street in 1909 to show a *Herald* reporter a cane-bottom chair-making operation. "The boys who bottomed these chairs were little fellows, hardly tall enough to stand up to the workbench," the reporter wrote. "The chief aim of all the lessons taught is to instill into each student some of the fundamental principles in woodwork, which have universal application."

Dean Street's Robert Alexander died suddenly of a heart attack at age 70 in February 1930. Among numerous tributes to him, the *Spartanburg Journal* reported that there were 20 teachers working in Spartanburg County classrooms who had been taught by Alexander at Dean Street School. At his death, local school superintendent Frank Evans called him "a man with no illusions as to the needs of his race" and praised the way he "consistently set his people a marked example of hard work and self-respect." All Black schools in the community were closed on the day of his funeral. Nine years later, the Spartanburg city school district renamed the school the Alexander School and embarked on a $15,000 renovation to clad the school in brick, removing its second story. The principals who followed him included Elvira Alexander, Eugene Rivers, Lula B. Sexton, Ada Bagwell Foster and Mary L. Copeland.

Robert Alexander's 37-year legacy on the northside, which ultimately led to added grades at Dean Street and a new city high school on the northside for Black students, was incontrovertible and long-lasting. The school that bears his name still stands on North Dean Street, housing the Epsilon Nu chapter of the Omega Psi Phi fraternity. A renovation of the school building began in 2024.

SPOTLIGHT

ST. LUKE'S LUTHERAN DAY SCHOOL

The earliest school located Back of the College was Saint Luke's Lutheran Day School, which served the neighborhood for more than three decades beginning in 1914. Initially located at 380 Evins Street, this parochial mission school began in what the Lutheran Church archives describe as "a poorly appointed house." Within three years 80 elementary and junior high students received their education there.

In 1917 the Missouri Synod of the Lutheran Church invested in the construction of a large wooden chapel, which also served as a schoolhouse. The L-shaped building had a belfry with bell, a sanctuary for 150, and large, arched windows. Attendance at the school increased to 177 students by 1920. Its first principal and pastor was the Rev. John McDavid, who went on to serve a church in Los Angeles, followed by the Revs. Frank Alston and John W. Fuller. Wilma Barnhardt was an early teacher, and early members included the Wiggins, Bobo, Rivers and Newton families. With the opening of Cumming Street School in 1926, attendance at the Lutheran School dropped precipitously. It served 80 students in 1932.

From 1932 until the mid-1940s, the church and its school were led by the Rev. Walter C. Hart. At that time, it was the only Lutheran Church serving Black congregants in South Carolina. Hart is best known for organizing Spartanburg's Black Boy Scouting programs in the 1940s and Kiddie Kollege in 1959. The Lutheran day school closed in 1948. The church turned its edifice over to Woodward Memorial Baptist Church in 1953, operated out of homes, then moved to Saxon in 1966. St. Luke's eventually merged with Lamb of God Lutheran Church on Fernwood-Glendale Road. The original chapel was torn down in 1976.

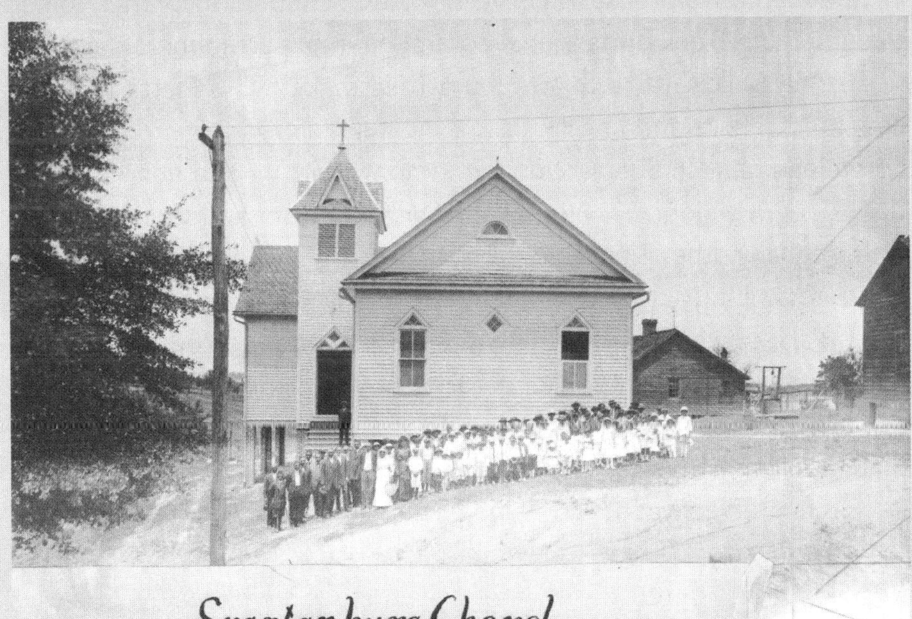

TOP: *A 1917 photo of students at St. Luke's Lutheran Day School, located Back of the College.*

BOTTOM: *St. Luke's Lutheran Church was dedicated in 1917. It was located on Evins Street near the site of the original T.K. Gregg Recreation Center.* Images courtesy of Concordia Historical Institute, Saint Louis, Missouri.

SPOTLIGHT

SPARTANBURG'S FIRST BLACK ATTORNEY

The first Black lawyer in the piedmont of South Carolina was Arthur Chester Platt (1892-1944), who lived Back of the College on Jefferson and Evins streets during his short and active life. Until the 1950s Platt was the only Black lawyer in the state to be granted permission to argue cases before the South Carolina Supreme Court. He won two of his four cases argued there.

Born in Marion, South Carolina, Platt moved with his family to New England before the turn of the century. His father, John, was a coachman in New Haven, Connecticut. While his parents never moved back South, their ambitious son Arthur did, attending North Carolina's Livingstone College, where he played on the college's first basketball team. He graduated from Boston University Law School in 1922, then joined the emerging Black professional community in Spartanburg. Platt married Anna Belle Gist, a Spartanburg dressmaker. The Platts had two daughters, Nellie and Lucille. In 1923 he helped organize the first Black home loan bank in Spartanburg, Piedmont Building and Loan Association, along with John W. Woodward, William Porter and W.M. Kirkland.

Like many other Black Southern attorneys of this era, he represented North Carolina Mutual Life Insurance of Durham, North Carolina, a large Black-owned firm that litigated throughout the country. Around 1930 Platt also represented Henry M. Cleveland, a prominent white businessman and major Spartanburg landowner, handling an estate of more than $1 million as well as some of Cleveland's banking litigation.

His first office was at 149 ½ North Church Street and later moved to 120 Short Wofford Street. Oftentimes Platt had to retain white co-counsel in his cases "because all-white juries preferred white lawyers," Anna Belle Platt once said. He was joined in Spartanburg in the mid-1920s by the city's second Black lawyer—Booker T. Smith of Cowpens—who in his early lawyering days was also a part-time bricklayer. Smith (1883-1948) opened an office nearby on North Church Street. He lived at 243 North Dean Street and was active in progressive Republican Party politics.

Prominent Lawyer

ATTORNEY A. C. PLATT

Attorney Arthur C. Platt, as pictured in the Afro-American *newspaper*

In September 1939 Arthur Platt stepped in to assist Black nurses at the Spartanburg General Hospital who were told they would be laid off and their jobs assumed by white nurses in training. Working as representatives of Spartanburg's Negro Civic League, Platt and local mortician John Woodward filed a protest and quashed the hospital's plan. "Mr. John Woodward and Mr. A.C. Platt are receiving a big hand from the Spartanburg folks for the stand they took in regards to the General Hospital," wrote a correspondent for the Columbia *Palmetto Leader* newspaper. "All colored nurses will be reinstated."

In August 1942 Platt defended a Black Camp Croft soldier from Philadelphia who was arrested for going into a Spartanburg drug store to get an ice cream cone. The soldier, Albert Carrish, was assaulted by the clerk and citizens, then thrown into jail. "Citizens in the town were called together and employed Attorney A.C. Platt to appeal the case," wrote *The Pittsburgh Courier.*

In the 1940s Platt was working 60 hours a week, making $1,500 a year, more income than anyone else living Back of the College. He owned his home at 230 Evins Street, and it was valued at $1,500. But Platt suffered from a "lingering illness," and passed away unexpectedly while visiting a sibling's home in Medfield, Massachusetts, on May 7, 1944.

The SOUTHERN INDICATOR

Entered as Second Class Matter May 8th, 1912, at the post office at Columbia, S. C., under the Act of March 3d, 1879.

C. C. SCOTT, Editor,
L MORGAN, Manager

Subscribtion Rates

One year.............................$1.00
Six Months........................... 60c
Three Months 35c

Advertising Rates Made Known on Application

The masthead of Laban Morgan's newspaper. In 1912 the Rev. C.C. Scott, formerly of Silver Hill Methodist Church, served as his editor.

SIX

THE NEWSMEN AND THE NEIGHBORHOOD

THE WALK FROM Laban Morgan's home on Evins Street to his newspaper office and print shop at the edge of Spartanburg's Morgan Square took about 15 minutes in 1897, perhaps 12 minutes if he walked briskly. The young publisher was often in a hurry. As the 20th century dawned, *The Piedmont Indicator*, the newspaper he founded in Spartanburg, had more subscribers than any Black-owned publication of its kind in South Carolina. Over the next 15 years Morgan would work himself to an early death with his single-minded focus to inform and advocate for Black people across South Carolina and beyond. He also would put a cadre of writers and editors to work for him, including his young Back of the College neighbor, Asa Thompson, and an important mentor, Spartanburg's the Rev. James A. Brown.

Why Laban Morgan chose to come to Spartanburg is a bit of a mystery. A native of Orangeburg, he was the oldest son of Shadrack Morgan, a Reconstruction-era state legislator who joined up with the 135th U.S. Colored Troops in 1865 when Gen. William T. Sherman's army blazed through the South. The younger Morgan bought a house on Evins Street in Spartanburg for $420 in early 1897. Laban Morgan was politically minded, just like his father. He rented an office for his newspaper venture on Spartanburg's North Church Street on a block that also housed several other Black-owned businesses: Charles C. Bomar's grocery, Henry Gaither's restaurant, H.S. Doogan's tailor shop, Dr. W.C. Rhodes' medical office, Octavia Nesbitt's restaurant, and the City Drugs pharmacy, owned by Dr. George K. Adams and Dr. G.W. Harry. Morgan's weekly *Piedmont Indicator*, of which no copies are known to survive, was the largest independent Black newspaper in the state by 1900, with 750 subscribers. By that time Morgan also was a major figure in his adopted hometown. In 1899 the young newspaperman served as master of ceremonies for the annual emancipation ceremony at the Spartanburg Courthouse where "a vast crowd had assembled in the courtroom and the outside space was also thronged and packed."

At the end of each day, Morgan, then in his late 20s, would return to his house at 137 Evins Street. In those days, Evins Street was unpaved, narrow and often muddy. Back of the College was a working-class neighborhood that was continuing to draw new residents from across the upcountry. The 1900 census shows at least 25 men who were day laborers, with another 12 listed as farm laborers and ten as brick masons. There were house carpenters, teamsters, railroad workers, draymen and gardeners—at least five of each. There were hackmen, coal passers, well diggers, waggoners and blacksmiths. Some Black men in the neighborhood were beginning to break into jobs previously held by whites: Hilton Glover and John Glover were part of Spartanburg's new Black city fire brigade. Five preachers made their home in the area, including Thomas Benson, who lived with his wife, Mamie, a school teacher, in a house they owned at 317 Evins Street.

Most women in the neighborhood held down domestic jobs to support their families. There were at least 70 women in the neighborhood who called themselves "washer women." Forty women were cooks. There was no public transportation in 1900, so these women either walked across town to white-owned houses or they hired a hack—a simple horse-drawn carriage, often driven by their Black neighbors—to get to work. Some women worked out of their homes: Corrine Thompson of Jones Street was a seamstress, as was Alice Jeffries of Evins Street.

When their children reached teen years, many of them were put to work, too. Financial circumstances were particularly tenuous for young women on the northside. Edith Button is recorded as being a "house girl" at 16 years old, living with her widowed mother, Charity. The two of them, with at least two other families, were lodgers in Henry Carson's crowded house at 97 Evins Street.

Turn-of-the-century street laborers digging water lines in Spartanburg.

One of the largest and most active early families on the northside was that of brick mason Jack Thompson, and his wife, Mary. The Thompsons raised at least a dozen children, many of whom became vitally involved in the growth of downtown Spartanburg and the lives of young people of their race. Jack Thompson, born into slavery in 1833, was a founder and central figure at Silver Hill Methodist Church, as was his wife. Jack's early history as an artisan is unclear. A team of enslaved masons helped build Wofford's twin-tower Main Building in 1854, and it's possible he could have been among them. A few years after emancipation, the Thompson family made their home on Jones Street, near the present-day site of Wofford's Gibbs Stadium.

This was a family that had close relations with its neighbor, Wofford College. Though his children would never be able to attend the then-segregated institution, Jack Thompson made sure his teenaged sons could circulate among the scholars and students next door. One son, Ben, was a "house servant" of English professor Dr. Whitefoord Smith. Another, Asa, worked both in the home of science professor Dr. Daniel A. DuPré and in general campus service for 10 years.

Jack Thompson also trained his sons in the art of brick masonry. At least three sons—Ben (1871-1927), Joseph (1874-1937) and Clifford (1888-1931)—were engaged as contractors for many of the brick storefronts going up in Spartanburg's rapidly growing downtown. As each of them passed away, local white-owned newspapers used the words "highly respected" and "well-known negro" to indicate their value to the local business community. Asa Thompson (1868-1935) was better known as an educator and journalist, but even he found time for masonry, serving as president of the Local 2 Bricklayers Union in Spartanburg.

Another Thompson son, Frank, became Spartanburg's first Black full-time postal service employee in 1898 at age 16. Henry, one of the youngest sons in the Thompson family, graduated from Howard University in 1907 and became a popular physician in Detroit for 35 years.

But it was the remarkable Asa Thompson who commanded the most attention in Spartanburg.

AFTER HIS STINT at Wofford College, Asa Thompson met newspaperman Laban Morgan, who lived around the corner from him. Morgan was politically connected, a big thinker and a fierce fighter for Black causes. His weekly newspaper covered activities throughout the state and even in North Carolina, where Morgan lobbied his readers in 1896 to invest in the first large-scale, Black-owned cotton mill in the town of Concord. One of the newspaper's earliest editorial stances was to warn its Black readers not to go to work in white-owned mills—assuming that opportunity ever arose—but to stay on the farm and work to become landowners. Textile work would breed ignorance and stunt their future economic prospects: "Once put the negro in the mills, and one generation will succeed another in ignorance. . . . There is nothing in the mills to inspire thought and stimulate activity," the Indicator editorialized.

Shortly after Morgan launched his newspaper, 28-year-old Asa Thompson became the Spartanburg editor for the four-page weekly publication. The Indicator was a huge advocate for the education of all Black children.

That mission was to become central to Asa Thompson's life. It was at the Indicator where he honed the opinion-writing skills that he would use throughout his life in frequent letters to the editor of the *Spartanburg Herald* and *Journal* to rally people to his causes. Thompson's voice, preserved on the pages of white-owned Spartanburg newspapers, provides the most important documentation of the issues that affected the Black community in the city's first three decades of the 20th century.

Asa Thompson and Laban Morgan were joined by another important figure in Spartanburg's early Black history: the Rev. James A. Brown, who served as the Indicator's editor at the turn of the century. Born into slavery in Union County, Brown came to Spartanburg after the war to attend the city's common schools. According to accounts of his life, Brown vividly remembered the closing scenes of the war. A graduate of Claflin College, he joined the Methodist ministry and was appointed in 1871 to serve beside the Rev. James Rosemond at Spartanburg's Silver Hill. There, he also served the far-flung Methodist congregations in rural Spartanburg County—Fair Forest, Tyger and Rio—areas where the Ku Klux Klan was indiscriminately terrorizing, and even murdering, the Black citizenry.

Brown's early Methodist service in Spartanburg also coincided with the start-up of Spartanburg's *New Era*, a Republican newspaper run by Anson Cummings and Dr. Javan Bryant. In an article later written about his life, Brown credited Javan Bryant—a former Confederate field surgeon-turned-Republican-newspaperman—as a key figure in his early education. Some 30 years later, the Black pastor also would take up the cause of journalism and his name would adorn the masthead of Laban Morgan's *Piedmont Indicator* as its editor.

The Spartanburg that this trio of Black journalists covered was a city on the move. Textile plants, and their villages of white families, were rising in Spartanburg's downtown and on all sides of the city. Four rail lines connected the city to Columbia, Atlanta, New York, Asheville and beyond. But for the Black population, which was heavily surveilled by law enforcement, economic acceleration mostly meant staying out of the way of progress. The white power structure expected the Black population to stay in its place. In October 1902 Police Chief A.B. Dean reported to City Council that there had been 2,232 arrests during the year and that 407 convicts had been sent

The Rev. James A. Brown, who served as editor of The Piedmont Indicator *in 1899*

to the chain gang, in a city whose population was roughly 12,000. Chain gang labor—which in those days was made up almost entirely of Black men—represented 6,862 days of work, Dean said.

In the police chief's mind, things were better for prisoners than they had been previously: "The days of beating, clubbing and other ill treatment of persons under arrest have passed," he told council. "It is the duty of the police to keep the criminal classes under such strict surveillance that it will be difficult for them to commit crime and avoid arrest and punishment. The criminal classes are the natural enemies of the police."

The Southern Indicator

The only Negro Journal published in the Piedmont section of South Carolina. Enters weekly without interruption one thousand homes of the best colored people, and is read by at least 5000 people every week. Advertising rates furnished on application

LABAN MORGAN, Manager

136½ N. Church Street **Spartanburg, S. C.**

An ad from the Spartanburg City Directory *after Morgan's newspaper had changed its name*

Despite purported progress in Spartanburg, there were still horrible crimes perpetrated against Black Spartans. Martin Hardy, who ran a blacksmith shop at 31 East Broad Street, was stabbed in the head at his business by an argumentative white man in April 1903. Hardy, a 58-year-old father of six children who had grown up in northern Spartanburg County as a free Black man during slavery times, died soon after. The assailant, George Blanchard, was given the minimum manslaughter sentence of two years in the penitentiary. Within a few months, Blanchard somehow escaped the prison and subsequently was pardoned by South Carolina's white supremacist governor, Duncan Heyward.

This was also the era that Spartanburg's new, segregated streetcars began operating downtown. This presented an opportunity for activism at *The Piedmont Indicator.* As Spartanburg's trolleys began rolling through the center of the city in 1902, Laban Morgan was well aware of what already was happening across the South: Black activists—in large cities such as Houston, Atlanta, Montgomery and Jacksonville—were boycotting the new forms of public transportation because of their Jim Crow segregation rules. Everywhere, Black riders were relegated to a few seats on such trolley cars or were forced to remain standing. A new generation of Black middle-class citizens resented the humiliation of racial separation. Domestic workers and porters often were unable to find seats at all. On Aug. 17, 1903,

Morgan called for a Black boycott of the Spartanburg trolley system. His directive was covered by *The Carolina Spartan*:

> "In today's issue of the '*Piedmont Indicator*,' a paper published for the colored people by a colored man named Laban Morgan, the editor advises the negroes of Spartanburg not to ride on the trolley cars. It is an invariable rule with the streetcar company here that colored people shall occupy the first two seats on each side unless standing on the rear platform. There has as yet been no friction or serious disturbances on account of this rule of the company, which has been in force since the first trolley made its trip on the electric car line."

The outcome of Morgan's call for a boycott is not known. In the years following, similar Black streetcar boycotts hit Richmond, Savannah and Nashville.

In 1906 a new controversy broke out that tore at the hearts of Black citizens in Spartanburg and infuriated them for years to come. That summer, Spartanburg City Council arranged to sell the Black community's longtime cemetery to the Charleston & Western Carolina Railroad for an expanded freight terminal, claiming that the burial ground was in a "neglected condition" and its location was no longer desirable. In a statement on June 26, 1906, the council said: "It is to the interest of the families of those there buried as well as of the city that this obstruction to its development should be removed."

Bodies in the old graveyard, generally located near the southwest corner of the modern-day AC Hotel Spartanburg, apparently dated as far back as 1849, the year attorney and former mayor Henry H. Thomson deeded one acre to the city to be used for a cemetery serving Spartanburg's enslaved people. Interred there were many of the early Black leaders of the city, including Southside founder Joseph Young and members of the Bomar family. Three or more generations of Black families had been buried there.

Asa Thompson, who had become a skilled editorialist, crafted a letter to the editor of the *Spartanburg Herald* on behalf of the cemetery trustees, pleading for the city to stop the sale to the railroad. He asked that instead the city erect a fence around the cemetery, preserving it forever as a Black

In today's issue of the "Piedmont Indicator," a paper published for the colored people by a colored man named Laban Morgan, the editor advises the negroes of Spartanburg not to ride on the trolley cars. It is an invariable rule with the street car company here that colored people shall occupy the first two seats on each side unless standing on rear platform. There has, as yet, been no friction or serious disturbances on account of this rule of the company, which has been in force since the first trolley made its trip on the electric car line. P. H. F.

The State *newspaper, Aug. 17, 1903*

burying ground. He protested the city's plan to have white undertaker John F. Floyd dig up the remains and move them elsewhere. On behalf of eight other Black leaders, including Tobe Hartwell, Thompson wrote, "The colored people buried there were your friends, and the friends of your fathers." Moving the bodies would be "a physical impossibility," he argued. "A part of these bodies will be left in one place and a part in another place, and when the excavations for the railroad are made, these bones will be thrown out in the fills and embankments."

His own family members were buried there, including his father, who died in 1885, and a brother in 1886. In a final, passionate plea, Thompson wrote, "We would rather by far have city council confiscate our homes, and turn us out of doors, without a shelter for our heads, than to disturb the resting place of our dead. . . . We are not children. We are grown and we know it would not be for our good or the good of our families to have these graves opened and the bodies removed."

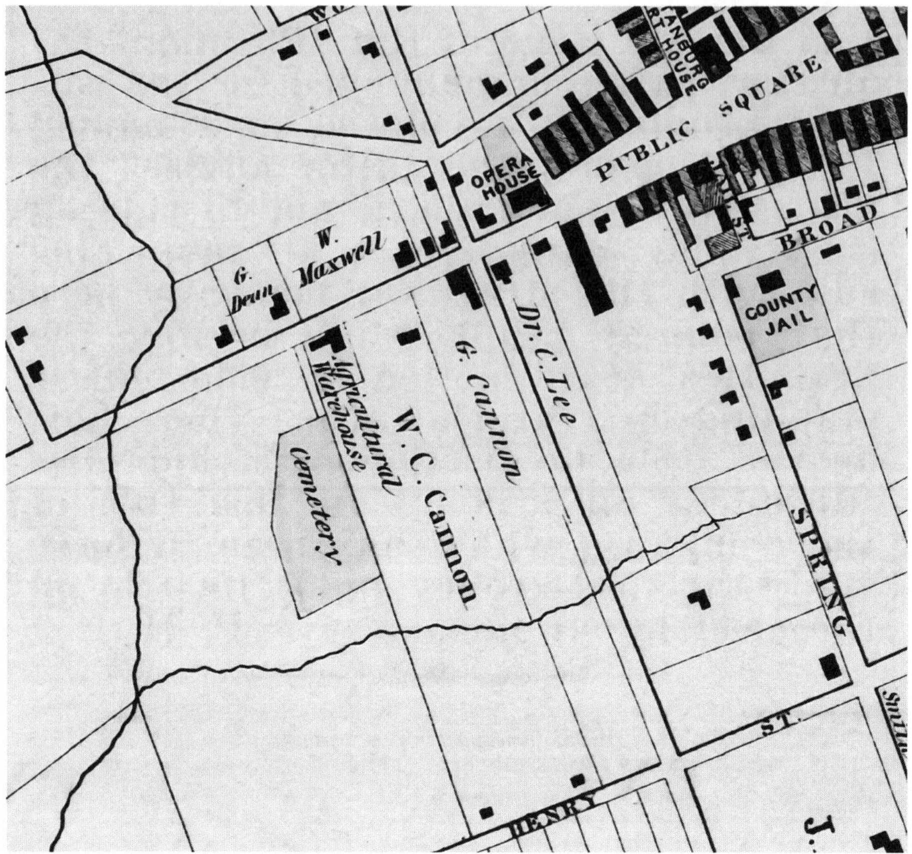

Location of the Black cemetery on West Main Street, relative to the public square. A railroad runs through here now.

His words fell on deaf ears. The cemetery was sold to the railroad for $5,500. In its place the railroad provided acreage for a replacement cemetery in a near-inaccessible area of the Southside and deeded plots to those who could claim their dead. Six years later the railroad finally laid tracks over the former downtown graveyard. "Steam shovels are at work obliterating the old negro graveyard," wrote a reporter. City Council vowed to spend the $5,500 on cemetery purposes, but it took a successful lawsuit by three Black citizens in July 1920 to force council members to spend the funds on additional burial grounds and maintenance of cemetery property on the Southside.

MEANWHILE, LABAN MORGAN was struggling to make ends meet at *The Piedmont Indicator*. Two years after he purchased his house on Evins Street, he sold it back to attorney Howard Bobo Carlisle for $500. For a while, he and his wife, Mattie, and their four boys moved to South Liberty Street, then to Thompson Street. He renamed his newspaper *The Southern Indicator* in 1908, replacing the more provincial "Piedmont" name. He added the Rev. C.C. Scott, a former developer of the Back of the College neighborhood, as editor. He was stretched thin, serving as a delegate to the state and national Republican conventions, a faculty member at the Summer Normal School for Colored Teachers of Spartanburg County, a member of the board of directors of the "Colored Hospital," and an officer of the South Carolina Colored Press Association. He carried mail for the post office for a while. He opened his newspaper office to local political meetings. In addition to his full-time newspaper duties, he became a Baptist minister in his 40s. Morgan grew increasingly frustrated with the Republican Party in South Carolina, then led by white men. In 1912 he joined with other Black political figures in forming an independent party. "This colored Progressive party," he said, "means we are not going to submit to domination by any faction in South Carolina. In other words we may vote for [Woodrow] Wilson four years from now, we may vote for [Theodore] Roosevelt, or we may vote for somebody else. We are tired of being ridiculed at national conventions."

In 1912 Morgan shifted his office to Columbia and began commuting back and forth to Spartanburg every two weeks. A few copies of the newspaper from this era survive and show extensive coverage of the Black colleges in the Midlands and Pee Dee, but little Spartanburg news. In declining health in 1915, he sold a half-interest in *The Southern Indicator* to Columbia's the Rev. J.C. White. At age 48, Morgan went home to Spartanburg for the final time, suffering from "a weakened system." His body filling with fluid from organ failure, Morgan died Oct. 12, 1915, at his home at 235 Thompson Street. *The Yorkville Enquirer* called him "one of the leaders of the colored race in the state." He was buried in the City Cemetery on the Southside.

Dr. John W. Sexton, owner of Spartanburg's Piedmont Drug Store, wrote a short tribute to the once-important journalist in 1921 in the pages of Morgan's former newspaper. Morgan, he said, "lived from hand to mouth for more than 30 years," and died destitute. "No greater service any man has given than Morgan, who stuck to this paper till the last breath was gone. Yes, died without clothes to be buried in. Yet he is dead and no one appreciates him. But thanks be to god that his widow and three boys are making good." Dr. Sexton noted that he had convinced a white Spartanburg banker to help Morgan's widow "at any time upon my request of many years ago, when Morgan was struggling, [and] lend her $50.00 with no visible means of paying back except my name upon the back."

Morgan's decline and death left Spartanburg without a Black newspaper. Yet Asa Thompson kept up his practice of sending regular letters to the editor of the *Herald* and *Journal*, spotlighting Black news and rallying people to Black causes. By then he was a respected educator. Beginning in 1908 the lifelong bachelor served as principal at Carrier Street School. In 1910 Thompson spoke up for Spartanburg's opportunity to land the new campus of Harbison College after its buildings in Abbeville were firebombed by unknown parties, resulting in a massive fire and the death of three students. When the national Presbyterian Church and the college's northern benefactor began looking for a new site for the historic Black college, Thompson wrote: "Should we succeed in having the college brought here it will supply a long felt want among our people," adding that the college's presence would save "$5,000 a year from the expenses of sending our children to colleges outside the city and state." Black leaders raised at least $1,260 as an inducement, but the college ultimately chose a 500-acre site in Irmo. The school lasted until 1958.

Thompson was one of Spartanburg's most vocal advocates for the annual Emancipation Day parade held on the first day of each year from the 1890s into the late 1920s. Hundreds of Black citizens would parade through the streets of Spartanburg, culminating in oratories and songs at the courthouse or, later, the Harris Theatre, located on the corner of what is now Church and St. John streets. In 1915 he was chairman of the publicity committee for the parade and announced to *Herald* readers that the parade would consist of Sunday Schools and societies marching with banners, a

Dr. John W. Sexton, who ran for Congress as a Republican in 1914, took care of Laban Morgan's family after the publisher's death.

rear guard of ex-slaves on horseback, as well as a line of "bricklayers, blacksmiths, carpenters, shoemakers, barbers, tailors and artisans of all kinds."

The parade got bigger every year. In January 1923 the line of marchers extended nearly a mile from the Confederate monument on Kirby Hill (current site of the U.S. Post Office) through the center part of the city, and around to Mount Moriah Baptist Church on the Southside. In his typical flourishing language, Thompson detailed the plans in a letter to the editor, describing how the marshal-in-chief, Art Martin, would lead the parade:

> "He presents a heroic figure, riding at break-neck speed up and down the lines, giving orders to his subordinate officers. He rides booted and spurred and wears a cocked hat with a feather floating in the breeze. The flag of the United States is draped over his shoulder, while he carries a drawn and uplifted sword in his hand. His friends stand in breathless awe, looking to see him dashed in pieces any moment, while his horse prances, kicks up, rears and tries to walk on his hind legs, while beating the air with his forefeet."

Back of the College students, with the Rev. Frank Alston and Fletcher Bobo at right

Except for a short stint in Asheville, Asa Thompson lived out his life Back of the College—usually sharing a home on Evins Street or Jefferson Street with multiple siblings, nieces and nephews. Sometime around 1915 he invented and received a patent for an automatic hoe and plow for cotton cultivation. The machine he created would be drawn by two mules and required two operators, taking the place of the old-fashioned hand method of plowing and hoeing cotton. While it may have seemed a miraculous invention, there is no indication the machine was ever put into production.

What really motivated Thompson was the idea of having a public high school for Black students in Spartanburg. While there were parochial and tuition-based Black schools in town after the turn of the century—including Carrier Street, Cedar Hill Academy, and at the Episcopal Church of the Epiphany, all located on the Southside—Thompson believed Black teens deserved more. He began an extensive campaign to convince white leaders that a dedicated school for secondary education was needed. Black families "have suffered an untold loss, both in money and in the intellectual advancement of their children by not having a high school," he wrote to the newspaper in April 1919. Noting that segregation prevented white people from knowing or understanding what Black families were experiencing, he walked readers through the psychological and financial effects of a community without access to a full education. He noted the financial loss to Spartanburg by Black students being sent elsewhere, but he emphasized pointedly the loss to Black students themselves: "The greatest loss, the cause that gives the most alarm, is the waning interest in education among large numbers of the colored youths. Having no opportunity to pursue their studies beyond the grades they drop out of school at the very time they need the guiding hand of the teacher the most."

While Thompson was always careful not to criticize white people, he made the consequences of their indifference clear, writing, "The white man has done nothing when he has educated his own child and has left the black child in ignorance. The ignorance in the negro child will become a magnet, a center of gravitation, and will draw everything to its level."

In a later letter he said, "The black man does not know, and has no means of finding out what thought or consideration the white man is giving to the cause of his education. When his anxiety pushes him forward to make enquiries he is considered bumptious and impertinent, and ulterior motives are ascribed to his actions." He pointed out that modern technology required a proper education to make for an effective workforce; that parochial or religious education was both unsustainable and fundamentally unfair when Black people's taxes were used to fund white schools; and that segregation necessitated the training of Black teachers, which required post-secondary training, the combined costs for which were affordable only to the very few.

Thompson kept up his campaign for a public Black high school for six more years. And then on Dec. 2, 1925, he picked up the newspaper, and there it was: in the bottom paragraph of a small article about school board business, was an announcement that trustees had purchased 3.5 acres in the

The trustees also are considering building a modern school for negroes in the northern section of the city and have acquired 3 1/3 acres for the purpose.

The Spartanburg Journal *announcement of Cumming Street School*

northern section of the city for a "modern school for negroes." Not only was there going to be a new Black high school, it was coming to his own neighborhood.

A joyous Thompson wrote a letter to the editor in response. "The issues of *The Spartanburg Herald* and *The Spartanburg Journal* carrying the announcement of the school board were thumbworn and passed from hand to hand and from house to house," he wrote. "The announcement was read and discussed around our firesides, causing the imagination of our people to run riot. In our mind's eye we could see the building completed, with school children thronging and crowding the classrooms. . . . The school will be surrounded by a thrifty, industrious, law-abiding people. Many of these people own their own homes, owning land measuring four thousand miles in extent from the surface of the earth down to its center. The negro people in this community are a proud set, but their pride is pardonable. They flatter themselves with the belief that their community is a peculiarly favored section."

The news was almost too good to be believed.

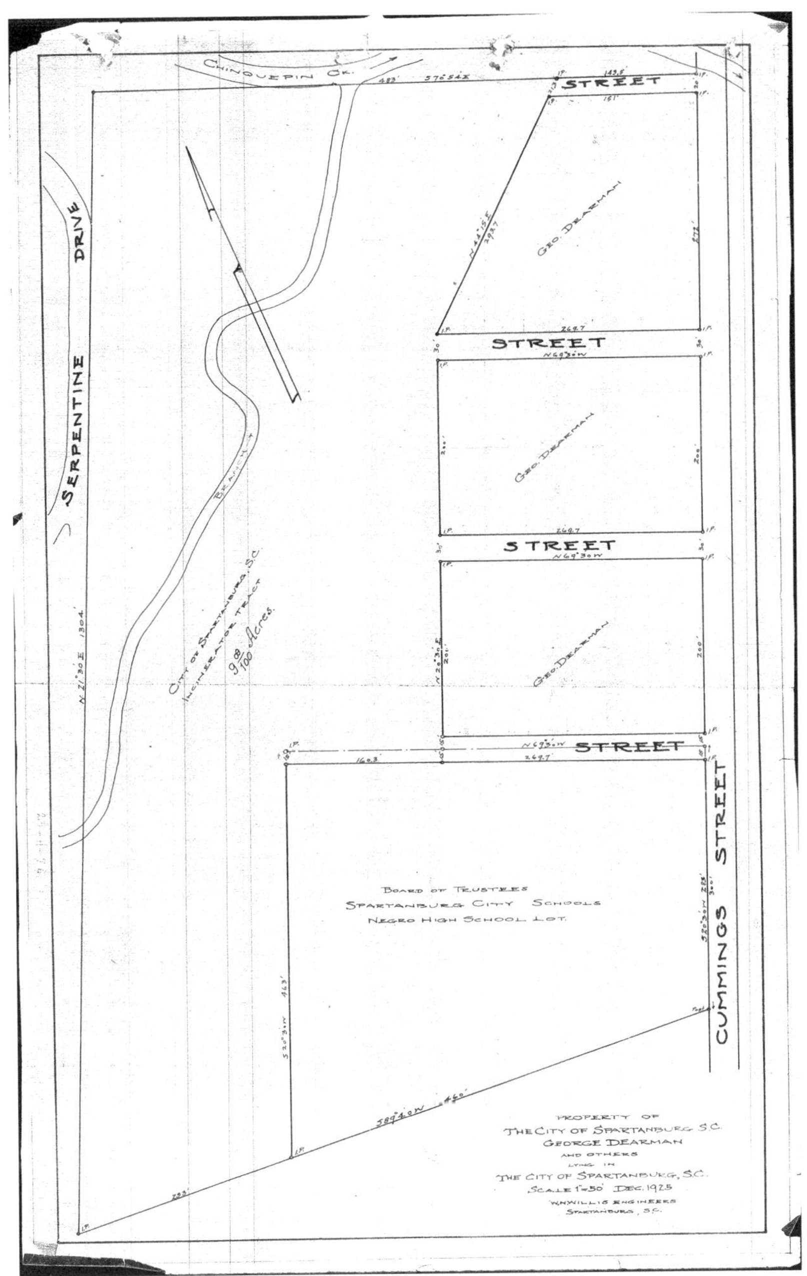

The original plat for Cumming Street School

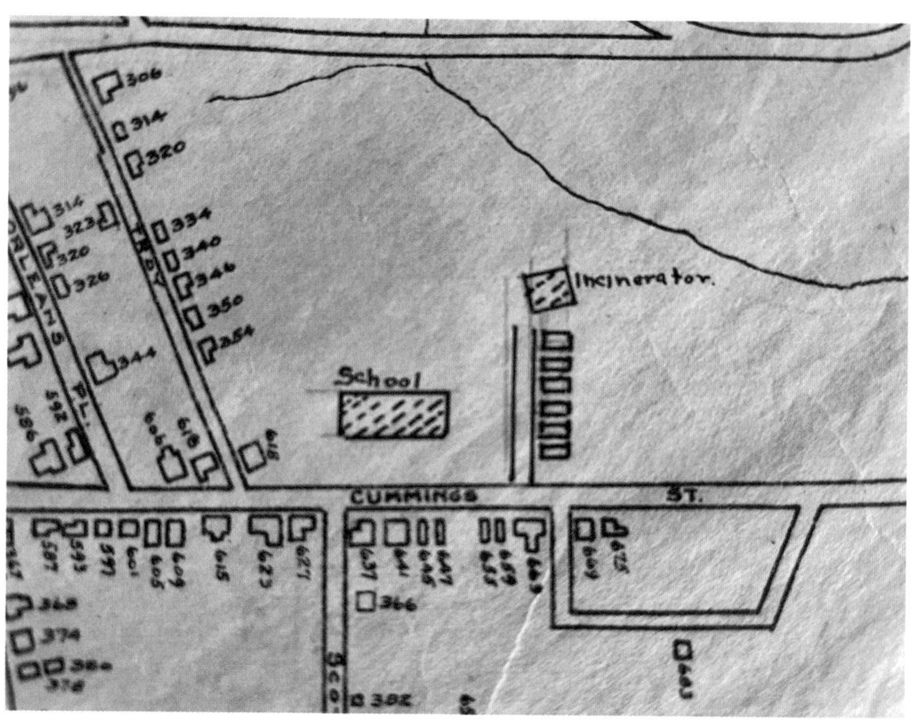

This city map, updated in 1926, shows the proximity of the garbage incinerator to Cumming Street School and nearby homes.

SEVEN

NOXIOUS AIR

BEFORE CONSTRUCTION COULD even be started on the new school, before any students would pass through its doors, another article appeared in the local newspaper announcing a more ominous addition to the Back of the College neighborhood: a major incinerator to burn all the city's garbage. The location that city leaders selected for the incinerator was in the backyard of the planned school on Cummings Street, literally adjacent to the school.

By the time the school opened toward the end of 1926, the furnaces were already firing at the city's $75,000 new incinerator plant. No one now is alive to recount the reaction in the neighborhood as the enormous smokestack began rising next to the school site. Spartanburg's white reporters were not inclined to interview Black citizens, so local response to the shocking development now is lost to history. But what is known is that for nearly 25 years, emissions from the burning of garbage—including tons of industrial waste, construction debris and hundreds of dead, stray dogs—drifted into the open windows of the school building and of the homes clustered around it.

Incinerators of the mid-20th century released a range of pollutants into the air that could contribute to asthma and other respiratory problems: carbon monoxide, particulate matter, sulphur dioxide and volatile organic compounds, among others. Incinerators in this era were noisy, and they emitted ash that rained toxic, heavy metals on the soil and kitchen gardens below. Recent soil testing through the Wofford College chemistry department has revealed a heavy presence of mercury in the soil in front of

Cumming Street School. Various studies have documented that mercury can cause damage to the nervous system, such as a reduction in strength. What residents noticed most at the time, though, were persistent, unpleasant odors.

What happened in Spartanburg would be a textbook case of environmental injustice, which was occurring throughout the South in this era. In his research on the "Dumping in Dixie" phenomenon, Dr. Robert D. Bullard—known as the father of the environmental justice movement—has documented the disproportionate siting of incinerators, landfills and other hazardous waste facilities into low-income communities of color. Bullard, who grew up in a Black community next to a landfill, pins the pattern on long-running, systemic racism.

Black residents of the northside had been dealing with incinerator emissions for years. The first Spartanburg incinerator—or crematory as they were called then—opened below Silver Hill Church, in the emerging Gas Bottom neighborhood, in the summer of 1914. It was located at the corner of Charles Street (East Daniel Morgan Avenue) and North Liberty Street, across and just west of a present-day Subaru dealership. This was at a time when new houses were going up quickly in that area of the city, as residents were attracted to the presence of Dean Street School. Like most other cities nationwide, Spartanburg calculated that an incinerator was a cheaper way of dealing with garbage than piling it on purchased land. The city board of health estimated that their small Nye Odorless Crematory would pay for itself within four years.

Most of the employees of the Charles Street incinerator were Black. They pushed garbage into the trapdoor of the furnace and operated the city's seven trash carts, which served an estimated 4,000 households in Spartanburg. "Because it has been set in a valley, all incinerator-bound carts will travel downhill, and the empty carts will travel uphill on the return to the business and residential sections of the city," wrote a journalist for the *Spartanburg Journal* in July 1914.

Spartanburg's original incinerator reached its capacity within 10 years, and city officials began looking for an alternate location. City Council briefly considered moving it to West Henry Street, but a delegation of a dozen prominent white landowners and businessmen, including the president of the Chamber of Commerce and two top officers of local banks, appeared at a 1925 council meeting to protest the location. Several owned property in the area and "declared that the proposed incinerator will cause a decided depreciation in the value of real estate holdings in that section of the city," The *Journal* reported. Mayor John F. Floyd claimed not to be aware that the incinerator "was causing so many complaints." Council instructed real estate men to scout sites south and west of the city.

In the meantime, the city school district bought four acres on Cummings Street on Oct. 10, 1925, for the new high school for Black students, spending $4,000. Six weeks after this purchase, the Spartanburg City Council—with three of its five members in their final meeting as elected officials—approved the purchase of a nine-acre lot adjacent to the school for the incinerator. The Nov. 21, 1925, purchase was for $4,999.

As soon as the new incinerator opened, 19-year-old Theo Thompson, a resident of West Lee Street on the Southside, fell into the fire pit and was burned severely.

Trucks came and went all day, stirring up clouds of dust on the dirt roads of the neighborhood. In March 1939, 5-year-old Frank McKain of 354 Simmons Street was struck by a truck near the incinerator. The *Herald* reported his condition as "fairly good" as he recuperated at the city's Black hospital. That year, a total of 26,230 loads of garbage was trucked to the incinerator—as many as 75 trucks a day passing down the street where children walked to school. The incinerator was expanded in 1940, and a new, 75-foot smokestack was added. Two more furnaces began operation, burning at more than 1,200 degrees.

By that time, even white neighbors downwind of the plant had begun to complain about the smell. Residents of the Beaumont Mill village voiced their disgust as early as 1940, saying the smoke settling over their community "had a very disagreeable odor." They presented a petition with more than 400 names demanding that the city take action to deal with a "smokescreen" drifting over their neighborhood.

In 1945 some white neighbors were at the breaking point. "I've lived here since 1925 and have been bothered by the smoke from the incinerator ever since they built it there," said Mrs. C.M. Cannon of 166 East Wood Street. "It is so bad at night that we have to pull down the windows to

Spartanburg's incinerator resembled this one, pictured in a 1929 magazine ad.

keep out the odor. We are bothered most when the wind comes this way. It smells like rags and hair burning." Mrs. Cannon lived in a house built on the old Evins estate where there were deed restrictions prohibiting Black buyers. Mrs. Fleet F. Clayton, a white woman who lived on the opposite side of the plant on North Liberty Street, chimed in: "Nearly every night it is so smoky you can hardly see." Gracie Daniel, a white woman in the Beaumont Mill village, said, "I couldn't sleep for the smoke. It keeps me awake all night."

An anonymous contributor living near the Spartanburg hospital wrote to the *Herald* in January 1946: "Imagine seating yourself before a golden brown meal of fried chicken, and just as you start to raise it to your mouth, a smell that is a cross between a dead rat and a dead horse comes between your mouth and the chicken. Maybe it is impossible to correct this, but I wish the one in charge of such things would try a little harder."

Apparently, the incinerator was not burning at a hot enough temperature to actually incinerate the garbage, which was often wet when taken to the facility. Each morning, crews would remove the ashes and the unburnt garbage from the incinerator and dump it in a pile next to the building—a pile that had smoldered for 19 years. Between the smoke from the inciner-

Firemen Attempt to Put Out 19-Year-Old Blaze in Trash Pile at City Incinerator

By WILSON HARRISON
Journal Staff Writer

Following numerous complaints about the nuisance created by smoke from the city incinerator behind Cummings Street School in the northeastern section of Spartanburg, the Fire Department yesterday afternoon began playing a stream of water on a 50-foot deep trash pile where a fire has smoldered ever since the incinerator was built 19 years ago.

Fire Commissioner L. T. Cothran said that he had received complaint after complaint from residents in the vicinity of the incinerator about the smoke and odor from the trash fire.

About 1,600 feet of hose were laid by firemen from the nearest hydrant on Cummings Street to reach the smoldering trash pile at the incinerator.

After playing water on the trash pile all yesterday afternoon and last night, the Fire Department reported that it was still smoking this morning. Efforts to soak the debris sufficiently to relieve the smoke nuisance were being continued this morning.

Judging from a survey of residents of the area the smoke reached a height this summer, Wednesday night. One eyewitness who investigated the smoke in North Liberty Street section Wednesday night said smoke was "thick enough to cut with a knife."

A newspaper report of the 1945 incinerator fire, which produced smoke "thick enough to cut with a knife."

ator itself and the smoke from the unburnt garbage and ash deposit, residents were dealing with a lot of obnoxious smog.

But as bad as it was for white residents of the area, most of them did not live next door to the incinerator. Cumming Street School students and staff did. They had to choose between closing classroom windows during hot weather or leaving them open to the smoke. Students and staff with asthma or other health problems were at risk as they entered or left the property. After-school activities were compromised. An outside report on Spartanburg schools by the George Peabody College of Teachers in 1948 was unequivocal: "The incinerator is a health hazard to the children attending this school. The investment in the school building is too much to justify abandonment; yet school children deserve a more desirable environment."

In 1951 there was yet another problem. The city's animal control and local Humane Society chose to use a dirt-floor building at the incinerator as a makeshift dog pound. A reporter who visited the site wrote that 20 dogs were crammed into the 6-by-8-foot building. Sick dogs were finding their way out into the neighborhood. "Another dog lay dead in the pound Thursday afternoon, while five other dogs tried to dig their way out of the place."

By the early 1950s, the incinerator finally was abandoned, and the city chose instead to landfill its garbage on a 25-acre site close by. Students at Cumming Street School could look out of their classroom windows and see an enormous pile of rubbish rising at the end of Twitty Street, just across Chinquapin Creek. Fires, started by spontaneous combustion or vandals, were frequent. Firemen often battled the blazes for a day or two before getting rid of the smoke. When School District 7 superintendent J.G. McCracken began speaking out about the inappropriateness of having a landfill so near a school in 1954, City Council ultimately relented and began a search for a new location for the dump. Years later, a Kmart would be built on the site, then a Food Lion grocery.

On Sept. 11, 1957, a demolition crew set off dynamite at the site of the old incinerator, and the giant chimney came crashing down beside Cumming Street School. A cellphone tower stands on the site today. Meanwhile, a replacement city dump began rising across town in the historic Black neighborhood of Sims Chapel Road, next to an old fertilizer plant, in the community of Arkwright. Some 40 years later—after a cluster of cancer cases and a series of mysterious health problems emerged to plague residents there—a young former college football player named Harold Mitchell would embark on one of the most significant and innovative environmental justice missions ever to take place in the United States. His nationally recognized ReGenesis project would force an $8 million city cleanup of the waste that had once plagued Gas Bottom and Back of the College, and now had helped turn his own Black neighborhood into a Superfund site.

OPPOSITE: *It took two days to bring down the incinerator chimney in 1957.*

Chimney Rocks, Rolls But Stands Her Ground

Spartanburg's old incinerator chimney near Cummings Street School rocked and rolled Monday but she wouldn't fall down at all.

A demolition crew pulled and tugged at her with cables, then blasted her with dynamite. But the old chimney stood pat, disrupting the best laid plans of Hollis Brock, who contracted to tear her down.

City Council let the contract to the firm several weeks ago. Monday, work crews using a cable, tried to pull the chimney down.

A worker climbed the 75-foot chimney via an iron ladder on the outside and attached the cable. The other end of the cable was attached to a tractor which attempted to pull down the chimney. The chimney rocked a bit, snapping the cable clean in two.

Using six sticks of dynamite, the crew tried to weaken the old girl. They fastened another cable to the top of the chimney first so that if the dynamite toppled the chimney, the tractor could pull the falling monster away from a house about 50 feet away.

With a mighty blast, the dynamite blew out a hole big enough to walk through. When the dust settled the chimney still stood.

Workmen tried again to pull the chimney down with a cable. Again the cable broke. The workmen packed up and went home.

They plan to come back today. But the big question is, who is going to climb up the partially dynamited chimney to hook on another cable?

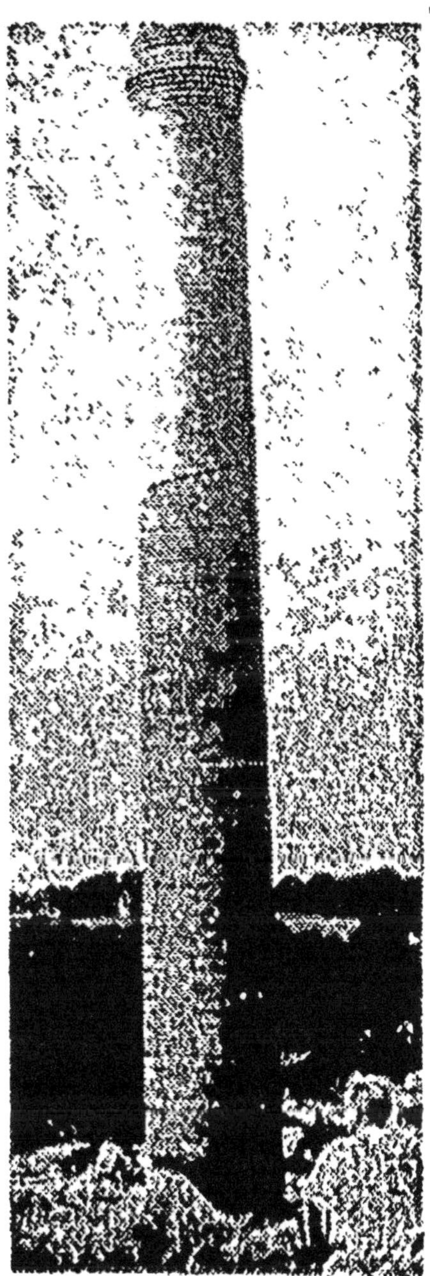

INCINERATOR CHIMNEY
Withstands Dynamite

Students at Cumming Street School in the late 1920s with Principal William Dendy

EIGHT

A HIGH SCHOOL AND A COMMUNITY CENTER

ON A DAY NEAR the end of 1926, some 600 Black students in grades 1 through 9 arrived at the doors of their brand-new public school. Waiting to greet them was Cumming Street Principal Palmer G. Brewton, who had come over from Cedar Hill Academy, the Southside's private school. A cadre of 11 teachers, all women, awaited them too. The school itself was a marvel—a two-story, red-brick temple to education, perched atop a rise at the far end of the neighborhood. The older students hustled up the stairs to eight spacious classrooms on the second floor, while the younger ones drifted into their rooms on the first floor. There was a large cafeteria in the basement, where the students eagerly ate their first school lunch. On this school day—and on most days during the four decades to come—there were more Black students at Cumming Street School than there were white students at neighboring, 100-acre Wofford College.

Designed by architect J. Frank Collins (1883-1969), Cumming Street School's simple, institutional design was accentuated by 16 large window bays, with each holding 45 smaller window panes. Over the course of his nearly 60-year career in Spartanburg, Collins designed more than 53 local buildings and facilities, including downtown's Masonic Temple, the original Spartanburg General Hospital, Duncan Park Stadium, the Coca-Cola Bottling Co. on West Main, as well as Andrews Field House at Wofford College. The new school building sat on about 3.5 acres where Cummings Street came to a dead end.

Cumming Street School, around the time of its opening. There were 500 students in the late 1920s.

Carved in granite at the roofline of the new building was CUMMING STREET SCHOOL, which, of course, did not match the spelling of the street below, named more than 50 years earlier by the neighborhood's original developer, Anson Cummings. The mistake apparently was caused by a lack of attention, and it has created confusion ever since. Regardless, even a journalist at the *Herald* was impressed, calling it "one of the best buildings for colored children in the South" and noting that Black families in Spartanburg heretofore had been "sending their children off to school at great expense."

A grateful Asa Thompson wrote a letter to the editor: "The colored people are justly proud of the school, not with a false and foolish pride but a pride that has grown out of a deep sense of appreciation and gratitude to the trustees, superintendent and all who are responsible for the school's establishment and maintenance." In typical fashion, though, Thompson had another agenda wrapped in his platitudes—he noted that after more than a year, the grounds around the school had not been graded, and the promised walkways, trees and flowers had never been added.

During the vacation months between the first and second years of the school, Professor Brewton suddenly passed away. The *Herald* wrote that Brewton had "laid a good foundation for the work and his influence is still felt in the school and his life and work will linger long in the memory of his pupils." His shoes were quickly filled by William P. Dendy, who also came over from Cedar Hill School. Dendy and his wife, Lillian, made their home near the new school at 250 Evins Street. Dendy also served as a correspondent for a short-lived weekly Black newspaper in town called *The Spartanburg Times*, which operated in the early 1930s and was managed by Howard L. Neale of Northview Street.

Dendy's teachers came from throughout the city: Fordham Foster, Carolyn Snetters, Elva Lowery, Edna Drake and Lillie Brewton came in from the Southside, while Louise Brown, Ethel Carter, Georgia Talley and Allie Ferguson lived on the northside and had a much shorter walk to school. Students came from all across the city. Many disenrolled from the Southside's tuition-based Cedar Hill Academy in favor of the free education at Cumming Street, eventually leading to the demise of that school after a 25-year-run. Over the next two years, 10th and 11th grades were added at Cumming Street. The first graduating class was in 1929.

Just because parents now had the high school building they had sought for years it did not mean they were satisfied with the way public schools dollars were doled out in Spartanburg. In 1929 the Colored Civic League published a list of requests in the Black-owned newspaper *The Hub City Observer* to the chairman and members of the Spartanburg School Board that addressed their grievances. Their requests included hiring more Black elementary schoolteachers and paying them the same wage as their white counterparts; standardizing curriculum at Cumming Street School so graduates could matriculate at area colleges; building laboratories at Cumming Street; adding an auditorium to Cumming Street and planting trees and beautifying school grounds; and "[calling] attention to the unimproved condition of the streets leading to the Cumming Street School."

TOP: *The 1929 graduating class at Cumming Street.*

BOTTOM: *Cumming Street fielded a championship football team in 1928.*

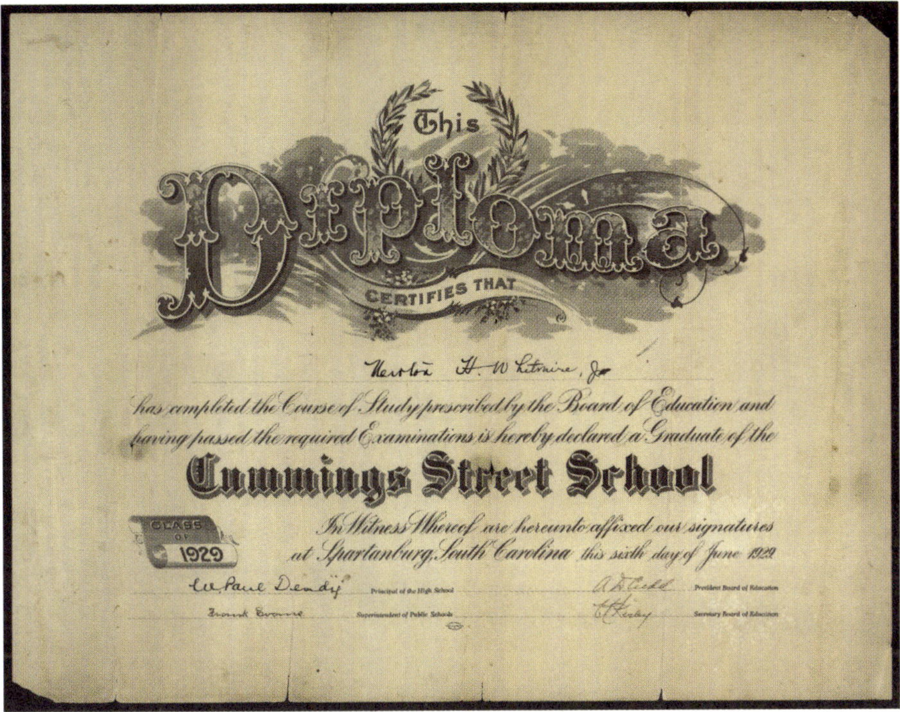
This
Diploma
CERTIFIES THAT

has completed the Course of Study prescribed by the Board of Education and having passed the required Examinations is hereby declared a Graduate of the

Cummings Street School

CLASS OF 1929

In Witness Whereof we hereunto affixed our signatures at Spartanburg, South Carolina this sixth day of June 1929

Principal of the High School — President Board of Education

Superintendent of Public Schools — Secretary Board of Education

Newton Whitmire Jr. graduated from Cumming Street in 1929. Principal William Dendy signed his diploma.

This would be the opening salvo of an endless battle for equitable education in Spartanburg.

In 1932 Dendy was succeeded by Camillus C. Woodson Jr. (1901-1975), a towering figure in Spartanburg educational history. He was born into a family with distinguished service in education—his father, C.C. Woodson Sr. (1868-1932), had served as principal of Carrier Street School. The younger Woodson attended his father's school and Dean Street School before eventually earning a graduate degree in secondary administration at the University of Michigan. He supported his undergraduate education at Benedict College by working as a Pullman porter and hotel waiter, then spent several years in the insurance business in Philadelphia.

Woodson served in the lean years of the Great Depression, but these were some of the best years at the school. Students were attending college regularly by 1930, including Ernest Collins (Johnson Smith University), Newt Whitmire and Claiborne Carter (Livingstone College) and Vincent

Principal C.C. Woodson Jr. with his school's float in a local parade

D. White (Negro Agricultural and Technical College in Greensboro, North Carolina). Other Cumming Street students went on to Benedict College, Allen University, Claflin College, South Carolina State and Voorhees. In 1934 a large football field was added next to the school; its stadium had a seating capacity for 1,500. A day nursery was added in 1935 with Genevieve Woodson and Carrie Bomar Perry in charge. New teachers included neighborhood favorite Stacey Whitmire, and, for the first time, male educators, including Arthur Benson, Willie Lewis and David Nicholas.

In the mid-1930s Hattie B. Penland moved over from her teaching position at Dean Street School and began a 30-year career of educating the youngest children at Cumming Street. Penland, who had been born behind the college in the winter of 1902, had a fascinating life story and enjoyed sharing the events of her childhood with her students. As a child, her mother, Millie, had been employed as a cook at the home of Wofford College's ancient languages professor, Dr. Joseph A. Gamewell, in a

Carrie Bomar Perry, who helped run the Cumming Street nursery after operating the Provident Hospital

brick house that now houses the college infirmary. "Hattie Bell," as she was called, spent many days in the Gamewell home, absorbing the culture of the scholar and his wife. "They told me this was my palace and all of this was my yard," she recalled in a 1995 interview recorded for Wofford. "I could play in it. Then they said, 'Come in the house.' Then they showed me a room and they had books from the floor to the ceiling. I knew as soon as I saw all of that that he was rich." The Gamewells would lend her books, and she discovered a love of reading. One day, Williams Jennings Bryan, a former U.S. presidential candidate, visited the college, and he spoke with her in the Gamewells' study. That was one of her favorite stories to tell. She liked to say, "I was a freshman at Wofford College when I was 4 years old."

Penland, who became the valedictorian of her high school class, attended Claflin College and received her bachelor's degree from South Carolina State. Knowing she could make more money with an additional degree, she followed the advice of two childhood friends and traveled to Indiana University for her master's. She never married and never had children of her own, living out her life on Jones Street, sometimes taking in pregnant teens to care for them. But in her three decades at Cumming Street, she taught almost all the Black men and women who would rise to positions of prominence in the late 20th century, including Mayor James Talley and School District 7 Superintendent Tyrone Gilmore.

The school's original advocate, Asa Thompson, continued to live Back of the College. He commuted each weekday to Whitney, where he held the position of principal and teacher at a three-room Black school established with the financial assistance of Julius Rosenwald, a Jewish-American businessman and philanthropist out of Chicago. Thompson was instrumental in the founding of the Bethlehem Center, a social outreach center, in the Highland neighborhood in 1930. Thompson died at home on Jefferson Street Sept. 29, 1935, at the age of 70. "Quiet, unobtrusive, yet a man of sound character and exemplary habits, he became a leader of his race, one whose advice and counsel was sound," wrote the *Spartanburg Journal* two days later. The tribute was somewhat ironic as Thompson had been a man of strong and passionate opinions delivered by pen much of his life. The newspaper noted that he was largely responsible for procuring Rosenwald funds for many of the nearly two dozen Black schoolhouses in the county. "His passing marks the end of a useful, well spent life."

His Whitney schoolhouse, located at the current site of Cleveland Chapel Baptist Church, was renamed the Asa Thompson Colored School and operated about 13 more years.

MEANWHILE, THERE WAS another community improvement idea taking shape through the persistent efforts of a young Black physician who was a relative newcomer to Spartanburg—the legendary Theodore "T.K." Gregg. With federal dollars beginning to flow to cities and towns as part of President Franklin D. Roosevelt's New Deal programs, Gregg saw an opportunity to bring a community center to the neighborhood behind Wofford College.

Raised on a farm in Marlboro County in a family of dedicated Methodists, Gregg (1902-1939) was introduced to Spartanburg in the late 1920s when his father, the Rev. Lexington Grant Gregg, was named pastor of Silver Hill Church, a position he held for four years. Because of the size of the Gregg family—there were 11 children—the Methodist congregation built

The Rev. Lexington Gregg brought his large family to Spartanburg when he served Silver Hill Church.

them a new, eight-room, brick parsonage on North Converse Street. T.K.'s mother, Eliza Jane, capably led the Ladies Aid Society at Silver Hill and encouraged and challenged her children to make the most of themselves. Every Gregg child earned a college degree and most went into professional careers, either in the ministry or in medicine.

T.K. Gregg, the fifth child in his family, graduated from Claflin College in 1925 and completed his medical degree at Meharry College in Nashville in 1930. He moved to Spartanburg to join his family and purchased a home at 237 Dean Street, a two-story, white clapboard house with a wide, brick front porch, which still stands near Barnet Park. Then 28 years old, Gregg began his medical practice as a general physician and surgeon, opening an office in the N.C. Mutual Life Insurance Building at 168 ½ North Church Street and often working from the "Negro Annex" of the Spartanburg General Hospital. He married Elizabeth Hardy, a former Baltimore school teacher.

In addition to his medical practice, Dr. Gregg led multiple efforts to im-

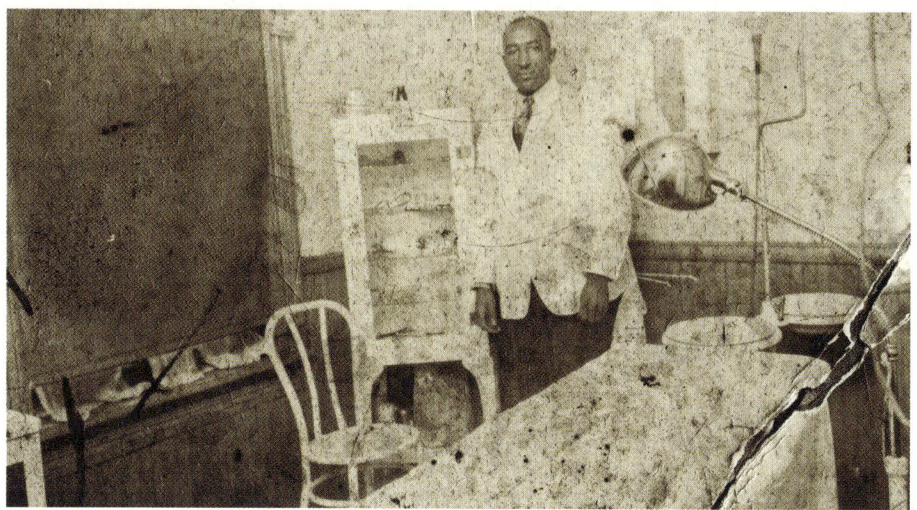

TOP: *Dr. Gregg in his medical office*
RIGHT: *Gregg was a resident of North Dean Street.*

prove Black life in other ways, most of which followed the model of cooperative organization prevalent in the northside's poverty relief efforts during the Depression. He was instrumental in the construction of a new Sunday School building for Silver Hill. He also was involved in a Depression-era relief project called the Negro Business College, which trained local Black women to be typists and stenographers and operated out of a North Church Street building near Morgan Square. When local administrators for the WPA hired white teachers there, Gregg traveled to Washington, D.C., in May 1936 to protest the discrimination against Black teachers. He was accompanied by three other Black Spartanburg leaders: pharmacist William H. Porter, Lutheran pastor the Rev. Walter C. Hart and businessmen William C. Dean. While there, they met up with journalist and Spartanburg

They Protested Discrimination

As representatives of a civic organization in Spartanburg, S.C., they went to Washington last week to fight discrimination in administra-

Dr. William Porter, Rev. Walter Hart, William C. Dean and Dr. T.K. Gregg traveled to Washington, D.C. in 1936. Photo from the Baltimore Afro-American

native William Nesbitt Jones who wrote about their visit in the Baltimore *Afro-American*. "They came with blood in their eyes," Jones wrote. "Conditions in South Carolina have created many good fighting men and women. You have to fight to live there." The outcome of their pursuit might be lost to history, but the business school operated until 1940 under the direction of Carrie Nell Hamilton, daughter of Mary H. Wright.

While in Washington, Gregg also lobbied for federal funding for a park and community center for Black children in Spartanburg. When he returned, he worked with Dr. J.B. Walker and others in the Colored Civic League to lobby city officials on such a project. The first success came when land was donated next to the Lutheran church along Evins Street by the Ernest Gentry Estate and, later, by Henry M. Cleveland, grandson of early

S. C. Community Center

This photo of the first T.K. Gregg Rec Center appeared in the Black-owned Journal and Guide *newspaper of Norfolk, Va. in 1938.*

Spartanburg merchant Jesse Cleveland. With nearly $50,000 in hand from the federal government and the city of Spartanburg, the two physicians vigorously fundraised through active solicitation of local residents and with special events, such as the "Spiritual Program" held Dec. 20, 1936, at the Carolina Theater in the Montgomery Building.

Construction of the three-acre park and center, which was coordinated and staffed through FDR's Works Progress Administration, began in 1937 and employed some 100 men. The new Evins Street community center—complete with a gymnasium, assembly room and game room—opened in the summer of 1938. Eunice S. Thompson (1904-1999) was its first director. She was the daughter of early Black attorney Booker T. Smith, who shared an office building with Dr. Gregg. Outside, there were tennis courts, a formal garden, picnic tables and a rock amphitheater big enough to seat hundreds of people. Brick masons from the neighborhood donated their services to complete the project. Rock was dug from the site for the foundations, and sand was hauled to the site in wheelbarrows from Chinquapin Creek, a quarter of a mile away.

Just as the new community center was becoming central to northside life, Gregg died of a long-running infection of the heart while at St. Agnes Hospital in Raleigh, North Carolina, where he served as an intern. He was 36 years old. In a short tribute, The *Herald* called him "a man of culture and vision" whose passing "leaves a vacant place which will be difficult to fill." Most Black businesses and schools closed for his funeral, and several thousand people, including white physicians and civic leaders, viewed his body as it lay in repose at Silver Hill. Gregg's body was taken to Orangeburg, where he was buried alongside his family members. Spartanburg memorialized his contributions by giving the community building his name: the Dr. T.K. Gregg Recreation Center. It would serve the Black population of Spartanburg for decades with after-school programs, athletic and educational events, social activities and much more. A modern-day community center on Howard Street still bears his name.

Former residents recall weekly sock hop dances held at the center under decorative streamers and lights, innumerable football, basketball and baseball games, home economics education, and committed leadership and instruction given by directors and staff. Doris Posey remembers the "joyful" environment there: "We learned to participate in the games regardless of the outcome," to "learn how to work together" and be "part of a larger group."

Many former residents recalled the importance of community at the T.K. Gregg Center. Will Westly's favorite memory of growing up in the neighborhood was spending time with friends at T.K. Gregg: "It's where all the youth at that time gathered. It was such a small place, but it was the center of the community. People looked after each other." Norma Pitts felt a sense of security: "People were safe there." Gwen Steen met her husband at the center. "He was in a jazz band that formed from Carver High School, but they would practice at T.K. Gregg. They were The Fabulous Dawbs. They were very well known here. The center was a place they could rehearse."

Cynthia Harris Logan remembered the variety of activities available at the center: "They had great summer programs—football teams, basketball, softball. They had dances if you were old enough or you could sneak in. You could play bumper pool, and they had all kinds of groups or little clubs like dance groups you could join." The T.K. Gregg Center had a large field next to it and a playground with swings, slides, tetherball and seesaws. Gwen Steen played and practiced piano at T.K. Gregg, and she also remembered a piccolo and other musical instruments that were available. Phillip Fant played many football and baseball games in the field behind the center, and he also remembered jumping the fence and taking "golden pears from a pear tree" nearby.

BACK OF THE COLLEGE in the late 1930s was a vibrant neighborhood serving hundreds of children with top-notch facilities. The school and the community center were magnets for new residents, as was the phenomenal leadership of school principal C.C. Woodson Jr., who served from 1932 to 1938, and his capable staff. Cumming Street School was so successful, in fact, that the Spartanburg School Board trustees decided to open a separate high school across town for Black students in grades eight through 11. When George Washington Carver High School—the "Pride of the Southside"—opened in 1938, Woodson was appointed principal and remained in that position for the next three decades.

Cumming Street was converted to a grammar school, serving grades one through seven. The elementary-age students moved to the top floor, with the older students downstairs. Eugene Rivers (1902-1973) followed Woodson as principal at Cumming Street, serving for 18 years. He was the grandson of one of the neighborhood's founders—Richard Rivers, who served as a Spartanburg alderman in the 19th century. Eugene Rivers, a graduate of the Colored Normal Industrial Agricultural and Mechanical Institute (now South Carolina State University), is remembered by his former students as a strict disciplinarian. Forty years after graduating from Cumming Street, JoAnn Frazier spelled out clearly what her principal expected: "With Mr. Rivers, you had to be on time." Eddie Bowman, a student at Cumming Street in the 1940s, recalled that students did not get a printed report card; instead, the teachers came to students' homes and met with their parents. "They gave your report in person. . . . I didn't enjoy it at the time, but as I got older, I thought it was a great thing that happened to me." Those in-person reports helped him learn "to do the right thing."

One of the most notable Cumming Street students of this era was Rivers's own son, Eugene Jr. After growing up at 476 Evins Street, the younger

After his career as cartoonist for the Nation of Islam's Muhammad Speaks, *Spartanburg's Eugene Rivers Jr. served as art director of the* Greenville News.

Rivers studied at the School of the Museum of Fine Art in Boston. In the 1960s he became the art director for the Nation of Islam in Chicago and was a close associate of Black separatist leader Elijah Muhammad. Over the years he produced hundreds of political cartoons for the weekly *Muhammad Speaks* newspaper, the largest Black newspaper in America at the time. Rivers Jr.—who changed his name during that period to Eugene Majied—is credited with introducing a young Cassius Clay to the Nation of Islam when the legendary boxer encountered a Rivers cartoon as he read a newspaper outside a skating rink in Louisville, Kentucky. "I liked that cartoon. It did something to me," the boxer who became Muhammad Ali once wrote. After more than a decade at the center of the Nation of Islam's messaging, the Spartanburg-born cartoonist moved back to the upstate, became Eugene Rivers Jr. again and finished his career as art director of *The Greenville News.*

His father eventually passed the baton in 1955 to Cumming Street School's final principal, Emerson Coleman. A native of Union, Coleman attended South Carolina State University, served in the U.S. Air Force during World War II, and then earned a master's degree in school administration from the University of Michigan. He continued his studies at the University of Pennsylvania before coming to Spartanburg in 1948, eventually becoming assistant principal at Carver High School and principal at Mary H. Wright Elementary School.

Coleman faced significant challenges at Cumming Street. With the winds of change blowing ever more forcefully after the 1954 Brown vs. Board Supreme Court decision outlawing "separate but equal" education, Coleman had to lead a school for which the writing was increasingly on the wall. Integration was in the wings. But the years under Coleman were some of the liveliest of the school's history. Between 1955 and 1964, Cumming Street's enrollments were its largest ever, with an average of 700 elementary and 300 junior high students, which required some of the most innovative and resourceful teaching the school had seen. An additional wing and mobile units were added to the school to accommodate the larger number of students in 1957. Among the students in that era was Gerald Dean Dawkins, who later became superintendent of the 45,000-student Shreveport, Louisiana, school district, and of the Saginaw, Michigan, public schools. An elementary school in Grand Rapids was named for Dawkins in 2023.

Teachers at Cumming Street were given a wide berth to develop their own curriculum and individual practices. Leotus Davis, an eighth-grade science teacher at Cumming Street, appreciated the freedom Coleman allowed him in the classroom: Coleman "would let us make our own decisions," Davis said. "He'd come in, sit in your room and observe for a period of time" to ensure all was well, but Coleman would encourage teacher autonomy.

A soft-spoken and carefully worded man, Davis's way of teaching science shows remarkable innovation for any junior high program. Davis offered classes on atmospheric science, mineralogy, oceanography and general science. In a unit on aviation, Davis decided it would be helpful for students to have their first plane ride. He believed learning about aviation was better done from an actual airplane, so took his students to the downtown Spartanburg airport. Students took turns riding in a Cessna and learned first-hand what it meant to fly. "The pilot would point out where their schools were, circle their neighborhoods, stuff like that," Davis recalled.

Emerson Coleman served as the final principal at Cumming Street School.

As was the case throughout the South prior to the mid-1940s, teachers and administrators at Cumming Street often were paid less than half of that of their white counterparts. Census records show that Hattie Bell Penland, first-grade teacher, was paid $540 annually in 1940. Another teacher, Stacey Whitmire, was paid $450. As comparison, two white public school teachers living near the present-day First Baptist Church—Beulah Johnson and Lillie Mae Werts—each received $1,350 that year. (Four years later the South Carolina NAACP successfully sued for equal teacher pay in a case argued by future Supreme Court Justice Thurgood Marshall, and the pay gap began to shrink.)

Supplies and resources were limited both at Cumming Street and nearby Alexander Elementary. As the buildings aged, especially as desegregation loomed, the district became more reluctant to invest in them. But that did not prevent Black educators from providing an excellent experience to their students, nor did it dampen Black students' desire to learn. Eddie Bowman was excited about going to Cumming Street from an early age: "I had a brother that graduated from there in 1938. I just couldn't wait to get there." Freda Byrd took no notice of what people told her: "They . . . told us that we had second-hand books or whatever the case was. But the teachers were really good at filling in information, things that they knew you needed to know."

Norma Green cited her classmate James "Jimmy" Douglas as an example of someone who went from completing an exhibit at a Cumming Street science fair to becoming a successful cardiac surgeon and medical director in Bellingham, Washington. Students learned French language from third through sixth grades, taught "by someone actually from France." They participated in numerous dramatic productions, operettas and festivals. They played in marching and concert bands. The Cumming Street Tigers fielded football and basketball teams, and in a couple of years, the basketball team won county championships. Students were able to make use of an extensive library. Freda Byrd would "take home six to seven books a night and read them." One tradition that many recall was the May Day festival. Students would dress in festive attire, a May Day Queen would be selected, and they would meet up with Mary H. Wright Elementary students to perform traditional dances and songs at Carver High School.

Seemingly everyone loved the cafeteria, where there was hot food cooked every day. Davis described lunch hour as one of his favorite times of the day: "We all enjoyed the good meals. We all would sit around and fellowship while we had our lunch, talk to the other teachers." Freda Byrd loved the "big ol' yeast rolls" available every day as well as the tradition of the entire class singing grace before they ate.

Community played a major role in the school's success. The practice of teachers visiting students' families contributed to a general feeling of mutual concern, but it extended further still. Norma Green pointed to the fact that students and teachers generally lived in the same neighborhood and went to the same churches, which meant that students were taught at school and at home: "If you got in trouble at school, chances are you were in trouble before you ever made it home!" Many Cumming Street teachers taught for years and knew generations of families: Norma Green said, "My second-grade teacher, Ms. Stacey Whitmire, taught my daddy in second grade. So she'd been there forever." This proximity and shared commitment led to life-long bonds that remained firm. An example of the

A classroom at Cumming Street in 1948, after it had become an elementary school.

feelings that teachers had for each other is illustrated by a memory Davis, the science teacher, recalled. One of his former colleagues died suddenly and tragically while cleaning her room at school. She lived in the Myrtle Beach area, about 240 miles east of Spartanburg. When her funeral came, every single teacher at Cumming Street was in attendance.

Difficulties existed, of course. One challenge to daily school life was the walk to school. For those who lived between busing zones, which were sparse for Black students during segregation, the walk sometimes took place in the rain and snow. Mildred Means recalled, "I had to walk three miles from where I lived to the bus stop to catch the bus to go to school. Yeah, I sure did. Better not be late!" Some had to face more than the weather. Linda Dogan's route in the 1960s obliged her to walk down two streets where the residents were predominantly white. "Pearl Street was all wooded up," recalled Dogan, who later served as a Spartanburg city councilwoman. "A few white houses were on there. And those people were hateful. They would throw things at us. And on Edgewood Street, the kids . . . would sic their dogs on us and just call us names and stuff like that. And it hurt."

The first wave of integration hit Cumming Street in 1968 when four white boys began attending the school. By that time, remembered Chuck Carree, "Cumming Street was a dingy school with poor lighting. We did not know to what extent because it was just a way of life." Carree, who became a sportswriter and was inducted into the Wilmington (North Carolina) Sports Hall of Fame, wrote about his experience years later for the Wilmington Star-News, describing how he sometimes reached out to the new white students for a game of basketball. Carree had wanted to attend Carver High School as his brothers did, but instead integration sent him to Cleveland Junior High School on Howard Street. "It was agony," he wrote. "The discrimination was blatant in the classroom and in athletic endeavors."

Forty-three years of Cumming Street School came to close in 1970. The district kept the building in use for another 13 years as an "individualized Learning Center," pre-vocational education center, office space for school psychologists and storage. It closed entirely in 1982 and later was condemned by the city for asbestos contamination. Twenty-six years later, Wofford College took ownership of the former schoolhouse in a property swap with District 7 Schools, ultimately moving its buildings and grounds operations there. In a unanimous vote of Spartanburg City Council on May 9, 2022, Cumming Street School was added to the local historic register.

Wofford has yet to declare its long-term intentions for the building, although college President Nayef Samhat said he hopes "to continue conversations with individuals and community partners regarding Cumming Street School. It would be appropriate and an excellent way to honor the community for that building, which played such an important role in our community's education, to be a part of Wofford's mission as well."

TOP: *The Littlejohn family at Cumming Street School, late 1950s. From left: Horace (June), William (Chuck), Val and Gaynell.* LEFT: *Cumming Street cheerleaders in 1969, the year before the school closed*

SPOTLIGHT

CAMP FRIENDSHIP

During the lean years of the Great Depression, the disease of tuberculosis was a serious threat, especially to undernourished children. In the summer of 1930, a group of Back of the College women stepped forward to create a "nutrition camp" that reportedly was the first of its kind in the nation to serve Black children. They called it Camp Friendship.

Madora Gist, Stacey Whitmire, Nina Littlejohn and others were motivated by Spartanburg County's lack of attention to poor Black children. White children had been receiving such services for three years at Camp Franklin, in a donated building on the west side of town. Such "preventorium" summer camps were popping up around the South to provide nourishing food, rest, fresh air and supervision to underweight white children in the poorest neighborhoods. It was believed that the children's undernourished condition made them susceptible to TB, a life-threatening and contagious disease affecting the lungs.

Madora Gist, a local educator, opened her home at 524 Jefferson Street for a nutrition camp on July 16, 1930, and ten Black girls, ages 6 to 14, moved in for six weeks. The *Spartanburg Herald* called it "the first negro institution of its sort in the US." Operations were supervised by representatives of the Spartanburg Tuberculosis Association, just as they were at Camp Franklin.

While the camp for white children was supported by donations from prominent citizens and local companies, Camp Friendship relied on charity from Black citizens. They came together to host various benefits, pageants and canned food drives to financially support the camp. Addie McWhirter hosted a singing convention on the courthouse lawn to raise funds. The Spartanburg Sluggers baseball team donated proceeds from ticket sales. One year, Trinity AME Church paid the ice bill

Participants in the 1930 nutrition camp held at the home of Madora Gist.

each week. Even with their enthusiasm, it was a struggle to keep the doors open each summer. But its success could not be denied: in 1933 the girls at Camp Friendship gained an average of eight pounds over a period of 28 days, compared to 1.5 pounds at Camp Franklin, according to health reports.

Camp Friendship eventually moved to the Bethlehem Center in the Highland neighborhood, where Dr. T.K. Gregg screened applicants, before closing due to lack of funds in the mid-1930s. The camp for white children continued until 1938 before it moved to Greenville, then to the YMCA camp near Columbus, North Carolina.

Norma Foster Greene and a friend on May Day 1967

NINE

HEYDAY

THOSE WHO GREW UP Back of the College after World War II remember it as a flourishing—and nourishing—community focused on lifting them toward success. According to its residents, the keynote of the Back of the College neighborhood was community. More than 250 Black households existed there by the 1950s, with the population of the neighborhood peaking above 1,000 residents.

"It was a loving community," remembered Judy Hutchinson. "Everybody was a family. Right? All of us stuck together. Just like they say, it takes a village, you know, to raise children. That's how it was back there. The whole village." There was a sense of security for many. The neighborhood felt like a sanctuary. "We were so safe. We were very safe," said Doris Posey, the daughter of a Wofford College janitor. "We have a lot of people to thank for that environment. We really do." Sherry Wiggleton agreed: "We used to sleep on our front porches. We could leave and go to town and come back, our doors unlocked. Nobody broke into your houses. I mean it was just such a lovely community back then."

Their parents, however, had lived through more difficult times. The Great Depression had brought some of the hardest years the Black population in Spartanburg had seen since just after the Civil War. The textile industry and cotton production could not weather the massive loss of market share after 1929's crash, and the industries that depended on and supported textiles dissolved. The First National Bank of Spartanburg, for which Tobe Hartwell had worked more than 30 years, collapsed in 1931, one year prior to his death, and the city and county saw more businesses and industries fail than many areas of the country. The work programs and rebuilding projects of Roosevelt's New Deal saved the Upstate both economically and psychologically by putting people back to work and stimulating revenue. But by every measure, both in terms of the severity with which the Depression hit and the relative degree to which New Deal programs helped people recover, Black people across the country suffered disproportionately.

As jobs disappeared, Black people lost more ground than anyone in the Upstate. By 1940 nearly 20 percent of all Black-owned farms in South Carolina were lost. Sharecroppers were especially vulnerable. Wages plummeted, debt increased, cotton prices collapsed, and the boll-weevil hit the cotton that had been planted. More than 100,000 Black farmers in the South lost their livelihoods by 1937. When farm workers looked for other work, they were shut out. Black people had long taken the jobs white people refused—garbage collection, delivery, street cleaning, "outside" work at textile mills, hotel jobs, railroad labor—but in the massive rush to the bottom for work, white people took whatever was available.

Skilled Black workers fared only minimally better. In 1930 as many as four percent of Black male workers were in skilled positions; by 1936 that dropped to less than 1 percent. Black men looking for work often faced outright discrimination or worse, including organized violence. Groups of white laborers attacked Black workers and forced them to leave their jobs. The Klan expanded and intensified the violence across the state, organizing around the creed that murder created vacancies. Now that industries were barely hanging on, and labor costs were often unsustainable, the value of free labor increased. Arrests of Black men accelerated and the numbers at the South Carolina Penitentiary grew from 528 in 1925 to 1,310 in 1941.

Black women stepped in to provide aid to their community. The Ladies Mutual Aid Society at Silver Hill Church, which had begun with the church's founding under the direction of Sophia McKinney, Winnie Pickenpack and Sophia Rivers, became one of the most effective relief organizations in the neighborhood. They organized hunger relief programs, job training programs, care for widows, burial services, sewing/quilting drives, and provisional lending programs that helped prospective property buyers. The Society collaborated with their peer organizations at neighboring churches to ensure that people did not go hungry, had clothes and quilts

Sophia and Walter Hart, 1930s. They met and married when he came to Spartanburg to become pastor of St. Luke's Lutheran Church.

for inclement weather, and were connected to employment opportunities as they emerged. It worked alongside the Daughters of Wesley Society, which focused on education.

As World War II broke out, dozens of men in the neighborhood headed off to war, both in Europe and the Pacific. When they returned, Back of the College was poised for its most propitious years. Doris Posey, born in 1932, attributed the stability of the neighborhood to the character of its residents. "I think the adults had the right state of mind," she explained. "They didn't have some big plan for the neighborhood or the children in the neighborhood to be just great children or come out right. They had good character. And it passed down to us. We had the benefit of their good character. A lot of them were uneducated, a lot of them were doing menial

Nellie Whitmire Barksdale, mother of Louvenia Barksdale.

jobs. A lot of them maybe had never left their own state, you know, but they were good character. And we were the beneficiaries."

Churches were the bedrock of the community. Over the years, various churches came and went, but by the late 1940s four stalwart churches remained: Cummings Street Baptist and Walker Memorial Christian Methodist Episcopal stood near to each other on Cummings Street, while Greater Trinity AME and Mount Zion Baptist Church held down the back of the neighborhood.

Cummings Street Baptist, located next to the school, had been organized in 1929 by 30 charter members and by the Rev. R.S. Sims, who lived at 550 Twitty Street. An outgrowth of a Sunday School class at the Southside's Macedonia Baptist Church, its services initially were held in an abandoned store before congregants built a modest, rectangular building during the Great Depression. This church had a dirt floor, plain wooden benches and seated about 200 in 1936. The church grew quickly, and in 1953, its members built the church that stood for the duration of its history.

Walker Memorial CME Church, at 532 Cummings Street, had been organized in 1883, with most of its charter members coming from North Carolina and Georgia. Led by the Rev. J.L. Moore, they met in homes on Jones Street until a Black woman named Ann Mintz sold them a lot. They named the first structure after her: Mintz Chapel. Later, the church was renamed Jones Tabernacle in honor of the location of the church's founding. When a storm damaged that building, a larger, wooden church was constructed in 1917, and the church was renamed again, this time for the Rev. C.T. Walker, president of the Paine Institute in Georgia, the precursor of historic Morehouse College. A brick church with belfry and bell—and seating for 300—was constructed during the Great Depression. This structure ultimately outlasted the neighborhood. In the 1990s its members moved to a building on Wofford Street and renamed it Bunton Institutional CME Church.

A small group of residents attended Mount Zion Baptist Church at 589 Charlevoix Street, founded about 1920. In its earliest days, the church was in a shotgun house. "You could see from the front all the way through the back door when you walked up to it," said Freda Byrd. "They took out the interior walls and put some seats in there so that you could have service."

TOP: *A Cummings Street scene, 1966. Walker Memorial Christian Methodist Episcopal Church is on the right.*

BOTTOM LEFT: *Cummings Street Baptist Church*

BOTTOM RIGHT: *Greater Trinity AME Church as it appears today. Now owned by Wofford College, it is used for art programs.*

Mount Zion moved to a small, block building on Chase Street, off what is now East Daniel Morgan Avenue. "I remember we used to have fish fries on Friday night," recalled Michael Hill, whose mother was superintendent of the Sunday School. "Sold fish, had lemonade. And that's how we made up to keep the church going." Church members constructed a small sanctuary in the early 1960s on Charlevoix Street. Future Spartanburg Mayor Jerome Rice attended this church as a boy. When Wofford College requested to purchase the church's property for its expansion in 1997, the congregation decided to move to the Arkwright area. It rechristened itself Mount Zion World Outreach Church.

Greater Trinity AME Church was organized and built in 1941 for $5,000 at 400 Evins Street. The congregation included numerous members of the Whitmire family. Over the years, it hosted several NAACP membership drives as well as other community social programs. The Rev. John "Bootsie" Wilson, who was the second lead singer for the classic 1960s doo-wop group The Silhouettes, served as pastor for a time. When he died in Spartanburg in 2009, he was the last surviving member of the group that recorded the mega-hit "Get A Job." The tiny brick AME chapel still stands and is in use by Wofford College as the "Cleveland Street Annex."

Neighborhood residents often visited each other's churches on Sundays, recalled Mildred Means. Norma Pitts fondly remembered walking to Cummings Street Baptist Church on Sunday mornings. "It was a lovely time because you see people sitting on the porch and waving and you come back by dinner. You don't see that anymore," she said. In the 1930s Gwen Steen would walk with a group of girlfriends and her grandmother all the way from their homes on Twitty Street to Trinity AME Church on Magnolia Street. "Church kind of made a pathway for our lives," Steen said. "One thing it taught us was respect—respect for yourself, respect for others." What Norma Foster Green remembered were the outfits. "People generally went to church every Sunday, and they dressed up. I'm talking hats, gloves, pumps, stockings, the whole nine yards, suits, ties, you know." Back of the College churches also offered enticing summer programs. Cynthia Harris Logan, a member of Cummings Street Baptist, often traveled with her church group to Frontier Land in western North Carolina.

THE WHITMIRE FAMILY, which established Greater Trinity AME, was one of the most active and familiar families living Back of the College. Teachers, businesspeople, promoters and activists, the Whitmires set a standard across generations for community involvement and achievement during much of the neighborhood's existence. The patriarch of the family, John Whitmire, was born into slavery around 1857. He farmed land around Union and Newberry before his growing family settled on Twitty Street sometime after 1900. Whitmire died early, and it was up to the matriarch, Ella—born about 1861—to raise a household of nine enterprising children. She was a cook and a home nurse and, despite having been born into slavery in a rural area, had achieved a fifth-grade education.

The first of Ella's children was Newton "Big Newt" Whitmire, who was in his teens when the family arrived in Spartanburg. He organized the Spartanburg Sluggers, an independent semipro Black baseball team that held games on a Wofford athletic field as early as 1911. Big Newt's Sluggers ultimately found a home at Duncan Park and played hundreds of games through their 50-year existence. He also ran a hotel and eatery on Short Wofford Street where he hosted numerous Black performers on the "Chitlin' Circuit." In 1946 his son, known as "Little Newt," moved back to Spartanburg from New York City to take care of his ailing father and to expand the Whitmire empire. Newt Jr. took over the Sluggers and also promoted major events at Duncan Park featuring such noted athletes as Jackie Robinson and Jesse Owens. He and his wife, Viola, assumed control of the family restaurant/hotel on Short Wofford and regularly hosted major touring performers, including Count Basie and Duke Ellington.

The oldest Whitmire daughter, Nellie, married an early Southern Railway fireman, A.B. Barksdale, and they made a home on First Simmons Street, raising one son and one daughter—teacher-activist Louvenia Barksdale. Nellie's sister Willie became a nurse and worked in the office of a local physician. Claude "Biggem" Whitmire, born about 1896, started what is believed to be Spartanburg's first Black taxi company, Deluxe Radio Cab, behind a sister's house in the late 1920s. The cab company had multiple drivers, including some of the Whitmire siblings and, later, an ambitious youth named Charles Atchison, who ultimately purchased the business.

He and his family turned it into Atchison Transportation Services, accumulating a large fleet of buses and cars and making it the leading chauffeured transportation business in the Upstate to this day.

Among the younger siblings were Stacey and Alberta Whitmire, each of whom had a high-profile presence in the neighborhood. Stacey Whitmire started a 47-year teaching career in 1923 and was one of the first female students at Johnson Smith University, where she received a bachelor's degree. She taught at Highland School, Cumming Street School and Carver High School before retiring in 1970 to become one of the first instructors at Spartanburg's Head Start program. Stacey Whitmire never married and lived on Evins Street most of her life, often making a home for her other siblings. She made time to serve as dispatcher for her brother's cab company, and, for a time in the 1930s, was director of the Friendship Camp, a summer nutrition program for neighborhood children. She had a tight relationship with Wofford College President Joe Lesesne from the 1970s until his retirement in 2000—they often were seen together visiting on her front porch, which faced dormitories of the college. Stacey Whitmire and Lesesne, a Democrat, worked together on voter registration actions and get-out-the-vote drives.

Stacey's sister Alberta Whitmire ran a popular beauty shop in the neighborhood from her home at 270 Evins Street and was president of a regional South Carolina beautician's association. She married Arthur B. Samuel (1898-1969), who began waiting tables in downtown Spartanburg as a teenager and ultimately rose to become the well-known head waiter at the Cleveland Hotel for many years. Samuel was responsible for training the well-dressed, all-Black wait staff at the hotel and had many friends in the white community.

Perhaps the most accomplished and highly regarded of the Whitmire family was a third-generation member, Louvenia Delores Barksdale. Receiving a master's degree from Columbia University in New York City, Barksdale had a 32-year-career as a language arts teacher at Carver High and later founded the Louvenia Barksdale Sickle Cell Anemia Foundation to take care of people of her race who suffered from the inherited blood disorder. A former student, Woodrow Brown, remembered her "as a premier teacher." She coached him on taking a test to get into the U.S. Navy and provided him a solid education. "And then when I got to the Navy, it was easy," he recalled. She taught each of her junior-class students to write poetry and short stories and each year published a collection of their work.

Another of Barksdale's students, Bertha Turley Johnson, grew up in a home where her parents had no education, and her mother could not read and write. When Johnson's parents moved to New Jersey, she went to Barksdale in a panic—she was ready to run away. "She said to me, 'That's nonsense about running away. We don't run away,'" Johnson recalled. "And she spoke to me that she was my mentor. She said, 'I watched you as a child. I watched you as you grew up in church, I watched you work in the church. And I even knew you when you were in your mother's womb.'" Barksdale received permission to take the teen into her own home to live, insisting that she improve her grades. "She says no Ds and Fs. 'That is not going to be happening.' . . . And during that time that I was in her home, she spoke of being a lady, you always have to be a lady. You have to act like a lady and make sure you carry yourself as a lady in any setting that you come into. She said, 'I want to teach you how to be anywhere. And don't be afraid to do anything.' I knew the nurturing part of Miss Barksdale. It was like everybody knew her as the educator, but I knew her as the mom."

For community activist Charles Mann, a stern look of the eye from Barksdale in March 1970 changed the course of his life. On the eve of school integration, Carver High students had walked out of their classes, protesting a lack of commitment from school district officials over Black representation in student affairs at the school they would attend in the fall, Spartan High. Mann had not joined them because of a fear of repercussions. In the Carver auditorium that day, Barksdale overheard him explaining his reticence to a friend. "She turned around and looked at me and didn't say a word," Mann recalled. "That look said, 'What's wrong with you?' I knew I was on the wrong side." He got right up and joined the pro-

OPPOSITE: (TOP LEFT) *Alberta Whitmire Samuel ran a popular beauty shop in the neighborhood.* (TOP RIGHT) *Arthur B. Samuel, husband to Alberta, was head waiter at the Cleveland Hotel.* (BOTTOM LEFT) *Entrepreneur Claude Whitmire with his taxi.* (BOTTOM RIGHT) *"Big Newt" Whitmire organized the Spartanburg Sluggers baseball team and ran a restaurant on Short Wofford Street.*

TAXI

Louvenia Barksdale, teacher, poet, mentor, historian and healthcare leader.

test. "I have been protesting for the rest of my life," said Mann, a founder of the Spartanburg Initiative for Racial Equity Now (SIREN).

Michael Hill remembered Barksdale from her days running the sickle cell resource center. His mother, Otis, worked alongside her. "They would travel around Spartanburg County, and they'd be trying to give tests to people they think may have that trait and then made sure that they get treated," he said. "And sometimes they would spend money out of their own pockets, just to make sure that [people] will get treated for that trait." About one in 13 Black people in the U.S. are born with the sickle cell trait, which can harden red blood cells, leading to pain and sudden death. Barksdale was one of them.

Barksdale never married and lived out her life in a house at 258 Evins Street, next to her aunts. She wrote poetry and collected historical information about her neighborhood. When she died Sept. 23, 1990, she was hailed as a once-in-a-generation mentor to hundreds of Black teens. Her obituary recounted 14 awards received in her lifetime and a dozen organizations served.

AS THE NEIGHBORHOOD GREW, so did Wofford College. By the mid-1960s there were more than 1,000 male students on campus from Septem-

Barksdale in her office at the Sickle Cell Anemia Foundation, which she founded in Spartanburg

ber to May. Children living Back of the College were curious about what went on over there. Some adults referred to the neighborhood as "Back of the Wall," said Norma Pitts and others, reflecting the feeling that they were not welcome on the campus grounds. Residents of Evins Street could see students on their way to class or returning to dorms but advised their children never to cross the street for fear there would be trouble with authorities. Remembering her childhood, Gwen Steen said it was "taboo" to wander onto campus. But Norma Foster Green said she often ignored the advice of the adults. "They used to always say, 'Do not cut through Wofford College campus.' Frankly, it was the quickest way to get to Krispy Kreme. So we crossed Wofford College's campus all the time. Nobody bothered us. You know, we skipped through. We talked to people. We knew most of the groundskeepers. We knew the maids because they all lived Back of the College."

Several former residents said they looked forward to Wofford College

ABOVE: *Wofford College with the adjacent neighborhoods in the mid-1950s. Cumming Street School is at the top. All of these homes are gone.*

football games on Saturday afternoons. Though they could not attend—typically only Black people with connections to the college were allowed entry—some nevertheless found a way to watch. Will Westly said one of his best childhood memories was sitting on a rooftop to look down onto the action on the field. Sherry Wiggleton remembered going through a neighbor's attic to get to the roof. "You know, it was just really exciting," she said. Sometimes there was money to be made. Neighborhood kids would suggest to football fans that they park on their streets. "We'd just tell people we'll watch the car for a quarter. We'll make some money off it. Yeah, we did," said Judy Hutchinson.

There was a big tree in the bend of Cleveland Street, and sometimes Wofford students would make the turn too fast in their cars, recalled Freda Byrd. "They would end up in that tree. So we were out there for a good number of times when police had to come and ambulances and whatever, you know, kind of get them down from that tree."

Donald W. Gibson remembered the story his grandfather, Ernest Long, told about being in charge of a furnace at the college. "You know it used

to get freezing cold, freezing rain, and Granddaddy got up every morning at 2 o'clock from that old, old raggedy house on 431 E. Cleveland Street," Gibson said. "He would shovel coal in there for about 30 minutes and then he would set a fire and turn up the thermostat. And this is what he said, 'Them boys will be warm when they get up.' You get up in a cold house and go make it warm for these little white boys and them be comfortable. I didn't understand [what it meant] then, but as I grew older I did."

When attorney James Cheek was a boy in the 1960s, he had a friend who wanted to see an exhibit at the college's annual science fair. But Cheek had been told that unless you were an employee of the college, Blacks could not cross the campus grounds. One day before school, they made up their minds to try it anyway. They saw two students on the campus, one of whom escorted the two boys to the science fair. "He stayed and waited while we went through the fair, and he escorted us back off the campus and waited for us to get on the school bus." Wofford College integrated in the fall of 1964; Cheek enrolled there in 1969 and graduated in a class with nine Black students.

In 1969 two Wofford students—Henry Freeman and Franklin Smith—

Children's Choir at T.K. Gregg / Evins Street, 1960

initiated a program called Happy Saturdays for neighborhood kids living Back of the College. They would bring children onto campus, play tennis with them, eat together in the cafeteria, and let them look through the microscopes in the science labs. In the fall there were hayrides; in the summer, opportunities for swimming; and at Christmas, visits with Santa. Within a few months, more than 100 children were participating as well as dozens of Wofford and Converse College students. "We couldn't wait till Saturday to get here," said Cynthia Harris Logan. "There were a group of students that took us under their wings and gave us the best times of our lives." Sherry Wiggleton remembered the M&M candy vending machines on campus and learning to bob for apples at Halloween. "They even came to our

LEFT: *Neighborhood resident John Shelton was a cook at Wofford College for more than 30 years.* RIGHT: *Walter C. Hart, pastor, Boy Scout leader, and Kiddie Kollege operator*

houses and ate dinner with us at times. My parents just really loved them."

Freshest in the minds of former residents were the ways they played together in the neighborhood. "We stayed out all day. We just had to be home when the streetlights came on," recalled Norma Foster Green, whose family ran a cafe on Bell Street called Foster's Lunch. After dark in the summer, they would play in the side yard under the streetlights. There was no air conditioning in those days, so it just made more sense to stay out. Cynthia Harris Logan remembered skating down Cummings Street hill. Plums, peaches, golden pears and blackberries grew wild in the neighborhood. "You can just go pick them and eat them. And nobody cared," Logan said. Phillip Fant recalled making scooters and derby cars out of broken skates. "You had to use your feet and guide them. Tie a rope on one side and a rope on the other side and steer it. So we were creative. You know you had to be." Fant later attended Wofford College, graduating in 1974, and owned his own menswear shop and insurance agency.

LEFT: *Cumming Street School operetta around 1962*
RIGHT: *King and Queen of Kiddie Kollege Kindergarten Homecoming, 1959*

ALL THE BLACK COMMUNITIES in Spartanburg—Northside, Southside, Highland—continued to grow during the 1940s. The Southside business district around South Liberty Street saw multiple businesses open. There were cafes, gas stations, a hotel, beauty shops, barber shops, liquor stores and repair shops. In Highland the Bethlehem Center opened in 1930 through a collaboration of white and Black community activists to provide poverty relief, pre-K and after-school educational programming, civic and social instruction, and general outreach for thousands of people. It continues its operations to this day. In the North Dean Street area, many of the businesses were white owned, though Callaham Funeral Home, Simpson Wheeler's upholstery shop, Gilbert Campbell's laundry and Wingo's Grocery were notable exceptions. Octavia Jones ran a boarding house at 225 North Dean Street. Her home was listed in *The Negro Motorist Green-Book* as was that of Lucinda Johnson at 307 North Dean.

Back of the College remained primarily residential, with small cottage businesses—groceries, liquor stores and a candy store—that came and went. These shops were vital community assets because Black residents sometimes were not welcomed in white-owned establishments, or it could be dangerous

LEFT: *Norma Foster Greene on Cummings Street*
RIGHT: *Robert Roston and Sheryle Atchison on Cummings Street*

to be there. As early as 1920, there was Littlejohn's Grocery Store at 553 Jones Street, operated by Emily Jones Littlejohn. She and her husband, Floyd, owned about seven houses in the Jones Street area. Many years later their great-grandson, Horace Littlejohn, would be elected as a commissioner of public works in Spartanburg. He remembered that there were silver coins embedded in the sidewalk outside the Littlejohn family home on Jones Street.

T.C. Charles ran an early florist business. Emily Martin ran a small store on Cummings Street. By the 1940s Eugene Marshall had a small grocery on Cummings Street, and there was a Jones Dry Cleaning on Evins Street. Several women operated beauty shops in their homes. A white man ran a store called McBride's that "was like a Winn-Dixie in your community," recalled Rose Thomas, who lived on Evins Street. "You could buy anything and then you get your little cart and go shopping. . . . He sold gasoline. I think you could buy coal. And a lot of people back then would give you credit. Didn't have credit cards." Norma Foster Green's grandmother ran a candy store, and her dad, a liquor store, which later became a record store. Norma Pitts remembered a little retail store in the neighborhood where she could get a bag of cookies for a penny, a soda for six cents, and a bag of pea-

James and Alice Foster in front of Foster's Lunch, founded by Sarah Foster

nuts for six cents. She would drop the peanuts into her soda. Will Westly remembered a little store called Julianne's, another called Blanco's and one he knew as "Larry's" just under the North Liberty Street underpass. "As kids we stopped in those stores with nickels and dimes every day," he said.

Former residents were crystal clear about the benefits of growing up in a place such as Back of the College. Despite the economic hardships of being Black in the South, despite the ongoing struggles for civil rights, despite the humiliation of Jim Crow, they had something very special. "Now with everything that I have experienced and seen since then, I know we were very lucky children," said Doris Posey. "And when I think about it as an adult, and not just an adult, but a senior, you realize how the framework of a neighborhood can actually shape a person's life . . . if you feel safe and secure, not just in your own home, but on your street. We could go wherever we wanted, as long as we were in before dark. And it was not because anything terrible would happen to us if we weren't. It was just the protective nature of adults. We weren't afraid that harm could come to us."

TOP: *A Jones Street family*
BOTTOM LEFT: *The E.B. Coleman family*
BOTTOM RIGHT: *A Jefferson Street family*

SPOTLIGHT

KIDDIE KOLLEGE

Many Back of the College residents fondly remember their experience at Kiddie Kollege, a privately run kindergarten, after-school program and day care center operated by two important figures in neighborhood history: pastor Walter C. Hart and his wife, Sophia Shelton Hart. The beloved nursery operated from the late 1950s to the 1990s at 552 Jones Street and, for a time, in two houses across the street.

"We actually functioned kind of like a tiny college," recalled Norma Foster Green, who attended when she was 2 to 5 years old. "We had a football team. We had cheerleaders, we had a band. We had a prom. We had this yearbook, we had graduation. . . . We had science fairs, we had anything that a normal school would have." In short, the center functioned like a miniature version of the growing Wofford College next door.

Sophia Hart, born in 1910, grew up on Evins Street and was an active Girl Scout leader in the early 1940s. Her grandfather, Ambrose, came from Woodruff to work at the Muckenfuss broom factory about 1900, and her father, John Shelton, was a cook at Wofford College for more than 30 years. She married the Rev. Hart, a Georgia-born minister, when he came to Spartanburg to serve the neighborhood Lutheran Church. He began a Scout troop for Black boys and served as a field secretary for the Spartanburg Scouting program in the 1930s. The Harts moved on to churches in North Carolina at mid-century, but ultimately moved back to their Spartanburg neighborhood and began new careers as operators of Kiddie Kollege. The Rev. Hart had a menagerie of animals for the children, including ducks, guinea pigs, reptiles and a parrot. Former student Vicki Coleman Hogan remembered the way Sophia Hart would begin each session: "She would sing this song. She sang: 'Good morning to you. We are all in our places with sunshiny faces, and this is the way that we start a new day.' I will never forget that song."

Sophia Hart oversaw harvest festivals, proms and operettas performed in the auditorium at Cumming Street School. Her husband ran

Sophia Hart, founder of Kiddie Kollege

the sports programs. "We always had a miniature football team here at the nursery," he told a local journalist in 1982. That was the year that one of his former players, Randy Anderson, was a three-sports star at Broome High School. Anderson went on to quarterback the Clemson University football team from 1985-1987.

The kindergarten program was a formative experience, recalled Ollie Brown Jenkins. "When [children] left Kiddie Kollege, they could read. And everybody knew their telephone number and their address." The days of Kiddie Kollege are fondly remembered by its attendees. "Most of the students that attended there I keep in contact with now, a lot of them," said Hogan. "We see each other from time to time so it was exciting."

The Rev. Hart died in 1986, and Sophia Hart in 2004. Both are buried at Lincoln Memorial Cemetery on Spartanburg's eastside.

SPOTLIGHT

THE SAINT OF SWAIN STREET

Rachel Glover thought she would take care of convalescing children for a month or two, then go on with her life. In 1938 a local welfare worker approached her with the idea of using her two-story residence at 245 Swain Street behind Wofford College as a temporary nursing home for Black children recovering from orthopedic operations at nearby Spartanburg General Hospital. As founder of the neighborhood's Sisters of Love Society—a benevolent organization begun at Saint John AME Zion Church on Cummings Street—she could hardly say no.

The assignment lasted far longer than a few months. For the next two decades "Mama Rachel" diligently attended to disabled and homeless children at her 11-room home on the eastern side of the thriving Back of the College neighborhood. Over the course of her lifetime, she nursed more than 200 children back to health, sometimes as many as 14 at once. These were invalid children who had been injured, burned or born with a disability. Once the arrangement was made official, the State Board of Health's hospital division sent her children from all over the Upstate to nurse and transport to the hospital for treatment and checkup. She was paid $1 to $3 a day to take care of the children, which was not enough. She put in a steam-heating system from her own funds to ensure that the children stayed warm in winter. Neighbors and the church contributed what they could. The Spartanburg Chapter of the Crippled Children's Society provided clothing, medicine, milk and the services of a teacher.

"I always loved children," she told reporter Hubert Hendrix in 1952. "Never had any of my own. But the Lord gave me children in my old age. It's hard to give them up when they are here a good while, and then the lady comes to take them away. Sometimes it almost breaks my heart." That day she was caring for 15-year-old Robert Logan, whose legs were crushed when lumber fell off a truck. He had 300 stitches in one leg, and a cast covered most of his body.

Of all her wards, Glover was most proud of her first two: Lucille Worthy, who came in as a burn victim, and Mildred Gaffney. She ended up raising them as her own daughters. Mildred married and moved to Asheville. Lucille attended South Carolina State and Benedict College on scholarship, then returned home to take care of "Mama Rachel," who worked her last few years from a wheelchair. "When you get into something like this you can hardly get out," Glover told the reporter in 1952.

Rachel Glover died Aug. 9, 1958. The Wofford tennis complex now stands on what was once her home's site.

The Kress store downtown, where lunch counter sit-ins were held in 1960 and 1962. This building still stands.

TEN

THE LUNCH COUNTERS

PRESSURE BEGAN TO BUILD in the 1950s for better economic opportunities and an end to Jim Crow segregation. The People's Citizens Committee, an organization formed to fight for inclusion, signed up 507 members at its mobilization event at Silver Hill Methodist Church in January 1950. Led by the Revs. Bruce P. Williamson and H.C. Young, the group lobbied the board of the new Spartanburg Memorial Auditorium in 1951 to provide designated seating in each section for Black patrons. They asked City Council to increase the number of Black officers on the police force from two to four and to provide them a patrol car. They also investigated complaints that Spartanburg General Hospital was using pickup trucks as ambulances for Black patients and was not providing telephones in their rooms as it did for whites.

A young Matthew J. Perry, future state NAACP chief attorney and U.S. District Court judge, arrived in Spartanburg in 1951. Then 30 years old, Perry opened his first law office on Short Wofford Street and began addressing local Black PTAs and churches on civil rights issues. In the wake of Brown v. Board of Education, Perry petitioned the Spartanburg School Board in 1955 for a hearing to determine "a definite time for the end of segregation."

In a rare confluence of civil rights heavyweights, the Rev. I. DeQuincey Newman—president of the South Carolina Chapter of the NAACP—was appointed pastor at Silver Hill in 1958 and moved into the parsonage on North Converse Street. His two-year period of service overlapped with Perry's final years in the city and allowed them to work together on key

Matthew J. Perry, a future U.S. District Court Judge

NAACP business. On April 17, 1959, Newman traveled from Spartanburg to Washington, D.C., to testify before the U.S. Senate Subcommittee on Constitutional Rights. He testified that there were parts of South Carolina, such as McCormick County, where Black citizens were afraid to talk about voting "above a whisper." U.S. Sen. Olin Johnston of Spartanburg argued with his premise and insisted Newman and other witnesses provide proof. The next day, the *Spartanburg Herald* ran a two-deck headline:

LOCAL NEGRO CLAIMS HIS
RACE BEING INTIMIDATED

The breakthrough moment for the civil rights movement in Spartanburg occurred in the summer of 1960 soon after 20-year-old Myrtle L. Williams came home from college to spend the summer with her parents at her childhood home at 327 North Dean Street. Then a sophomore at the historically Black Hampton Institute in Virginia, she had been an eyewitness to the birth of non-violent activism. On Feb. 10, 1960—nine days after the first lunch counter sit-in in Greensboro, North Carolina—students at Hampton Institute had initiated the first lunch counter sit-in in the state of Virginia. The following day, 200 Hampton students had shown up to continue the Woolworth protests. By the end of that month, some 600 Hampton students were participating in mass demonstrations, and the protests spread throughout coastal Virginia.

Myrtle Williams led lunch counter protesters in 1960.

Williams grew up in a home where civil rights were at the forefront. For more than two decades, her father, Julius Eroshell Williams, had led voting rights efforts in Spartanburg as well as discussions with local white leaders about fair pay for Black workers. Lunch counter protests were breaking out all over South Carolina in the summer of 1960 as Myrtle Williams waited to go back to college. On July 25 Spartanburg City Council passed an ordinance making it a misdemeanor for a person to stay in an establishment after an employee requested that he or she leave. Inspired by other protests taking place that week in other parts of South Carolina—and encouraged by NAACP officials in town from Columbia—Myrtle Williams and her young friends jumped into action the next day. "I didn't want her to do it," her father recalled to reporter Michael Leonard in an interview conducted 22 years later, "because I could see some guy going up and slapping her off the stool. And I know exactly what I would have done had that happened. I'm not going to tell you, but I wouldn't be here talking to you now if it

ABOVE: *Myrtle Williams with her brother, Julius, outside their North Dean Street home, mid-1950s* RIGHT: *Julius Williams Sr., chair of the Voter Registration Committee of the local NAACP*

had. It wasn't that I was opposed to what she did, I was just afraid of what could happen."

Julius E. Williams (1907-1987) was a longtime manager of the local office of North Carolina Mutual Insurance, the largest Black-owned insurance firm of his day. By the time of the 1960s sit-ins, he had served as a Boy Scout leader, president of the Carver High School Parent-Teacher Association and a trustee at Silver Hill United Methodist Church. He was keenly interested in voting rights. A native of Piedmont and a graduate of Claflin College, he and his wife, Lilla, had moved to Spartanburg in 1938 and encountered election officials who routinely prevented Blacks citizens from voting by claiming they could not find their names in the registration books. Finally, four years later, he was able to cast a vote after "a very genteel and nice white woman" let him and others into the booth. It was an important moment that led him to become the chairman of the Voter Registration Committee of the Spartanburg chapter of the NAACP.

Newspaper reports of Spartanburg's first lunch counter sit-in describe "a Negro boy and girl" taking seats at the Woolworth's soda foundation at 3:15 p.m. on July 26, 1960. They were later joined by nine other teenage boys. The Woolworth's manager ignored them, as was company policy in the South. The protestors sat there without being served for an hour or two, then went across the street to Silver's and browsed. A reporter on the scene asked "the young girl" whether there would be more demonstrations. She replied they had "no immediate plans." The newspaper account continued: "The Negro girl made a purchase, then the small band headed down Main Street again, again followed by the crowd of spectators. The Negroes went to 327 N. Dean Street where they were met by demonstrators who had taken another route to the house. Spectators broke up shortly before the group went into the house."

A B&B Studios photographer captured pictures that day of Myrtle Williams and three young Black men at the lunch counter. She was wearing a flowered, short-sleeved dress and glasses with cat-eye frames. The photos appeared on the front pages of both the morning *Herald* and afternoon *Journal*. In one, she looks directly at the camera, seemingly unphased. In another, three white policemen stand behind her. It was noted in the newspapers that none of the demonstrators would give reporters their names.

Photo by B&B Studio for The Journal

Young Negroes Sit But Not Served At Woolworth Lunch Counter Here Tuesday

They Refused To Give Names; White Patrons Seemed Undisturbed As This Photo Was Taken

(Photo by B&B Studio)

SPECTATORS FOLLOW AS NEGROES LEAVE STORE, HEAD FOR HOME
Entire Affair Orderly As Dozen Officers Stand By Quietly

ABOVE: *July 26, 1960*
OPPOSITE TOP: *Woolworth's lunch counter sit-in, July 26, 1960*
OPPOSITE BOTTOM: *The lunch counter at Kress with white patrons on a typical day in the early 1960s*

In the aftermath, the Rev. D.W. Roston, president of Spartanburg's NAACP, called the protest "a spontaneous" gathering and said his organization was not involved. There were, however, two young Black men on the sidewalk from Columbia who said they were with "a citizens group," presumably the state office of the NAACP.

The following day, a larger group of 18 to 28 Black protesters arrived at lunch counters in downtown Spartanburg, and fights broke out. Whether Julius Williams had allowed his daughter to attend is unknown, but a newspaper account refers to the leader of the protesters "as a young Negro girl wearing glasses." The demonstrators sat at the counter for about an hour as up to 100 white people milled about. As they got up to leave, "four or five jeers or loud noises came from the white onlookers," according to the local newspaper report. One of the white men knocked a Black youth off a stool. The Associated Press account of the event indicated that one Black man was struck and grabbed by the shoulders, while another was "slugged . . . behind the ear." In the fracas, two white men were taken into custody by police officers, along with two Black demonstrators, 17-year-old George C. Foster of 403 Caulder Circle and 20-year-old Willie Nathan Campbell of

Phyllis Goins Courts. All were charged with disorderly conduct. Assuming Myrtle Williams was there, she escaped prosecution. Foster and Campbell were defended in court by attorney Matthew Perry. They pleaded not guilty in a non-jury trial but were convicted and fined $100 by Judge E.C. Burnett. The two white men were acquitted in a jury trial after 15 minutes of deliberation.

City Council Mayor Pro-Tem Lachlan Hyatt urged peace in the city. He asked citizens to "use common sense and good judgment" in the event of further protests and said they should let police officers do their jobs. Julius Williams, meanwhile, was put in a tough spot. He had built a solid working relationship with Spartanburg Chamber of Commerce President Richard Tukey in issues of race, and now his own daughter was an instigator of unrest downtown. Years later he acknowledged that the events of late July 1960 strained the coalition that he and Tukey had forged.

Unfortunately, the lunch counter protests at Woolworth's and Kress stores in July 1960 failed to bring about change in Spartanburg, as they had in some larger cities, including Norfolk and Greensboro. So two years later, a second round of sit-ins was quietly planned. And this time, the influential Southern civil rights leader I. DeQuincey Newman was back in town for the day as state field secretary of the NAACP. On July 23, 1962, he and Rosyln Cheagle, a special NAACP youth field secretary, organized a return of the lunch counter protests in Spartanburg. The report Newman filed to his superiors of the action that day provides a unique Black lens to view the event. He described how about 40 "well organized high school students" arrived at the F.W. Woolworth's lunch counter at 9:15 a.m. They carried paper-bound copies of *Fight for Freedom*, the story of the NAACP. Again, they were denied service. Trouble broke out. "An assault on one student at the Woolworth's store by a white bystander marred the first sit-in for this year with violence," Newman wrote in his report.

The youths moved across the street to join others at the S.H. Kress lunch counter. The manager roped off the lunch counter, forcing them to leave. Outside, "a mob of 250-300 whites resembling mill hands gathered at the S.H. Kress store ostensibly to protest the pressure of the young Negroes at the lunch counter," Newman wrote. Police arrested an 81-year-old white man, S.M. Sisk Sr., for carrying a knife, as well as two other white men,

DeQuincey Newman, pastor at Silver Hill and field secretary of the South Carolina NAACP

Charles H. Bullman and Elbert Gunter, for disorderly conduct. The Rev. Harold Joseph Cox, the Black pastor of Garrison Chapel Baptist Church in nearby Tryon, North Carolina, was booked into jail "for investigation." Newman sought his release that night, but bail initially was denied. Four days later, Judge Burnett issued a directed verdict in the pastor's case—not guilty of disorderly conduct. The white men requested a jury trial in front of a routine all-white Spartanburg jury and were acquitted.

Newman also helped coordinate pickets at the same two Spartanburg lunch counters on Aug. 16, 1962. "Violence flared for a moment in connection with picketing activity when a youthful white passer-by assaulted Foster Gilchrist, NAACP youth leader who was serving as stake-out man at the time," Newman's account reads. "The victim of the violent attack was treated at the Bull clinic for contusions and lacerations. It is believed that Gilchrist's assailant used brass knucks." Gilchrist, a 20-year-old short-order cook, was arrested for picketing without a permit but later cleared of charges.

An early organizational meeting of the Spartanburg NAACP

Most lunch counters in South Carolina remained segregated into 1963, with outbreaks of violence continuing through 1964 in Charleston and Columbia as unhappy white patrons took matters into their own hands by attempting to remove Black diners. Julius Williams had a keen memory of how lunch-counter segregation ended in Spartanburg: one day Chamber President Tukey called him to report that 24 of the city's 28 restaurants had agreed to simultaneously begin allowing Black citizens to be seated and served. That was June 5, 1963, two days after a similar move occurred in nearby Greenville. The *Herald* reported that integration of Spartanburg's drug stores, restaurants, variety stores happened "quietly and without incident. . . . [Black patrons] were served promptly with very little conversation." An unsigned statement from a committee representing the stores and restaurants read: "We feel the business operators' decision is in the best interest of our citizens and the community."

Julius Williams was among those who were served. "I must have eaten three or four dinners that day," he recalled in a newspaper interview, "because places would call and say no Blacks had been there. To make sure we kept what had been gained, I and some others went and ate."

As for his daughter Myrtle, she graduated from Hampton in 1962 and received a master's in business administration degree from Ohio University. She married Howard University graduate Darnese Bell in a ceremony at Silver Hill Church in 1973. She got a job as a financial analyst with IBM in Endicott, New York, where she served on the executive committee of the Broome County NAACP and as adviser to the Broome County Urban League. She and her husband moved to Austin, Texas, in the 1980s. On April 11, 2023, she died at the age of 83.

Her husband, Darnese, said in an interview after her death that his wife "didn't really dwell on" activities from her younger years but was focused intensely on whatever organization she was serving, particularly the Delta Sigma Theta Sorority. "Whatever organization she joined, she was not just a joiner. I can see how she would have been pivotal." Her childhood home at the end of North Dean Street in Spartanburg was renovated in 2024 and remains standing as of this writing.

SPOTLIGHT

COURAGEOUS WYNONA DOUGLAS

Wynona Douglas put on her best pink and white dress on the morning of Aug. 27, 1964. As she left the comfort of her home at 294 North Dean Street, the 15-year-old felt sure she was prepared for what awaited her. That day she would become the first Black student in Spartanburg County to enroll at an all-white public school. Federal law already had established that children in the U.S. were entitled to equal education, and the Douglas family decided that Spartanburg High School was the best option in her hometown. The all-white Spartanburg school board, choosing to avoid a court fight, had agreed unanimously that she could enroll. She transferred in from a private boarding school in Camden.

A local photographer snapped her picture as she walked alone up to a side door of the local high school where a counselor awaited her, as did 1,800 white students inside. As Douglas calmly headed to her first class, plain-clothes law enforcement officers moved through the hallways. State troopers waited in their cars at Hillcrest Shopping Center in case of a riot. As Douglas stepped through the doors of the school where she would begin the 11th grade, newspapers as far as Tucson, Arizona, and Santa Barbara, California, took note of the moment. That day, about a dozen Black students in four South Carolina counties integrated public schools, but she was the only one who did it alone.

The trail-blazing teenager was the daughter of Dr. J. Marion Douglas (1909-1999), who began his medical practice in Spartanburg in 1946. Wynona's brother, James, was a few years behind her in school. He ultimately became the first Black medical resident at Duke University Medical Center and a leading cardiothoracic surgeon. Their mother, Gladys, had been a teacher at Cumming Street School. "I talked to her and she understood fully that somebody had to be a pioneer, somebody had to be first," Gladys Douglas said in a 1984 interview.

Wynona Douglas endured two extremely difficult years as the only

Wynona Douglas heads to a side door on her first day of class at Spartanburg High, August 1964.

Black student at Spartanburg High. "I was optimistic—I really didn't know people would be so rude," she recalled 20 years later. "People overtly were nasty. They made comments like, 'What is this we got in our school?' They threw things at me. They would do things like deliberately putting my name up for an office and nobody would vote for me." She was told she could not attend sports events because the school could not guarantee her protection. A skilled saxophonist, she was segregated from the rest of the band. Kids stopped eating with her at lunch. A white friend, C. Mack Amick, invited her to the prom, but the school nixed that too. In spite of all, she graduated in 1966 with an excellent attendance record and a scholarship to Ohio State University. She became a psychologist, worked in youth services and has lived in Ohio ever since. Court-imposed full integration finally came to South Carolina schools in 1970.

The gas plant, located where North Pine Street now meets the Southern Railway trestle, provided electricity to the city but emitted smoke and fumes into the neighborhood.

ELEVEN

URBAN RENEWAL IN GAS BOTTOM

THE NAME GAS BOTTOM first appeared in Spartanburg's daily newspapers in 1926. By that time houses had spread down the hill from Silver Hill Methodist Church through a low-lying valley, meeting up with those of Back of the College. In an area that ultimately became home to multiple auto dealerships, small, wood-frame houses—often constructed by white landlords—packed the valley, right up to the entrance of a coal-fired gas plant built in 1900 by the Spartanburg Railway, Gas and Electric Company.

The coal-gasification plant's purpose was to provide electricity to the city's new, segregated streetcar system and its electric streetlights, which replaced older gas-lit ones along the city's major thoroughfares. When it went online at the turn of the century, the plant also provided lighting to commercial businesses and to some residences, though only after the sun went down. Electric lines connected it to the trolley system, which by 1906 had 15 miles of track and 10 cars.

Over the years, Black residents complained about the smoke and fumes drifting into their homes from the electric plant. Coal was the primary fuel used to produce electricity, and when burned, it created a visible haze. Gas plants such as these typically emitted hazardous sulphur dioxide, nitrogen oxides and other pollutants now known to create respiratory problems, cardiovascular disease and other health issues. Back then no one kept track of the impact on the human body of the gases settling in the valley.

A Converse College professor brought the issue to the attention of Spartanburg City Council in late 1925. Smoke from the gas plant was surrounding the college and the adjacent neighborhoods in "offensive, unhealthy clouds," Belgian-born Dr. Adolphe Vermont said in his remarks to council. The dense smoke was a menace to the health of the people residing in the area, Vermont said, asking that the city pass an ordinance forcing the gas plant to attend to the nuisance. Council referred his complaint to its health department, and there was no later update. The plant churned out thick smoke for three more decades.

Another issue in the neighborhood was flooding. Gas Bottom developed at the convergence of several creeks, and when it rained, water rose in the area, making the dirt streets impassable by automobiles. Rental houses went up in a hurry, and usually without indoor plumbing. Among the first of these were the homes along Fowler's Row, which developed at the doorstep of the Muckenfuss broom factory, near where North Liberty Street cuts under the Southern Railway. Throughout the neighborhood, homes were tiny, sometimes shotgun-style and often poorly built.

Despite that, the neighborhood just kept growing. It not only spread north, it spread east, from Lizzie Judd's Chasander Hill to the edge of Converse College. Homes for Black residents ran down a wide gully just off St. John Street, past white-occupied Oakland Avenue, and over to the site of the new Golden Street Baptist Church, where in 1958 the state highway department would blow North Pine Street Extension through. New streets and alleys whose names ultimately would disappear filled the area: Cherry Street, Frazer Street, Humber Street, Jolly Street, St. John's Alley, Chase Street, among others. Many of the new residents worked in the electric plant. The so-called "power house" employed Black workers and, over a period of six decades, provided jobs to as many as 200 Black men. One of those was Arthur Beatty (1896-1956), grandfather to South Carolina Supreme Court Chief Justice Donald M. Beatty. He moved into the neighborhood from Union County sometime after 1910.

The newly named Gas Bottom area became one of the densest and poorest in the city. It also was often a battleground between the city's white police force and Black residents. Law enforcement officers routinely burst into homes to break up gambling games and to haul players off to jail. Newspaper accounts sometimes made fun of the arrests. In September 1926 a reporter bragged that the city had "won" $135 in a "skin game" in

Shotgun-style rental houses, built on pillars, in Gas Bottom.

Gas Bottom when nine "cullud genius" men were fined $15 each. On New Year's Eve 1932, police officers arrested a record 21 men when they stormed a house in Gas Bottom. On July 13, 1941, they raided a gambling game in a Gas Bottom home and shot a fleeing Willie Fowler to death. Fowler, 25, went running through heavy brush and was attempting to take cover behind an outhouse when he was struck by a police bullet in the back of the head. Fowler was dead on arrival at the Black hospital. A coroner's jury quickly absolved City Detective W.C. Hayes of blame, saying the death occurred "in the performance of his duty as a police officer."

One of the most notable people to come from Gas Bottom was longtime educator and state legislator Hudson Barksdale Sr. (1905-1986). Barksdale grew up on Charles Street and, later, on North Liberty Street, after his parents moved him and his siblings from Laurens County sometime prior to 1910. He lost his father early, and his mother, Mary, was a laundress who took in boarders to help pay the bills. At age 15 Hudson was a delivery employee for a local clothing store and later worked at the Camp Croft military training camp south of the city in a tailor shop and laundry.

In 1974 Educator Hudson Barksdale Sr. became the first Black representative from Spartanburg County to serve in the S.C. State Legislature.

Rising from difficult circumstances, Barksdale received a bachelor's degree from South Carolina State University, a master's degree from Columbia University, and had an illustrious career in the education field, teaching at Carrier Street School and Mary H. Wright Elementary School, and as principal at Zion Hill School in Pacolet. There, he was known as "Mr. B." Along the way, he served as president of the South Carolina Colored Teachers Association and the American Teachers Association, an all-Black organization. In November 1963 Barksdale participated in a conference on education with President John F. Kennedy three days before the president's death. Intensely focused on civil rights, Barksdale also served as president of the Spartanburg NAACP in the 1950s and was instrumental in pushing the city to hire its first two Black officers, Thomas "Fox" Abrams and Francis Dogan.

After a 27-year educational career, Barksdale was elected in 1974 to the South Carolina Legislature as Spartanburg County's first Black state representative, serving House District 31 until 1982. Barksdale never left the larger northside neighborhood. He and his wife, Geneva, moved to 331 North Dean Street in the mid-1930s, where they raised two children. Among his myriad accomplishments, he is credited with helping to preserve the historic Alexander (Dean Street) School, located down the street from his home, once telling the District 7 School Board, "The Alexander School is as much a part of our heritage as is Morgan Square in downtown Spartanburg." A few years prior to his death on April 13, 1986, the city renamed South Liberty Street—site of a massive urban renewal project—for him: Hudson Barksdale Boulevard.

THE GAS BOTTOM AREA was full of musicians who went on to great fame. Metropolitan AME Zion Church, located on North Dean Street, encouraged the blossoming music scene in the neighborhood, often sponsoring popular gospel concerts. In 1928 it hosted the Silver-tone Quintet from Chicago, an event so anticipated that seats were reserved for white people. Victor Records artists the Livingstone Quartet also appeared that year. The church hosted singing conventions and had its own "old folks chorus." Prince Chester Wilburn, "scion of African royalty" and a graduate of a German music conservatory, performed there in January 1931.

Grammy-winning vocalist Ira Tucker, lead singer for 70 years of the Dixie Hummingbirds soul-gospel group, grew up amid a burgeoning music scene in Gas Bottom. He was born in 1925 in a rented shotgun house on a dirt road called Golden Street (also known as Golding Street), which ran along the eastern edge of the neighborhood near Converse College. The Tucker house, like many others in that poorer section of the neighborhood, was propped on pillars to keep it from flooding.

Tucker's grandfather, Ed Moore, lived with them and played an old German accordion. The front porch of their home on Golden Street would be "full of people," when Moore performed, Tucker said. His grandfather sang bass and his mother sang soprano in the choir at Metropolitan AME. During the 1930s singers often gathered under the streetlight at the intersection of Crawford and Golden streets or at the Jolly Street home of Belton Woodruff. There, Tucker met other Spartanburg singers who would go on to great notoriety: Julius "June" Cheeks of the Sensational Nightingales, William Bobo and Arthur "Bob" Beatty of the Heavenly

Gospel Singers, and R&B stars Arthur Prysock and Red Prysock. On other days, Tucker went door-to-door offering to sing for spare change. At the age of 13 he joined the Dixie Hummingbirds, never to live in Spartanburg again. Among those influenced by his hard-charging gospel sound forged on the streets of Gas Bottom were James Brown, Stevie Wonder and Jackie Wilson. Tucker's Grammy for Best Soul Gospel Performance came in 1973 for the Hummingbirds' recording of a Paul Simon hit, "Loves Me Like a Rock." In his later years, he returned home to play at the Bethlehem Center in 1995, then at Barnet Park in 2008.

ABOVE: *Ira Tucker as a boy in Spartanburg. Later in life, he sold these autographed portraits at his concerts.*
OPPOSITE: *Ira Tucker, about 1950. Courtesy of the Smithsonian National Museum of African American History and Culture.*

Blind Simmie Dooley cut this record with Pink Anderson in 1928.

One of the South's great Piedmont bluesmen also made his home in the Gas Bottom neighborhood. Simeon "Blind Simmie" Dooley (1881-1961), a Columbia Records recording artist, lived on Fowler's Row toward the end of his life. Dooley performed on the streets of Spartanburg with fellow bluesman Pink Anderson, and, according to most accounts, taught the younger man to play the guitar. Dooley was instantly recognizable for his Vaudevillian-style, nasal tenor voice. Dooley and Anderson recorded songs together in Atlanta in 1928 with music historian Samuel Charters, including "Papa's 'Bout to Get Mad" and "C.C. & O. Blues," a song about the Clinchfield Railroad, which sliced through the Back of the College neighborhood beginning in about 1910. Dooley sang, "The C.C.&O the best train I do ride . . . That's the train to ride to pacify your mind." Those songs featured dovetailing guitars and Dooley on the kazoo. He died of heart disease, generally unheralded, Jan. 17, 1961, and was buried without a grave marker at the East Spartanburg Cemetery. After Dooley's death, Ira Tucker said of him, "For the blues, he was the greatest."

DECADES HAD PASSED since the nightly raids of the Ku Klux Klan in Spartanburg County, but that did not mean the terrorist organization had disappeared. In fact, on the night of Oct. 24, 1940, carloads of masked Klansmen sped through Gas Bottom, intimidating and menacing everyone they saw. Three teenagers from the neighborhood—Frank Caine, James Fowler and Paul Beaty—saw them coming. Two ran directly to their homes. Another took refuge in a nearby beer garden. More Klansmen were spotted on Morgan Square and Magnolia Street handing out circulars. City police, who were on high alert because of an earlier Klan beating of four Black men near Wellford, later said as many as 100 were in the city that night wearing pointed hats, white robes and dark glasses. Police arrested 15 men, most from Greenville and Anderson counties.

Eight months later, the three Gas Bottom youths testified in court against the Klansmen in a trial that devolved into a circus. The KKK defendants were represented by Depression-era Gov. Olin Johnston of Spartanburg, whose brother, Edwin, had been swept up in the arrests of the Klansmen. Two city police officers took the stand and made the startling claim that Spartanburg County Sheriff Samuel M. Henry was himself a member of the Klan and had once marched with them in a Klan parade—a charge the sheriff vigorously denied.

As the trial wrapped up, the grand dragon of the South Carolina Ku Klux Klan applied for a permit for his followers to parade through Spartanburg's downtown. This cast a pall over Black Spartanburg and threw city officials into a frenzy. One of them appealed to sitting Gov. Burnet Maybank, who then sent a telegram that the parade should be stopped, adding that he believed the Klan was supported by the German Nazi government. Maybank then abruptly changed his mind, and city leaders decided the Klan could assemble, but only if they refrained from wearing their hoods.

Gas Bottom and the North Dean Street neighborhood in 1959. South Pine Street, stretching left to right, had just opened.

As many as 5,000 Spartanburg onlookers lined the streets on June 24, 1941, as 35 cars packed with robed Klan members—men, women and children, some perched on the fenders of their vehicles—drove slowly through the northside from Wofford Street to Cleveland Park as the sun set over the city. From his perch at the Cleveland Park pavilion, KKK Grand Dragon Ben K. Adams looked out over the 150 Klan members around him. He shouted, "The people of Spartanburg and the Ku Klux Klan will not be put on an equal social and economic basis with the negroes of South Carolina!" Meanwhile, some anti-Klan Spartanburg residents who had followed the parade attempted to drown out the grand dragon by honking the horns of their cars. Adams ratcheted up the tension. He condemned Maybank and accused him, too, of being a former Klan member: "He took the same oath the rest of us did!"

The Klan melted away that night but left its mark on a nervous community. The three Klansmen on trial received sentences of one and two years. Life went on in Gas Bottom. Frequent raids for violations of the city's whiskey and "tipboard" gambling ordinances continued unabated. People tried to make a living as best they could. Paul Smith, a Gas Bottom poet who lived at 287 Cherry Street, submitted a verse to the *Spartanburg Journal* and it was published in August 1946:

A PORTER'S DREAM

Day in and day out the floors I must clean,
And the windows sparkling with a bright and radiant gleam.
Though as I work and to clean
My thoughts are filled with a porter's dream:
To be the boss, the one in charge,
To bark the orders like an angry sarge,
To dictate the hiring.
To command the firing,
To inspect and supervise,
To command and watch my powers rise,
To be important and don't give a care,
To be recognized anywhere.
But all these things are so untrue,
And I must stop for there are things to do
Back to work and work to clean,
And long for the things of a porter's dream.

AS EARLY AS THE 1940S, Spartanburg city leaders began talking about "slum clearance." In truth, many people in Gas Bottom were living in grinding poverty. Some lived in homes without heat or stoves, toilets or running water. Often they were paying rents wildly beyond their means to landlords. Eighty years after emancipation, large numbers of women in Gas Bottom still worked in the kitchens of white owned homes. Jim Crow employment laws, based on white supremacy, shut Black men out of textile manufacturing jobs that would have paid them living wages. Even when Gas Bottom residents tried to rise above their circumstances, they

Homes in Gas Bottom, just prior to urban renewal.

were sometimes thwarted: a Black man tried to open a hotdog stand at 220 Crawford Street in 1942 but was denied when City Council determined "that the location of such a business would be undesirable since Converse students often walk in this area."

In the mid-1950s local politicians sought state funds to extend Pine Street from its then-terminus at Main Street to Beaumont Mill and beyond, steering it right through Crawford Street. The new, wide, four-mile section displaced multiple Black homes on Crawford Street, along with Golden Street Baptist Church and a Presbyterian Mission building that served as a kindergarten. The city named the new street James F. Byrnes Boulevard in honor of the former governor and U.S. senator from Spartanburg. Byrnes also happened to be an active and staunch opponent of racial integration of South Carolina's schools.

On Jan. 26, 1957, the city of Spartanburg announced it would seek a federal planning grant for an urban renewal project that would raze large numbers of Gas Bottom residences and rehab others. This was to be the first urban renewal project in the state, an outgrowth of the 1949 federal Housing Act, which provided funding for communities to clear blighted areas and construct public housing. Spartanburg city planners drew lines around a wide area bounded by St. John Street, Converse College and the Southern Railroad. The 20-acre demolition zone was centered in the "Grand Canyon area," a wide gully that dropped off St. John Street and ran to the electric plant. Everything west of Northview Street was to be spared, including Dean Street School, Callaham Funeral Home and dwellings on North Dean, Keene, Silver Hill and North Converse streets.

As plans took shape, the number of substandard houses to be demolished crept up, from 83 to 162. The city's contract engineer told the all-white City Council: "New houses this project will cause to be built will bring in twice the amount of taxes [that] property in the area is now bringing," adding that Gas Bottom residents "are in general agreeable" to clearance of the area. "We have encountered no serious objections, not even from those who own homes there." One reason: the poverty in Gas Bottom had led to crime—break-ins, shootings, stabbings and some gang activity. Black and white residents who owned homes closer to St. John Street that could be rehabbed were OK with seeing some of their neighbors relocated.

Spartanburg Mayor Neville Holcombe used his regular "City Hall Report" newspaper column to explain the urban renewal project to the community and to warn people in Gas Bottom that "unscrupulous" persons were trying to buy up their houses before the project could get off the ground. Much of Gas Bottom would become a park and a recreation center, he said. At this point, state law prohibited cities from selling urban renewal property to developers. There would be picnic areas, flower gardens, a baseball field and tennis courts. Those who owned homes would be paid a fair price. They would be given $200 federal moving allowances.

In the last paragraph of his April 19, 1959, column, Holcombe announced there would be no new public housing built in Spartanburg. Gas Bottom residents were on their own in a city with insufficient housing stock. City rehabilitation director Marion Bryson warned council: "There are not enough houses with low enough rent to accommodate these people." There were FHA home loans for those who could afford to buy, but at one point, 75 families had no place to go.

Spartanburg City Council surveying plans in 1960. Mayor Neville Holcombe is at the head of the table.

Holcombe worked to keep white public opinion on his side. The $300,000 the city would spend in order to get matching money from the federal government was a steep price in the eyes of some. The mayor argued that city residents needed "decent, clean and safe homes." But he also wrote that Gas Bottom needed to be cleared "because the people who live in these unsanitary surroundings work as servants in the best homes and can very easily carry disease into those homes." Another time he wrote: "We could not forget that slums breed crime and disease and that people who live in these slums cook and serve our food, launder our clothes and nurse our children." This was a pretext that other municipal officials across the U.S. used to displace people in vulnerable communities in the 1960s. While it is true that there were outbreaks of cholera and tuberculosis in the overcrowded neighborhoods of the nation's largest cities during the 19th and 20th centuries, more often it was an attempt at crime control—even fear of race riots—that was the silent, but primary, motivator of urban renewal in the 1960s, argues University of Michigan scholar Amanda Rowe Tillotson.

In the end, 110 Gas Bottom residents received stipends to move as their dwellings were taken by eminent domain. Another 148 homeowners received some form of rehabilitation of their properties, shoring up part of the remaining neighborhood for the decades to come. Shortly after the project was complete, Converse College decided it, too, would do some clearance. As part of the college's 75th anniversary celebration in 1963, Converse raised $150,000 to buy and demolish a long row of Black-occupied homes on its western border that had stood since the 1920s. Roughly 18 more bungalow-style houses that had survived the Byrnes Boulevard construction and the Gas Bottom clearance quickly disappeared. The families who lived there joined the northside exodus in search of new housing elsewhere in the city.

City officials, under the leadership of new Mayor Bob Stoddard, deemed the Gas Bottom project so successful, they applied for federal funds to clear 87 acres in Highland in the mid-1960s and move its residents to the new Cammie Claggett Courts public housing. They then moved onto the Southside and its thriving Black business district in 1970, clearing 40 square blocks in and around South Liberty Street and uprooting some 2,000 people. In all, Spartanburg's per capita urban renewal tab reportedly was among the highest in the country.

In 1974 money from the federal Model Cities program built the Brotherhood Recreation Center on Oakland Avenue in the heart of the Gas Bottom clearance. The name was borrowed from that of an earlier Gas Bottom park: Brotherhood Park, a place with swings, slides and a merry-go-round that had been built and operated in the 1950s by a group of white Wofford and Converse college students and was staffed by the city. The new rec center, located above the new community baseball field in now-cleared Gas Bottom, carried the Brotherhood name until 1979 when the Spartanburg Black community renamed it: the building would be the T.K. Gregg Center. They named it for the late, prominent physician Dr. T.K. Gregg and for the former Back of the College rec center, then gone, that once bore his name. One of its key employees was Jesse James Carter, known as "King of Gas Bottom," who was inducted in the Softball Fast Pitch Hall of Fame and drafted by the Boston Red Sox.

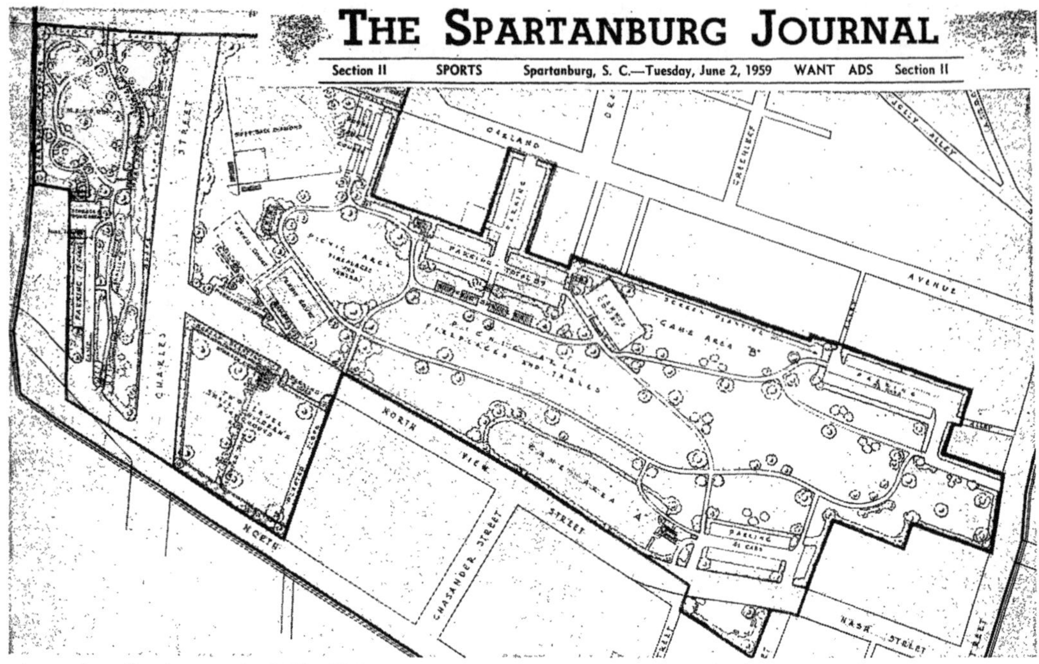

THE SPARTANBURG JOURNAL

Section II SPORTS Spartanburg, S. C.—Tuesday, June 2, 1959 WANT ADS Section II

Gas Bottom Park Would Have Recreation Areas, Picnic Grounds And Flower Gardens

SPARTANBURG'S PROPOSED, 23-ACRE Park in the Gas Bottom Area would feature recreation areas for both young and older children and include a softball field and tennis courts. A main feature of the park would be botanical gardens adjacent to the Southern Railway property on the north end of the park Picnic areas would have outdoor fireplaces and tables and parking facilities for about 200 cars. The city's share of the entire Gas Bottom Rehabilitation project would be about $250,000. Other plans for the over-all project would connect N. View Street with Nash Street and close up Jolly and Crawford Streets to N. Pine Street traffic. The project relies heavily on Federal aid and is the first of its kind in South Carolina. Initial plans were drawn by Prather and Thomas, Spartanburg Engineers and Architects and William Pitkin, land planner from Asheville. Park plans call for only one entrance to the area from Oakland Avenue. City planners estimate about 158 "dwelling units" or a total of 100 houses would have to be removed from the park area. The remaining houses in the Gas Bottom project would comply to the City's Urban Rehabilitation standards. The State Highway Department would be expected to finance about $45,000 worth of streets adjacent to the Park to connect with the State Highway System.

ABOVE: *Residences along North Pine Street, demolished in 1963. Their backyards faced Converse College.*
OPPOSITE TOP: *An early map of the Gas Bottom clearance area. Ultimately it was larger than this. This area is now greenspace and car dealerships.*
OPPOSITE BOTTOM: *Urban renewal beginning in Gas Bottom*

Turmoil arose again in the North Dean Street area in 1985 when city officials secretly agreed to sell the community ballpark to a development company led by George Dean Johnson Jr. After signing a contract with the developer to close the end of Northview Street—cutting the neighborhood off from Daniel Morgan Avenue and turning it into a cul-de-sac—Mayor Lewis Miller and City Council set up a public hearing. "You had a public hearing to close the street, but you had already sold the street?" asked an incredulous Patricia Reed. "You had a public hearing after the fact?" Eunice Thompson, a North Dean Street resident and former T.K. Gregg Center employee, asked, "Why do you want to uplift our community and spirits and make us feel like somebody, then close us up and put us back in an alley?"

The vote was 4-1. Mayor Lewis Miller apologized for the city's secret actions. The one vote in opposition came from James Talley, the first Black person on council since the 19th century and a future mayor. The city proceeded to sell the ballpark for $401,000, and the development group sold it to Vic Bailey for the first of many car dealerships along East Daniel Morgan.

An exasperated and angry Harold Miller, longtime advocate for the North Dean Street neighborhood, reacted with a scorching letter to the editor. He had lived at 330 Northview Street since his birth in 1929, and his parents had lived in that same house two decades before that. "It is a shame that a Mayor can use the words revitalize Main Street and at the same time devitalize every area possible in the black community," wrote Miller, a courthouse bailiff and former head waiter at the Piedmont Club, a private dining facility in downtown. "All a developer has to do is drive through a black neighborhood and say, 'I want this property.' A 4-1 vote is waiting in the closet to approve it."

On Oct. 21, 1985, Harold Miller came to the podium at a City Council meeting on behalf of his neighborhood. In his signature baritone voice, Miller asked the councilmembers a very important question: "When are we going to be totally consumed?"

OPPOSITE TOP: *The Brotherhood Center opened on the lower end of Oakland Avenue in 1974 and was later renamed the T.K. Gregg Center.*
OPPOSITE BOTTOM: *Neighborhood advocate Harold Miller among children at the T.K. Gregg Center in 1993.*

MODEL CITIES BROTHERHOOD PARK CENTER on Oakland Avenue was opened to the public on Monday featuring a gymnasium, craft shops and general recreation facilities. The lower level of the center will house a 90-child Day Care Center under the direction of the County Department of Social Services while the top level provides office space for representatives of the police department's Community Relations program, the Office of Economic Opportunity and Model Cities representatives. The facility is staffed by four employes from the old T. K. Gregg Center which was closed when the new facility opened. The Day Care Center is expected to open in the near future. Shown are front (top photo) and rear views of the facility. (Photos By Sammy Hughes Of B&B Studios For The Journal.)

SPOTLIGHT

GOSPEL GREAT BOB BEATTY

While the Beatty family is deeply connected to the Southside of Spartanburg, the family originally came from Union County and settled in Gas Bottom, the springboard of several soul-gospel pioneers.

One of the great early Black musicians to emerge from Spartanburg was Arthur Lee "Bob" Beatty Jr., whose singing career spanned 80 years and landed him in the Gospel Music Hall of Fame. Born in 1914, Beatty—who became known as "the Black Angel"—came to Spartanburg as a toddler when his father, a minister, took a job in the gas plant that gave the neighborhood its name.

As a boy, Bob Beatty dreamed of becoming a professional boxer, but that was not to be his future. In the mid-1930s, a group of Spartanburg singers who had moved to Detroit and formed the Heavenly Gospel

Singers needed a tenor for their quartet who could hit the high notes. When they came back through their hometown, Beatty tried out. He knew their songs because he had listened to them on a hand-cranked phonograph, and his voice was just what they needed. Together, in 1937, Beatty and the group recorded "Precious Lord, Take My Hand," a Thomas A. Dorsey song that is considered today "one of the most significant in the whole development of gospel music," according to music writer Tony Cummings. Suddenly, the Heavenlys were the "pinnacle of gospel quartets," said Dave Lindy, radio host of "The Gospel Train."

Beatty's style contained a touch of old-time spirituals, some blues and an early form of doo-wop. "Everybody was using what we created back then," he told the *Spartanburg Herald* when he came to town to do a concert in 2008. Beatty went on to perform with the Sensational Nightingales, the Trumpets of Joy and—for 40 years—with the Soul Lifters Quartet. He sang on the stages of Carnegie Hall and the Apollo Theatre. He performed on Art Linkletter's radio show. He toured with boxing star Joe Louis to raise money for research and treatment of infantile paralysis. Fellow Spartanburg gospel star Ira Tucker called him "the legend."

Other than touring and service in World War II, Beatty never left Spartanburg because his wife, Ruth, wanted him home. He held down a job with the Spartanburg County Department of Maintenance and Transportation. He and Ruth had nine children, including South Carolina Supreme Court Chief Justice Donald W. Beatty and Spartanburg School District 7 Trustee Vernon Beatty. Another son, Willie, became a gospel singer.

When Beatty died Jan. 8, 2011, at the age of 96, the South Carolina State Senate passed a resolution honoring him and expressing their sorrow at his passing, noting that not only was he a master musician, he was also a champion chess player and a fine fisherman too.

OPPOSITE: *Bob Beatty, a member of the Gospel Music Hall of Fame*

Hattie Bell Penland at the dedication of the Back of the College monument in 1993.

TWELVE

DEMOLITION BACK OF THE COLLEGE

IT WAS THE TENNIS COURTS that pushed Nellie Platt and Sylvania Level over the edge. The two old friends had watched Wofford College slowly encroach upon their neighborhood. There were grassy spaces where there used to be houses. There were houses with no one living in them anymore. There were college kids swearing and yelling outside their homes. Ten tennis courts had come first, and now there was a new team clubhouse going up on the site. "I think they are trying to close us out of here," Platt protested in 1991. At age 62, she was the youngest daughter of the late Arthur C. Platt, Spartanburg's first Black attorney. "They did this because this is a Black community and they think they can run rampant over us."

Tempers boiled over in the neighborhood that fall as the students came back to campus. Residents along Evins, Jefferson and Littlejohn streets took their indignation about the tennis building to a news reporter and to Black attorney James Cheek—himself a Wofford grad—in an attempt to halt construction. Cheek argued in front of the city's Zoning Board of Adjustment and Appeals that the neighbors had not been property notified of the zoning change. A Wofford vice president argued they had. The vote came down 3-2 in

Nellie Platt discussing the college's incursion into the neighborhood where she was born.

favor of Wofford in a technicality over the start date of a new city public hearing ordinance. In the end, the protests had all been futile. The liberal arts college, barreling toward a day when it would have more than 1,800 students and Division 1 athletics programs, was on a path that ultimately would displace the entire Back of the College neighborhood by the end of the decade.

From its very beginning, Wofford College needed more land. Since the moment it opened its doors in 1854 on 36 acres offered by wealthy Spartanburg merchant Jesse Cleveland, the college sought to expand its borders east, west, north and south. Shortly after the Civil War, the campus had 80 acres, and at the turn of the century the college began creating a front entrance by buying lots along North Church, College and Evins streets. The college was not always pleased about having neighbors. Professor David Duncan Wallace said as much in his 1951 *History of Wofford College* book: "The trustees showed lamentable lack of foresight by requesting a tract so

Back of the College, 1963. Everything here, except Cumming Street School and Wofford's Joe Taylor Athletic Center, has been replaced.

small that within a few years it was necessary for the college to purchase adjacent tracts to prevent the establishment of undesirable neighbors, virtually at the doors of its buildings, not to speak of the needs for expansion," he wrote.

For the first century of its existence, Wofford had taken baby steps into the surrounding neighborhood, picking up a lot here and a lot there as property became available for purchase. Wofford was not a wealthy college in its early days. Its leaders were ministers, its boosters financially decimated by the Civil War, and its alumni pool small—the college graduated no more than 100 men a year until 1920. The college's fortunes changed dramatically in 1954 when New York textile magnate Roger Milliken relocated his family-held company to Spartanburg and joined the Wofford College Board of Trustees. Milliken, whose net worth was once estimated at $1 billion, believed in the accumulation of land, especially when it meant creating a buffer around valued assets like manufacturing plants, colleges and, later, the Greenville-Spartanburg Airport. Except for three brief periods when board policy required him to roll off, he served 50 years as a Wofford trustee, many of them as field general of the college's real estate vision.

The ultimate disappearance of the Back of the College neighborhood was at once complicated and simple. As testimony and documents show, Wofford officials wanted to move north since at least the late 1940s, and they worked through a combination of planned and opportunistic property acquisition to do so over a period of about 70 years. While college officials did not consistently acquire property based on a specific expansion plan, they were always willing to buy as funds allowed, and they consistently conceived of the neighborhood as fertile expansion ground. The college was aided by favorable city policies and practices as well as homeowners in the neighborhood and landlords who managed properties from as far away as California and were willing to sell for a variety of reasons.

As the country turned away from World War II and the G.I. Bill took effect, Wofford began to reconsider its place in the landscape of liberal arts colleges in the South. What had been a distinguished pre-professional, liberal arts school with a limited geographic scope began to see itself as an institution that could expand its reach. Milliken, Wofford's principal benefactor and most salient voice among its trustees, personally funded the college's acquisition of properties north and east of campus as they became available. In February 1966 the college bought 17 properties, totaling six acres, on Charlevoix Street for intramural sports fields, including an area that was used as a neighborhood playground. In August 1969 Wofford asked the city to rezone seven additional properties from residential to institutional. A public notice in the local newspaper identified the land as part of "a plat for C.C. Scott," the Black pastor from the 1890s who kickstarted the neighborhood's development.

Former Wofford College President Joab M. Lesesne Jr., who served from 1972 to 2000, explained that the college would buy a house or a lot if the price was right, typically when vacant. If no one was living on the property, the college would have the house demolished and leave it as "green space;" if someone lived there, Wofford would sometimes assume landlord

Hattie Bell Penland's home on Jones Street. Kiddie Kollege also was on this street.

responsibilities and raze the house after the tenants left. In this way, slowly at first, houses began to disappear. Some homeowners began contacting college officials with a desire to sell in the mid-1960s, which became increasingly the case into the 1970s and 1980s.

These actions contributed centrally to what ultimately became the neighborhood's decline. The opportunistic acquisition of property loosened the soil for the college's taking possession of all the land that was once home to the people who built together the first Black neighborhood in Spartanburg. As houses disappeared, property values decreased. Young people began to think twice about settling there. Older residents increasingly felt trapped. Those who could, either moved or sold to Wofford. As more properties became available, Wofford bought them and cleared the land.

MEANWHILE, URBAN RENEWAL came to the Southside of Spartanburg, and Back of the College residents watched in increasing anxiety as South Liberty Street was bulldozed in the early 1970s. What they did not know was that city officials were working quietly on a plan to dismantle their

Bertha Johnson, left, with Louvenia Barksdale at the Barksdale home on Evins Street

own neighborhood in exactly the same fashion, along with the neighborhood around Silver Hill Methodist Church. These discussions were going on behind the scenes at City Hall in 1973 at a time when Wofford Vice President of Business Ed Greene had just been appointed to the all-white Spartanburg City Planning Commission, the board that reviewed urban renewal proposals.

Unlike many other universities around the country that were confiscating Black neighborhoods for campus expansion during this era, Wofford College could not seize any houses by eminent domain. It was a private entity, and only public entities could take private property for their own use. For instance, in the 1960s the University of Oklahoma dismantled a Black neighborhood of 713 families to create a new medical center. The University of Georgia demolished a Black neighborhood of 50 families for student housing and parking. Likewise, the University of Pennsylvania in 1969 forced nearly 600 Black families from their homes to make way for its new science center. This was happening with great frequency in the 1960s, but without a public body such as the city of Spartanburg leading the effort, there could be no taking of houses Back of the College by eminent domain.

By 1973 the city of Spartanburg had completed or initiated the destruction of four Black neighborhoods—Gas Bottom, Highland and two large areas of the Southside—with $19 million in federal funds. Back of the College was the largest remaining Black neighborhood in the central city, with some 300 houses. That year, a young John G. Baehr was elected mayor of Spartanburg, succeeding outgoing Mayor Bob Stoddard, who had overseen three of the four projects. Baehr, who was white, ran on an anti-urban renewal platform. “The wholesale bulldozing of entire city blocks in the name of urban renewal is not renewal—it’s destruction,” he said at a public forum days before the election. Baehr, a 36-year-old Navy fighter pilot and sitting city councilman, swept into office, winning by wide margins the voting precincts of majority-Black neighborhoods on the northside and southside. Almost simultaneously to his election, the administration of U.S. President Richard Nixon shut down federal funding for urban renewal, a program that novelist and activist James Baldwin notably had called “Negro removal.”

About two years later, people living in the vicinity of Wofford College began to wonder why they still did not have cable TV service when it seemed everyone else in the city was being served. The situation just seemed strange. One resident reached out to the regular Ask-the-Mayor newspaper column in the *Spartanburg Herald* to find out why there was an “island” with no cable TV in the Wofford College area. In what appears to be the only public mention of urban renewal plans for Back of the College, Mayor Baehr took the occasion to reveal what had been going on. “The particular area your letter describes broadly falls into a portion of the city that has been targeted for renewal,” Baehr wrote. “Somewhile ago the timetable seemed fairly short and it appeared the work would be started in the near future. Such a project would mean considerable clearance of substandard housing and a redevelopment of the neighborhood.” Baehr noted that the end of federal funding had thrown future urban renewal projects into uncertainty: “Major change in the area described is now not within view,” he wrote. Cable TV lines now could be installed, and he hoped that would begin soon.

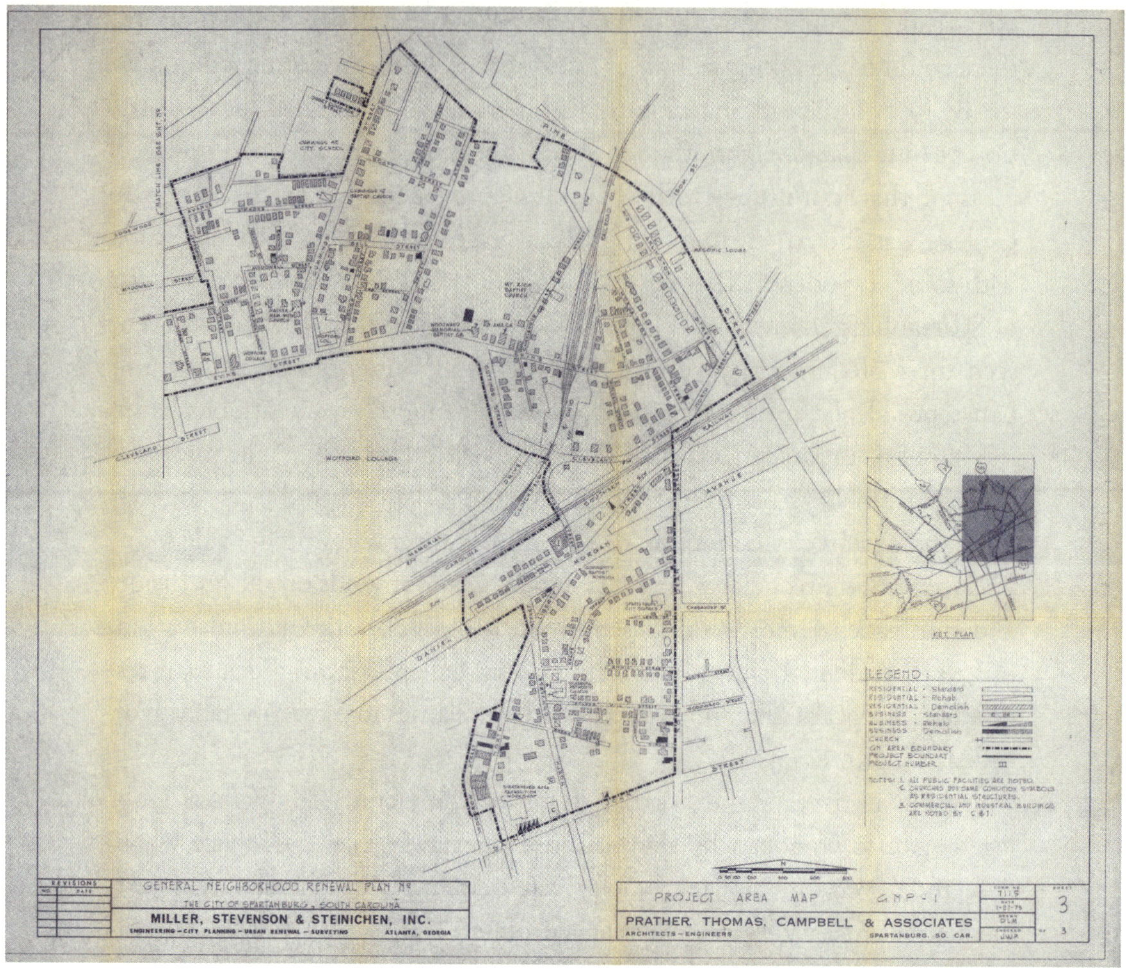

The proposed urban renewal clearance of 450 homes in the Back of the College and the Silver Hill Church area. Federal money ran out before this could be implemented.

Unbeknownst to residents, the city of Spartanburg had hired surveyors and engineers in 1972 to develop sweeping plans for the wholesale obliteration of hundreds of houses around Wofford College and Silver Hill Methodist Church. A plat of the proposed Back of the College-Silver Hill urban renewal project—dated Jan. 27, 1973, and never introduced in public—shows approximately 450 homes to be demolished, almost all of them Black occupied. Among them were the substantial, well-kept homes of longtime neighborhood residents. The proposed demolition zone stopped at the white-occupied homes of Beaumont Mill workers on Arlington Street. It also stopped at the white-occupied homes closer to North Church Street. Virtually the only structures to be left standing in an area of nearly 200 acres were Cumming Street School, Dean Street School, Cummings Street Baptist Church, Silver Hill Methodist Church and Mount Zion Baptist Church. Everything else was to be wiped out, including all the homes along Evins Street, Cummings Street and half the homes along North Dean Street.

Then-City Planning Director Tim Kuether said in a 2023 interview that urban renewal plans for Back of the College could not advance because the spigot of federal dollars had been shut off. Besides, he recalled, city fathers believed that Wofford already was doing its part to remove substandard housing in the area.

Most of the neighbors in this area got a reprieve, but it would last at most 25 years.

For Wofford, this was a lost opportunity to purchase at a discount the property it desired, according to a letter Ed Greene sent to Spartanburg City Manager William Carstarphen in 1981. (Carstarphen arrived at the city after urban renewal, in 1975.) "At a time when the area was scheduled for urban renewal, and there was the possibility of building housing elsewhere, Wofford was interested in acquiring a portion of the area," related Greene, who served the Planning Commission from late-1972 to mid-1976, the last year as its chair. "On that basis the college could have acquired the land at a relatively low cost, but, as you know, the urban renewal program was closed down."

If Wofford still wanted the neighborhood, the college would have to buy the property itself.

THE WRITING WAS CLEARLY on the wall by that time. Cumming Street School was no longer functioning as an elementary and junior high school, and many properties were empty or in decline. The number of owner-occupied homes behind the college—in areas white and Black—had dropped from 430 in 1952 to 328 by 1970. City directory records show multiple listings being vacant by 1970, numbers that increased into the decade.

Several studies in urban sociology have pinpointed contributing factors to such urban decline: red-lining, white flight, urban renewal, declining

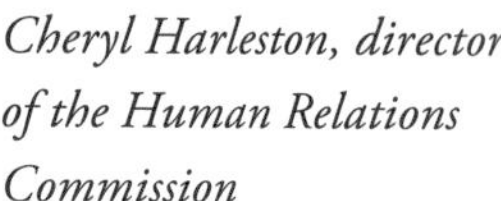

Cheryl Harleston, director of the Human Relations Commission

condition of houses, residents' lack of access to home improvement funds, geographic limitation or isolation and loss of community cohesiveness. As Mindy Fullilove has shown in *Root Shock: How Tearing Up City Neighborhoods Hurts America, and What We Can Do About It*, one of the principal causes of predominantly Black neighborhoods being ruined in cities such as Pittsburgh and Roanoke was the systematic acquisition and razing of land by local institutions. "Reclaiming land" for "progress" is a central tenet of institutions that look to increase or improve their condition by expanding into areas already owned or occupied. People who resist incursions into their land or neighborhood, Fullilove wrote, are said to be standing in the way of progress, and local government, often in lock step with local developers, develops policies that favor progress.

In 1981 Cheryl Harleston, the city's first Black director of the Human Relations Commission, requested a meeting with Wofford officials. The longtime advocate of Black heritage and civil rights in town wanted residents to have an opportunity to air their concerns about what was happening to their neighborhood—houses were beginning to disappear at a faster rate. Afterward, Ed Greene wrote a letter to City Manager William Carstarphan dismissing the grievances of the residents. "It was obvious to me that citizens really do not understand what the city can and cannot do," he wrote. "Even when programs are understood, citizens do not understand how priorities are set. They do not understand, for example, why they cannot get low-interest loans while homeowners in the Hampton [Heights] area can." He added, "It was inferred that city personnel have excused a lack of city response to concerns, complaints and requests for city services because Wofford and the hospital-medical complex were buying property on the north and south sides of the neighborhood."

Assumptions that residents "do not understand" property law and municipal finances were common pieces of the destruction of Black neighborhoods across the United States throughout the 20th century. Such thinking was "debilitating" to the people who were dismissed, said Tony Thomas, community engagement coordinator for Spartanburg's Northside Development Group. "That goes back to Jim Crow," said Thomas, longtime leader of a team of Black "Voyagers" participating in an ongoing revitalization of the mixed-race neighborhood surrounding Spartanburg's VCOM-Carolinas Medical School. "There were a lot of assumptions going on that were not based in fact. You don't assume people don't understand. You sit down with them. You'll find pockets of knowledge that are untapped and unused." He looks back and is saddened by the diminishment of early neighborhoods of Black and Brown people. "There was this desire for our communities to fail. 'We're going to allow them to implode.'"

LITTLE DID RESIDENTS KNOW, but Wofford College had been planning an expansion for some time. An early strategic plan—called "A Plan for the 70s"— named expansion north of Evins Street as a primary college goal. The 1970 Plan spelled out that "if Wofford is to achieve its objectives," it must "[a]cquire land north of campus" and budgeted $300,000 to do so. The minutes of the meeting of the board of trustees on May 11, 1971, include a report provided by Roger Milliken that two residences owned by the college, at 152 East Cleveland and 214 Evins Street, were demolished with $1,600 from the "Milliken Fund." Milliken also reported that $15,000 was set aside to purchase Elva Carter's house at 215 Evins Street. Four years later, a facilities sub-committee chaired by Milliken reported that "progress [was] made in planning the conversion of the recently acquired property adjacent to the campus into playing fields."

Ed Greene, the vice president, checked in by letter with the Spartanburg city manager in 1981: "We continue to purchase property as it becomes available at an attractive price.... Most of the property we have bought either faces Evins Street or, if north of Evins, is adjacent to property we already own." In 1982, when the college was between major long-range plans and was doing its best to survive an economic downturn, it nevertheless committed $5,000 from the depreciation fund to tear down three houses on East Cleveland Street and one on Jefferson Street and to fill and clean up the lots.

Another long-range strategic plan in 1986-87 recommitted the college to expansion inside the neighborhood. Co-chaired by Lesesne and then-chairman Russell C. King, the "Master Plan" received input from a wide range of Wofford's community members, including board members, administrators, faculty, staff, students and alumni. Multiple committees were created, and individuals worked for at least an entire school year to develop recommendations. A subgroup called the Physical Facilities Committee urged the college to continue buying homes along Evins and Cleveland streets:

> The properties in these areas are a natural extension of the Wofford campus since the campus is physically confined by the railroad tracks to the east and North Church Street to the west. It is conceivable that as property becomes available, the area between the Clinchfield tracks and Cleveland Street can be acquired within the foreseeable future. Such an acquisition would enable Wofford to have an entrance from North Pine Street if this is found desirable. The Committee has contacted the City Manager and other officers of the City of Spartanburg to secure information regarding future development in the area near Wofford's present campus. We strongly recommend that Wofford designate a staff person to maintain a continuous relationship with the City so that any future land acquisition and development can be coordinated with the plans of the City of Spartanburg. In order to purchase property as it becomes available, we recommend the creation of a fund from which the President, and/or a small committee designated by the

A house scheduled for demolition on Charlevoix Street

> Board of Trustees, can quietly and quickly purchase property as it becomes available. In order to develop the ownership of land, we recommend that an ownership and appraisal map be developed of the areas in which Wofford has an interest.

Larger societal issues then accelerated Wofford's land acquisition. In the 1980s crack cocaine distribution and its oft-associated violence moved into some low-income neighborhoods in Spartanburg, including Charlevoix Street behind the college. This unnerved college administrators as well as many members of the neighborhood. Older residents were frightened of crime, so they would ask Wofford officials to protect them, recalled Lesesne. "After the mid-70s, there were real problems in that area in terms of vandalism and drug sales," he said. "So there were a number of people who asked our maintenance people to watch out for their houses." The fear was real. In August 1987 the partially clothed body of 52-year-old Arthur Griffin was found in a field off Charlevoix Street, and a man living on Evins Street was charged with his murder. A little over a year later, an 18-year-old Charlevoix Street resident was arrested in the beating death of a man in Greer.

The worst was yet to come. A 22-year-old man was found burned, shot and badly decomposed under his Charlevoix Street duplex on April 5, 1989. His brother said he had been a drug runner for the so-called Boston Boys, a group of six men from Massachusetts who briefly set up shop in Spartanburg to enlist locals—often teenagers—to distribute crack cocaine. The Boston Boys publicized their identity by wearing Boston Celtics jerseys and driving cars with Massachusetts plates, according to then-Sgt. Randy Hardy of the Spartanburg Police Department. The transplanted gang reportedly shot and killed a man found lying face up on a sidewalk at Tobe Hartwell Courts. They sprayed a house on Baltimore street with bullets. A 14-year-old boy on Carpenter Street was dead, and his mother blamed the shooting death on the gang. With uncertainty about crime creeping into the neighborhood, Wofford's opportunistic land purchases proceeded apace. "There were lots of people in the neighborhood who were getting old and they would come to the college to see if they would buy it," Lesesne said. "It was getting rough for old people to live back there."

Wofford's 1986 Master Plan had recommended relocation of the tennis courts to the north side of Evins Street, and bulldozers began preparing the site in 1990. The territory behind the tennis site was still a viable, mixed-race neighborhood of neat, wood-frame bungalows, some occupied by the same families for 60 years. This was the move that riled up Nellie Platt and her neighbors, whose homes faced the construction area. Platt recently had moved back to the area after a career in the finance industry out of state. She reached out to attorney James Cheek, then 30 years old and working out of a law office on Evins Street, to represent a group of 12 neighbors seeking to slow down Wofford's incursion. "Nellie Platt was a class act," Cheek recalled many years later. "She was an African-American Jackie Kennedy Onassis, designer handbags, designer clothes. She was confident in herself, secure, intelligent, articulate. She made me more of an astute attorney. . . . I was young and angry."

Wofford tennis coach Ben Varn tried to keep the peace by offering to allow neighborhood children to play on the new courts as his guests. But Mildred Littlejohn, a resident at 531 Jefferson Street, claimed that college security guards and a Spartanburg City Police officer had escorted two neighborhood boys off the courts just two weeks earlier. A frustrated Varn

Jerry Richardson, Wofford College football star and benefactor

could not understand why the tennis facility would bother local residents. "What is the objection?" he asked newspaper reporter Melinda Mooty. "The thing is, who's next door to them now? If a person sells out and Wofford buys their property and puts something up, is it any worse than what was there?"

Nellie Platt said indeed it was. Sitting on her front porch was no longer a pleasant experience. The college's chain-link security fence around the courts made the area "look like a prison," she said.

AT 8:05 P.M. ON OCT. 26, 1993, the telephone rang in hotel room 2206 of the O'Hare Airport Hyatt Regency Hotel in Chicago. Jerry Richardson, then a food-service executive at Spartanburg's Flagstar Corp., had been waiting anxiously for the call. The 6-foot-3-inch former Wofford College wide receiver was told to walk down the hall, take the elevator to the hotel kitchen and come to a meeting room where 28 National Football League owners were gathered. The owners had voted unanimously to give the 1958

Wofford graduate an NFL franchise for the Carolinas. This was a moment of great elation for the Richardson family, for the city of Charlotte and for hometown boosters in Spartanburg who had enthusiastically supported Richardson's six-year campaign for the team.

It also was the death knell for what was left of the neighborhood known as Back of the College.

Within a few months it was clear that Richardson, 57, would bring the football team's summer training camp to Spartanburg. There simply was no way Wofford College was going to pass up an opportunity like that. It meant a dazzling new workout building for the campus, a kickstart to a long-desired new football stadium, new athletic fields for college sports teams, and national exposure each summer as the upstart Carolina Panthers and thousands of tourists came to town. The alumni and students were fully on board, as was the Spartanburg Area Chamber of Commerce and Spartanburg's Black mayor, James Talley. Wofford and its donors would pay whatever it took to make the training camp happen. The college sent its agents out into the neighborhood to negotiate prices on the homes in the path of the Panthers.

The number of houses in the place where Anson Cummings, C.C. Scott and the Bobo heirs had first launched the neighborhood had declined steadily. In 1960 there had been more than 150 Black-occupied homes on Evins, Bell, Jones, Twitty, Scott and Peachtree streets—the designated site for the training camp facilities. By the early '80s, about one-third of those had slowly disappeared. As plans were unveiled in 1994 for Gibbs Stadium, the $5 million Richardson Physical Activities Building and two new practice fields, the count was about 50 homes.

"It was good to get rid of that property at the time, because it had fallen pretty well into disarray," maintained Mayor James Talley, a former star football player for the Carver High Tigers and a former wide receiver coach for the Wofford football team. "And it had gotten to the point where it would cost more to fix it up than it would to sell it." He said Wofford made a special effort to pay more money for homes occupied by longtime residents of the neighborhood. He continues to believe the changes were for the better. "So a lot of them sold and had enough to buy a house somewhere else. So in that manner, that was the way in which Wofford worked

Linda Dogan as a city councilwoman fighting for her neighborhood

on them. They didn't put anybody out and force anybody out. They made everybody a fair offer." He said he encountered no one in the neighborhood who was unhappy about the NFL coming to Spartanburg.

"The community was changing," said Norma Foster Green, who grew up on Bell Street with her mother, Sarah, and father, Clifford, and grandmother Lily next door. "You know, it wasn't that 'family feel' anymore in a lot of different ways." Many families had sold their homes to landlords, or they rented them themselves. "You know, people complain about Wofford taking their property, but the reality was, they didn't own the property. So it was easy to get it."

The loss, though, was hard to stomach. "I didn't like it at all," said Cynthia Harris Logan. "They just took our neighborhood away from us. And we got divided. Because when they start taking the neighborhood, people start moving in different directions. They had to move. We still stay in contact with some of the people, but not everybody—everybody just scattered. Just a whole neighborhood. And it's just—it's gone."

The first tangible sign of what was to come occurred in April 1994 when city officials announced the forthcoming closure of several roads through the neighborhood: Jones, Bell, Twitty and Pee Dee. When the issue came before Spartanburg City Council, newly elected councilwoman Linda Dogan cast the lone dissenting vote, saying she felt the area had too much history to destroy it. Even after her losing battle, she worked to help her former schoolmates, church members and neighbors by negotiating directly with Wofford's Ed Greene, noting that she and the white vice president often butted heads. In one case, she convinced Wofford to swap one elderly resident's home for a better one elsewhere.

Norma Pitts remembered the trauma. "They just start separating people. 'You gotta move, you gotta move,' you know. 'We selling out.' So it was a lot of people they had to uproot. Can you imagine? That's the way they did Southside, they just uprooted it. They just came through and you got to go." All the property once owned a century earlier by the Rev. C.C. Scott went to Wofford: the Honeycutt family sold its piece of Scott's former parcel on Peachtree for $20,000; John S. Woodward and Palmer Miller did the same with theirs.

As the mass purchases proceeded, many in the neighborhood saw it as "a racial thing," Norma Green recalled. "A lot of people will say that they got cheated. But again, they didn't own their homes." Her family's former home was now rental property. Wofford's first offer was "lowball," she said, and they negotiated to get a better price. "So we did get a little more than I think they had offered originally. But because we weren't living there, it wasn't as traumatic as it was for some people. . . . If everybody had owned their homes, they could have stood up against it. But once the people who were renting started selling their houses . . . pretty much there's nothing left you could do. You pretty much had to go." On the other hand, she said, proceeds from the sale of her home did have a positive effect on her family. "The money we got from selling to Wofford sent my son to college without a student loan," she said.

A CONTROVERSY AROSE when the college applied for grant funding from the Appalachian Council of Governments to support construction of the stadium. In order to qualify for $1.25 million in federal funding, Wofford

Gibbs Stadium construction, 1996. These homes were ultimately removed.

had to designate the site as the center of a high-poverty area, which raised eyebrows among people who questioned why federal money was going for a private college football stadium rather than to Spartanburg's economically distressed. Wofford had to meet a requirement to provide 20 jobs for people of color in the target area, which stretched from North Dean Street to Farley Avenue, but that seemed decidedly insufficient to some. Members of Spartanburg's Black community argued that a portion of that grant should more directly benefit them. "I think they should at least give us some sidewalks," said Carrie Henderson. "We need sidewalks and we have never had any. But they are going to do whatever they are going to do in the end." Even the boosterish *Spartanburg Herald-Journal* was skeptical about the grant funding, arguing in a February 1996 editorial that the allocation illustrated why the federal program should be shut down: "This county is one of the most economically booming areas in the nation," it said. "Why should we be pulling in federal money for economic development assistance?"

Some neighbors hung on as long as they could. Then 84 years old and disabled, Icie Hamilton had lived her whole life in a home her father built on Twitty Street. She turned down Wofford's initial offer, but her family knew she could not remain there without the help of neighbors. There was no one nearby to help her if she fell. Her relatives negotiated a price of $75,000 for the house and an adjacent lot. “She is doing well, but she is living in Boston against her will,” a family member told *Herald* reporter Linda Conley in 1997.

A bulldozer arrived at the former Jones Street home of 80-year-old Sophia Hart, who had operated Kiddie Kollege for more than three decades. It plowed over the two ponds on the property and the tiny log cabin where her late husband, Walter, once had kept a menagerie of animals to entertain the children. “She didn’t want to go. They literally packed her up and moved her to Lucerne Drive,” said her grandson, Keith Harris.

Bertha Turley Johnson would call her father in Connecticut and tell him what was happening. “I’d have to say, ‘Dad, no, no, that does not exist anymore. Wofford College has that. You cannot go into the area like that, that is private now.’ This is what I have to tell my dad. So that’s the part that kind of got to me a little bit—that how I could not go back over into Littlejohn Court or Edgewood Avenue, even down to Twitty Street.”

Hattie Bell Penland, who had lived and worked Back of the College her entire life, was not ready to move either and turned down multiple offers from Wofford for her Jones Street house. Pressure to begin building the stadium was intense, remembered Lesesne, the college president. He worried that Spartanburg would lose the training camp to Rock Hill if they did not finish the acquisitions. But Penland was steadfast, and Lesesne—who had known her for 30 years—was sympathetic. “So we wound up moving the stadium a little bit,” Lesesne said. “We didn’t want to, but we did.” Ultimately, Wofford made special accommodations for Penland and her longtime best friend, Stacey Whitmire, both in their 90s. They could stay in their homes as long as they needed. Everything else would be cleared, but those homes would stand as long as the women were alive and desired to stay.

A year before she died at age 97, Whitmire sold out for $116,000 and moved in with family in Daytona Beach, Florida. Penland negotiated a $175,000 price for her home plus two rental houses on Jones Street and stayed on site until Whitmire left. She moved to an assisted living center on Skylyn Drive, before dying in 2000 at age 98. She was buried in the Old City Cemetery on the Southside along with other greats of Spartanburg’s past. Their houses came down.

Jeanette Wiggins held out the longest. Her home had been built by her grandfather, William Robinson.

Jeanette Wiggins hung on without selling until May 1996. By that time, the new Gibbs Stadium was on the verge of opening, and the Carolina Panthers already had spent one summer session at the college. A huge football fan herself, Wiggins had watched the NFL players practice from the shady backyard of her Twitty Street home, then surrounded by a chain-link fence. Wofford officials made a series of offers for her five-bedroom house—built a century earlier by her grandfather, William Robinson—but Wiggins had refused. As the weeks went by, Roger Milliken lost patience, Lesesne recalled, and declared that he would not provide the money to purchase the property. Finally, a $154,000 price was right, the college found another donor to cover the cost, and Wiggins gave up the last structure still in the way of Panther practice facilities. The *Spartanburg Herald* trumpeted: RED-LETTER DAY FOR WOFFORD. Wiggins wasn't quite as effusive. "It's hard when you have to leave the memories," she told a reporter. "You think about all the good times I had here. If it was possible for me to take this house with me, I would."

Back of the College, post clearance, 1999. Wofford College and the Memorial Auditorium are in the foreground.

Some former residents moved in with families out of state. Others went to the west side of Spartanburg, to South Converse Street, to the Plainview Drive area, or to assisted living centers. Meanwhile, tens of thousands of Carolina Panthers fans began descending on the area each summer. There were shuttle buses, national TV crews, autograph lines, food trucks, inflatable playhouses and souvenir sales.

ON A COLD, MISTY DAY in February 1998, artist Winston Wingo stepped up to a microphone that had been placed outside Wofford College's new Gibbs Stadium. A group of about 100 people, Black and white, were there

The day of the monument dedication. L-R: Jonathan Metcalf, James Cheek, artist Winston Wingo, Wofford College President Joab Lesesne.

for the dedication of a bronze relief monument Wingo had created to honor the people who had lived Back of the College. Attendees huddled under umbrellas and pressed tightly together to stay dry. As the 44-year-old Black artist began describing the imagery of his piece, he was overcome with emotion. He paused. His voice cracked. Tears rolled. What he felt that day was both grief and gratitude, Wingo said in an interview 25 years later. While he had not grown up in the neighborhood, he remembered the dances he had attended as a teen at the T.K. Gregg Center. He remembered front-porch visits with Louvenia Barksdale. He also remembered three white Wofford professors who had mentored him in the 1960s, allowing him access to the college's science labs, setting in motion his life as an artist who works with metal.

When the somber ceremony was over, the participants dispersed and headed back to their cars and their offices. Thousands of people would take their place that fall, funneling through the gates of the football stadium in high spirits, wearing the Wofford colors of black and gold. That same year, Wofford began a second push into the last remaining residential section north of campus, this time buying houses from both white and Black families. The college cut a wide swath north toward Spartanburg Medical Center, buying what was left of Swain, Jefferson, McDowell, Osage and Thomas streets and demolishing more than three dozen houses. The hospital, meanwhile, bought property along Pearl Street, forming a common border with the college. The former Evins estate, which began as an all-

Houses coming down on McDowell Street to make way for Wofford's senior student Village housing.

white neighborhood in 1907 but ultimately had integrated, vanished. In its place was colorful, apartment-style housing for the Wofford senior class, now 400 students strong. The college christened it "The Village." A new fraternity row stood where Louvenia Barksdale and Stacey Whitmire once lived. In all, Wofford purchased 275 parcels for its expansion.

In the years after the Panthers camp opened, Jerry Richardson would bestow upon his alma mater a blizzard of philanthropy—more than a quarter of a billion dollars in the last years of his life. The funds paid for three more buildings bearing the Richardson name, scholarships for needy college students, study abroad opportunities, and a new minimum wage of $15 an hour on campus—a boon to employees who maintained the buildings and grounds.

For the people who once lived where the Panthers then practiced, it all had happened so fast. "I can still see Miss Barksdale's house on the street," a mournful Linda Dogan said in an interview 20 years later. "I can still see Nellie Platt's house on the corner next to the tennis court. They were beautiful houses. I can still picture."

Demolition of Cummings Street Baptist Church

Nellie Platt lived out her last years in an assisted living center on the east side of Spartanburg. In 2012, 90 years after her father arrived in town to become Spartanburg's first Black attorney, Platt passed away at age 83. By then, all the houses were gone, and the people scattered. There were no remnants of a 125-year-old neighborhood built by people who had been freed from slavery. Just like Spartanburg's Southside neighborhood and business district 20 years earlier, it had been wiped from the face of the earth.

In the summer of 2023, the NFL players packed up and left for good too. The new Panthers' owner, a hedge fund billionaire from New Jersey, consolidated the team's practice facilities to Charlotte, officially severing ties to Spartanburg and Wofford College.

SPOTLIGHT

THE LOSS OF A LANDMARK

Lisa and Monica Thornton are daughters of the Rev. James D. Thornton (1924-2002), longtime pastor of Cummings Street Baptist Church. Here they describe their reactions when they found out that Wofford College was tearing their childhood church down:

Lisa Thornton*:* I got a phone call from the friends that we had when we were little. She called me and said, "Guess what? I passed by Cummings Street today, and all the stuff that was inside is outside, and they're tearing into—it's going to be torn down." We knew it was in transition, and we weren't sure what the situation was, but we knew something was wrong. I went by there and I saw the pews are outside. [The next week] there were workers outside, on heavy equipment, pulling up trees and doing stuff outside. I went to the front, and the door was standing wide open. And I said, "Well, that's my invitation to go inside." All the ceiling tiles were gone, no electricity, all the fixtures were torn out. The carpet was torn out. It was empty. I walked through and I went all the way to the back. I tried to look for some kind of souvenir to take back with me, and I found a hymn book. It's like I could see moments in my life in my head. I could see Easter programs and Christmas and funerals and weddings. I think I stayed in there maybe 10 minutes. I stopped at the bottom of the hill where the steps were and I got three bricks. And that's what I put in my car and I took that on with me. And it wasn't long after that, that it was gone. That was hard. It was a big part of your life.

Monica Thornton: All I have to do is use the word "traumatized." The way that I found out was my sister informed me. I told her that it was almost like Dad had died again. At the time that my father accepted the pastorship of Cummings Street, I was about to be born. He had his maiden sermon on May 3, 1964. And I was born the next Monday. So really, his life with the church, in our mind, is running parallel. And you have to understand, he was not the first pastor there. He was the fifth. But he was the first one to really build it out and to establish it and to start programs there and just create the modern phase of the church. Before he passed away, he left the church on an excellent financial footing. On top of that, he bought property around the church knowing that Wofford College was encroaching on the church itself. They were just getting closer. All of the houses right around the church were owned by Wofford College. People were renting houses. So when they wanted to take control of the property, they had the right to do it. But he bought the little plot right behind the church, right next to the church, so whatever Wofford decided to build, whatever parking lot they decided to build, it wouldn't be right upon the church. He had the foresight to do that.

OPPOSITE: *The Rev. James D. Thornton of Cumming Street Baptist Church*

SPOTLIGHT

THE LOT FARROW HOME

For more than three decades, an old log cabin has sat in a secluded, wooded spot at the back of the Girl Scouts' Camp Mary Elizabeth on Spartanburg's westside. Neither the girls who visited it over the years, nor the local preservationists who arranged to have it moved there in 1992, nor the Scout leadership who accepted the gift had any idea of its real significance.

In 2022 Danice Meunier, an amateur historian in Greenville, began looking into the history of the house. Her daughter was a Girl Scout who wanted to take on the repair of the cabin as her Gold Award project. Meunier noticed something interesting in 1960s newspaper clips about the cabin's original Magnolia Street address. They clearly identified the cabin as the 19th century childhood home of noted Spartanburg educator Mary H. Wright. Wright had grown up there in the 1870s along with her formerly enslaved parents, Lot and Adaline Farrow, and two sisters.

In 1992 the Magnolia Street house had fallen into such disrepair that it was scheduled for demolition by the city. Covered with clapboard and added onto over the years, it had been occupied by renters, then abandoned. White families had lived there much of the 20th century—Mary H. Wright had deeded it to Henry Cleveland in 1904 for cancellation of a mortgage. Without knowing its early history, the cabin's 1992 owner brought it to the attention of the Spartanburg County Historical Association, which set out to save it, because it appeared to be one of the county's oldest structures. Tammy Whaley, who served the Girl Scouts at the time, said she recalls hearing nothing about the house's original owners. Newspaper articles written at the time of the relocation do not mention it.

The virgin pine logs were dismantled carefully over a series of days in June 1992. Inside, the workers found a six-pound cannonball, a 19th century women's boot, an 1817 coin, and a marble carving of a Bible dated 1871. The logs were hauled to the back of the Girl Scout camp where a crew reconstructed an 18-foot-by-20-foot cabin that resembled the Farrow home, though its flooring, windows, chimney and roof were newly constructed. And there it remains.

TOP: *The Farrow home covered with clapboard before its removal*
MIDDLE: *Dismantling the beams of the original cabin, 1992*
BOTTOM: *The Farrow cabin reconstructed at Camp Mary Elizabeth*

Consecration services at Silver Hill Memorial United Methodist Church at its new location on Reidville Road, Aug 9, 1998.

THIRTEEN

THE RENAISSANCE PROJECT

ROUGHLY 185 YEARS after 19th-century merchant Jesse Cleveland rode into Spartanburg and bought huge swaths of land north of the public square, his great-great-great-grandson Arthur had a novel idea to revitalize the city, which by the 1990s had become depressingly moribund. Arthur Cleveland, a 48-year-old successful local real estate developer, called his ambitious plan the Renaissance Project. First quietly, then publicly, the lifelong promoter of downtown Spartanburg began assembling 40 acres in 1996 in a big rectangle bordered by North Dean Street on the east, St. John Street on the south, Church Street on the west, and East Daniel Morgan on the north.

The plan he presented to City Council and state legislators would cost upward of $120 million, a cost to be borne by private investors and government funding. This massive development, Cleveland said, finally would bring into reality the luxury hotel and conference center that had eluded Spartanburg leaders for decades. It also would include a nine-hole golf course with a "golf learning center," an amphitheater, a renovated Montgomery Building, office buildings, a daycare center, and a brand new neighborhood of low- to moderate-income housing. He vowed that his development would bring about a rebirth for a lackluster downtown then peppered with empty buildings, empty lots and empty promises.

While there were several problems with Cleveland's plan, among the serious ones was that part of a Black neighborhood—located there for more than 120 years—lay in its path. This was the area that Spartanburg city leaders had sought to take by eminent domain in their unsuccessful 1973 urban renewal project. There were far fewer houses now—many had been purchased and razed, others abandoned or collapsed from age. But as the plans for Renaissance were revealed, at least 20 Black families lived in its footprint. As Cleveland and his team moved through the neighborhood making offers for homes, lots and landmark institutions, the price tag of his Renaissance Project ballooned. Several people in the neighborhood were not happy about having to move. After three decades of watching other Black neighborhoods in Spartanburg disappear to promises of progress, there was a resolve in the North Converse Street area that "we won't get fooled again." Black City Councilwoman Linda Dogan captured the feelings of many in the North Dean Street area when she told a newspaper reporter, "People still have a lot of questions. They are not as trusting as they were 10 years ago with Vic Bailey [car dealerships] and two years ago with the Panther Camp."

The homes in the path of the Renaissance Project were located on North Converse, Keene, Annie, Lewis, Silver Hill and North Liberty streets, a gently sloping hillside area thick with trees behind present-day Barnet Park. In the center of it all, venerable Silver Hill United Methodist Church still stood on a site it had occupied since the early days of emancipation.

Cleveland met with a group of residents at the T.K. Gregg Center in January 1997 after news of his plans leaked in the newspaper. An earnest and courteous man, he apologized for not meeting with them earlier. He promised to provide new housing opportunities onsite for displaced residents as well as a daycare center to serve the neighborhood. His golf training center would be open to Black children from across the city, he said, invoking the example of Tiger Woods.

Community representative John W. Goodwin was the most vocal about opposing the plans. "We want to make sure that people are not pushed out of their homes," he said at the time. "Some of the tax dollars that are used in this project belong to us and we need to have our say in the matter." Knowing that they were up against strong headwinds in favor of the project, Goodwin, James R. Thomas and others began pushing for improvements to the T.K. Gregg Center, then located on Oakland Avenue. In a letter to the editor in March 1997, Goodwin presented a litany of Black neighborhoods that had been wiped out: Gas Bottom, Northview Street,

Silver Hill Church members in their sanctuary about 1940. Educator Mary H. Wright is at bottom right.

South Liberty Street, Cemetery Street, Golding Street, Glendalyn Avenue (now East Henry Street) and Highland Avenue. "And don't forget the back of Wofford College," he wrote. "We lost two churches and lots of homes."

Meanwhile, Cleveland's allies followed his activities with growing trepidation. They watched as the money he was spending and the loans he was taking out reached levels that threatened his ability to pull off the Renaissance Project. They looked on as he confidently purchased the historic Duncan-DuPré mansion—built in 1885 on Church Street—for four times its assessed value and afterward spent at least $500,000 of his own money relocating it five blocks away to Howard Street, next to present day VCOM-Carolinas. They saw him purchase the crumbling Montgomery Building for $3 million and announce a $6 million renovation of its theater. They watched him boldly buy a former car dealership, an electronics store, an office supply store and an old armory.

Cleveland's friends knew that when he publicly promised to build a new neighborhood for low-income residents in Renaissance Park, he had likely convinced himself that he could.

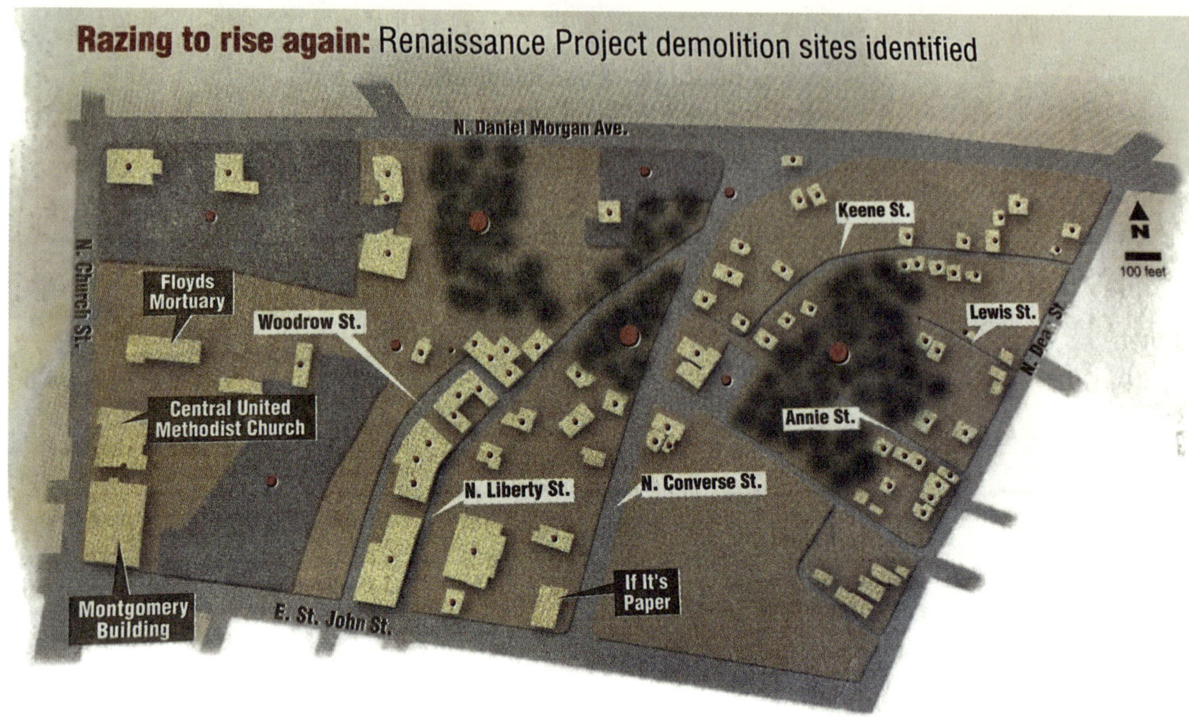

A Herald-Journal *map identified structures to be razed with a red dot.*

Cleveland worked his way down Keene Street, buying every lot and every home, some viable, some dilapidated, some vacant. This soon-to-disappear street had been named for Black barber Alfred Keene, who had bought land there in 1889. For the most part, Keene Street homes were small, one-story structures, often located on lots that were as tiny as one-tenth of an acre. Jerome Davis sold his parents' house on a quarter-acre Keene Street lot for $110,000. Bennie Johnson's house was located on a piece of property originally developed in 1890; he sold his house and half-acre to Cleveland for $85,000. Donna McJimpsey sold two properties on Keene Street, one for $48,000 and another for $32,000. Genevieve Fuller Robinson, a graduate of Carver High School, sold a house on North Converse Street for $80,000. She had owned the home for at least 35 years. Raymond Floyd sold a North Dean Street home for $95,000. The Knuckles family, which had lived in its little house on Keene Street for 55 years, sold

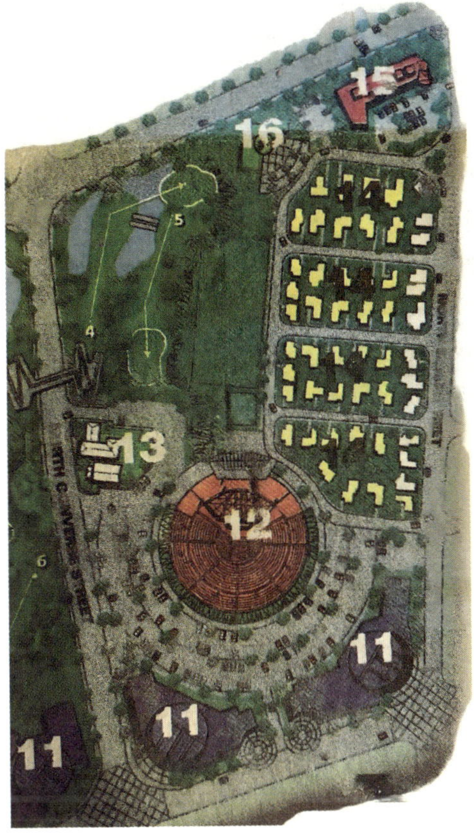

Early plans for Renaissance included a new neighborhood of low- to moderate-income homes (labeled 14) behind what became Barnet Park (12). Originally, Silver Hill was to stay (13).

out for $65,000. Among the homes Cleveland purchased on Keene Street was one that had housed beloved midwife Phyllis Goins until her death in 1945. In the end, Cleveland purchased about 20 homes, some of which had emptied in advance of the final sale.

For two residents, Cleveland found replacement homes on nearby Rudasil Street. Lillian Gilmore and Frances Perry swapped their current residences for newer ones. He assured Councilwoman Dogan that 50 new, affordable homes would one day be part of Renaissance.

Members of Silver Hill Church looked on warily. Things were proceeding quickly, and they worried about people such as Dorothy Boyd on Lewis Street, who told the *Herald-Journal*, "We're senior citizens, and we're on a fixed income." Curtis Boyd noted that they had lived in the neighborhood for 40 years: "I'm 68 years old, and I finally bought my house. I'll fight it to the end. I'm too old to start over."

Silver Hill Church member Bernice Garner Lewis recounted in an interview in 2023 that her congregation often stepped in to help residents negotiate a fair price. Lewis had spent her girlhood on Keene Street in the late 1930s and remembered playing under the streetlights and splashing in the creek when it flooded. Though she described Arthur Cleveland as "a good man, an honest man" in those negotiations, she said, "We fought to get him to give these people more than he was going to give them." One of those property owners was retired Cumming Street teacher and community icon Harriet Dawkins, born in 1907 and blind with old age.

The members of Silver Hill had a big decision to make themselves. In the beginning, they voiced a desire to preserve their church. Early renderings of the Renaissance Project showed the church still standing. Yet the Renaissance Project master plan was a troubling glimpse into a potential future for the church: landlocked by unfamiliar development, unable to expand and wedged between a concert venue and a golf course. Many in the congregation initially worried about the financial impact of a move. "I was really against moving," recalled Willamae Mackey, a member since 1964. "I didn't like debt." Some wondered whether the church could be used as a Black history museum. Cleveland's original offer for the church at 269 North Converse St. was rejected.

The consecration service at the new church, 1998
OPPOSITE: *Alice and Dorthy Bomar at a Silver Hill Easter Service at the old church, 1997*

The Rev. George Ashford Jr. knew that his congregation no longer was anchored in neighborhoods just north and south of Main Street. A diaspora caused by the destruction of the city's original Black neighborhoods had sent large numbers of his members west of the city. When Park Hills Baptist Church on Reidville Road went up for sale, an answer emerged. Cleveland raised his offer to $750,000 and the church accepted. The church received a $150,000 grant from the United Methodist Church and purchased its new location for $975,000. "I will miss the old structure and neighborhood, but most of what's there is leaving and has been leaving for years," Bernice Lewis said at the time.

On Aug. 9, 1998, a "leave-taking service" took place at the old church on the corner of North Converse and Silver Hill streets. Members stripped the altar and gathered flags, the baptismal bowl and the pulpit. A police

The historic Callaham Funeral Home before the fire

escort led them to their new Park Hills home, two and a half miles west. Awaiting them was a new piano organ donated by 91-year-old Harriet Dawkins, who was considered "Mother of the Church." A truck moved the historic old church bell to the new front lawn. In a nod to their storied history, they added a new word to the church name: they would now be Silver Hill Memorial United Methodist Church.

Meanwhile, one of the oldest Black businesses in Spartanburg was dealing with an offer of its own. The city wanted to purchase property from Callaham-Hicks Funeral Home on North Dean Street for amphitheater parking. Owner Leonard Hicks told city officials that his 85-year-old building—which had housed the John-Nina Hospital in 1913—was not for sale. In fact, he planned to expand. "I have gotten phone calls asking me if I was selling, and I am not," he told a reporter. "This renovation is a doable project that will allow me to preserve this structure, and I plan to be here for many more years."

Demolition of 63 structures on the Renaissance Project site began in earnest in 2000. Mounds of debris, asphalt and trees rose more than 20 feet high. Barnet Park opened with a major gift of open land from a group of local investors, including Bill Barnet, who had intended to build an arts center there a decade earlier. The Zimmerli Amphitheatre rose roughly where George and Lydia Hardy, once-enslaved, had built their homestead not long after the end of the Civil War.

City officials, solidly behind the Renaissance Project, allocated $12 million to repurchase land from Cleveland for other public amenities—the golf course, new streets, development sites—and had an agreement to be repaid over 50 years. But roadblocks emerged in the Statehouse in Columbia. State legislators and Gov. Jim Hodges balked at the huge financial requests coming from Spartanburg. The chosen hotel operator strung out its negotiations with Cleveland. The loans Cleveland needed from banks and the federal government did not come quickly. He scrambled to raise $11 million in private equity from family and friends. City Manager Roy Lane, an important steward of the project, died unexpectedly. There were issues with the titles of homes Cleveland purchased. Vagrants moved into empty buildings and some homes caught fire.

Finally, in April 2002, a 175-foot crane moved onto the site, and the prom-

Later plans for Renaissance no longer included a new residential area along North Dean Street though many homes had been cleared.

New, high-end homes along Woodward Street, just off North Dean

ised luxury Marriott and conference center began rising at the opposite end of Renaissance Park. The 10-story hotel opened to great fanfare in January 2004, seven years after it was first announced. That day would be the zenith of Arthur Cleveland's Renaissance efforts. Three months later, BB&T Bank filed foreclosure papers on Cleveland's Montgomery Building and a shopping center he owned on Garner Road, signaling the collapse that was to come. He missed the deadline for his first $400,000 land-lease payment to the city.

In letters and comments to the *Herald-Journal*, Cleveland's many friends rallied to his defense, expressing their deep appreciation for the construction of the Marriott Hotel. But as the months progressed, Cleveland forfeited much of his significant real estate empire to pay his debts. Shopping centers, office buildings and family land scattered across the county slipped away in a cascade of quick property sales and loan defaults. The Marriott fell into bankruptcy in 2007 and ultimately sold to a partnership that included local industrialist Jimmy Gibbs. With Cleveland sidelined, the city moved forward on the project with construction of the Chapman Cultural Center, the George Dean Johnson School of Business and a parking garage. A sprawling, 200-unit apartment complex went up in 2022 called The Charles, invoking the road name that once ran through Gas Bottom. Its rents topped out at $2,400 a month.

The new Renaissance neighborhood of low- and moderate-income houses never got built.

In March 2019 a Greenville development company called the Terranova Group announced that it would develop 24-single family homes at the long-cleared site of Silver Hill Church. In a discussion of development incentives, two Black members of City Council—Erica Brown and Ruth Littlejohn—made an unsuccessful plea that the neighborhood include affordable housing. A development spokeswoman responded by saying that $275,000 was intended to be the "upper end of the price range" for homes. The council proceeded to sell the developer 4.5 acres for $100 with no stipulations attached. In the end, the houses that went up on the site were some of the most expensive new homes in the city, listing for as much as $699,000. A slick sales video beckoned people to come live in a new urban neighborhood called Silver Hill.

A couple blocks away, a Charleston developer purchased two Rudasil Street houses in 2022 in the heart of the North Dean neighborhood. The little houses were bulldozed quickly, and up went seven colorful new homes on tiny, one-tenth acre lots, with listing prices of $400,000 to $450,000.

Gentrification officially had arrived in a 150-year-old neighborhood where generations of Black families once lived, worshipped, played and attended school. A historically Black neighborhood was becoming home to affluent whites.

Residents share memories of the Back of the College neighborhood.

EPILOGUE

2024

DRIVE DOWN THE 200 and 300 blocks of North Dean Street in Spartanburg and you'll see what remains of a Black residential district that once stretched nearly a mile north and included hundreds of homes. Along these blocks stand 15 century-old, Black-occupied bungalows and two-story homes, including those once inhabited by revered physician Dr. T.K. Gregg and integration pioneers Myrtle Williams and Wynona Douglas. You'll see the now sparsely attended Metropolitan AME Zion Church, whose story goes back to 1866. You'll see a street sign for Lewis Street, now dead-ended, named for a successful, post-emancipation Black builder. You'll see the historic Dean Street School building that has become the Omegas Of Spartanburg Uplift Center and now hosts gatherings for Black residents. You'll see the last remaining Black-owned business in the area: Callaham-Hicks Funeral Home, rebuilt around the fire-damaged vestiges of the John-Nina Hospital. One block over, on Northview Street, there are about 10 more historic homes, most of them built by Black owners prior to 1920, most still with Black occupants.

This now-tiny Black neighborhood clings to life after other enclaves of the original northside have been dismantled. Back of the College perished at the hands of Wofford College. Gas Bottom's demise was executed by city government, its eastern edge by the state highway department and Converse College. The adjacent Silver Hill area was cleared by developers. Today, there are new gentrification pressures on both sides of this remnant

North Dean Street neighborhood—just as there are for other Black neighborhoods across the city of Spartanburg.

You only have to look to the neighboring city of Greenville to see the dramatic racial population swings that can be brought about by gentrification. In a phenomenon that has been called "the new urban renewal," gentrification occurs when neighborhoods are transformed through an influx of more affluent residents, leading to the displacement of long-term, lower-income residents who no longer can afford to live there. In Greenville thousands of apartments and condos for high-income city dwellers have been built in and around its historic Black neighborhoods. In the three decades between 1990 and 2020, approximately 21,000 white residents moved into the city of Greenville, and 3,000 Black residents disappeared—many because their homes were bought by developers, others because they could no longer afford rising rents, property taxes and housing prices. Black population in the city just 30 miles to Spartanburg's west dropped from 35 percent to 19 percent in three decades. Suddenly, there were fears that no Greenville City Council district could reliably elect a Black representative.

A well-established body of research indicates that diversity in American cities improves the competitiveness of the workforce and can lead to a better quality of life for people of all races and income levels, said Dr. Ken Kolb of Furman University, author of a study about racial displacement in the city of Greenville. Diverse cities often experience higher levels of innovation and creativity as people with different perspectives educate, collaborate and inspire one another. Diverse cities can promote empathy and understanding, leading to a stronger democracy. A diverse city is resilient for the long run, Kolb said. Having a healthy mix of residents ensures that a city will not be hollowed out by major cultural shifts that have happened before. Gentrification, which usually boosts the tax base, "might seem fine now, but we don't know when white flight is going to occur again," said Kolb.

For now, the Black population in the city of Spartanburg remains relatively stable at about 45 percent. Spartanburg in 2024 has—for the second time—a majority-Black City Council, its second Black mayor, a Black fire chief and its second Black police chief. Its largest university has a Black president. In recent years there have been two Black city school superintendents. A colorful mural with the words "Black Lives Matter" fills the street in front of City Hall. The city now celebrates the Juneteenth holiday with several days of activities.

In September 2020 Spartanburg City Council even confronted the specter of urban renewal and neighborhood destruction. It unanimously passed a resolution acknowledging there had been systemic racism in the past, formally apologizing for racial injustices and their resulting long-lasting inequities. In a meeting held at the new T.K. Gregg Recreation Center at the height of the COVID-19 pandemic, Black residents cheered as the council acknowledged that "communities of color have borne the brunt of social, environmental, economic, criminal justice policies, practices and investments." As the only city government in South Carolina to pass such a resolution, the council pledged to do a better job in the future ensuring that policies and funding decisions focus on racial equity.

That sincere gesture notwithstanding, the legacy of racism and indifference to the value of Black neighborhoods haunts the city of Spartanburg. Black families of all income levels struggle to find affordable housing in the city. In the places where Black families relocated during the era of neighborhood clearance, poverty levels are achingly high. In Highland, where the Black population approaches 90 percent, median family income was $11,189 in the 2020 census. In comparison, in the heart of Converse Heights, where the white population is 96 percent, it was $98,545.

Over the past two decades Spartanburg City Council has worked with its partners to replace decaying, first-generation housing projects and older recreation centers in Black neighborhoods. It has assisted with the development of new, privately owned Section 8 housing where occupants receive federal vouchers to make rents more affordable. A new neighborhood of moderately priced single-family homes is gradually rising on the footprint of the old Spartan Mill village thanks to a partnership between the city and the Northside Development Corp. These actions, however, have not been enough to meet the great need. The waiting list for public housing in Spartanburg continues to hover at 3,300 families; the housing voucher program has nearly 5,000 waiting to be served. Stable, majority-Black neighborhoods such as Collins Park, Park Hills and Forest Park rarely see new construction of affordable single-family homes. Residents of these middle-class neighborhoods recently have confronted the same economic pressures that have impacted neighborhoods across the United States in an era of high inflation—rent increases and rising home prices.

IN THE MIDST of these difficulties, however, there has been a new effort in Spartanburg to capture and elevate Black history. A $1 million monument now graces the entrance to the Southside neighborhood, celebrating the people and places important to Black history. A plaque honoring lunch counter protestors adorns a building on Main Street. An effort is underway to erect a statue of Mary H. Wright outside the doors of a former elementary school that once bore her name. The new Spartanburg High School opened in 2019 with an expansive "history wall" and outdoor sculpture dedicated to the experience of students who attended segregated schools. The Omegas fraternity has begun a renovation of the historic Dean Street schoolhouse and is contemplating a Dean Street museum room.

Sentiment remains strong among the elders of the Black community for the preservation of Cumming Street School, the lone remaining piece of the Back of the College neighborhood. In response, City Council voted unanimously in May 2022 to add the building to the Spartanburg Historic Register. The ordinance ensures that the old school must be kept up to building codes and cannot be altered without approval of the city's Board of Architectural Design and Historic Review.

The long-term future of the Black history landmark remains unclear, but those who walked its halls and peered out its windows at a once-vibrant neighborhood have strong opinions. Norma Foster Green would like to see a museum dedicated to the history of the school and neighborhood—a place where "people can come back and see where they've been, where we came from, how we succeeded, despite, you know, that the odds were stacked against us." Wofford College will be the one to determine the future of Cumming Street School because it owns the building, noted former Mayor James Talley. "Something should happen to it that would depict that relationship between the Back of the College and Wofford," Talley

James Talley served as mayor of Spartanburg 1993-2001.

said. "I don't know if that's a museum or what, but something that could be done and let that remain there because the building is still a good building." Some point to the renovation and expansion of the former Booker T. Washington High School in Columbia, which shuttered in 1974, as an example. When renovations there are complete, the historic Black high school will house a research library and modern exhibit space to serve as a civil rights teaching space for the community and the University of South Carolina. The building will serve as a testament to the struggle for equality. Funds are coming from the National Park Service and other sources.

For Linda Dogan, former neighborhood resident, Cumming Street student and city councilwoman, there is opportunity to be grasped. "I just hope that at some point that the past and the present and the future can connect and embrace it and make it better not just for the students at Wofford, but for Spartanburg period."

THE RESIDENTS

In 2017-2019 student interviewers from Wofford College collected oral histories from these former Back of the College residents. Spartanburg photographer Mark Olencki was on hand to take their portraits.

VICKIE COLEMAN HOGAN

WILL WESLY

WOODROW BROWN

BERTHA JOHNSON

EDDIE BOWMAN

JACKIE MEANS PAYDEN

JOANN FRAZIER

MICHAEL HILL

MILDRED MEANS

NORMA GREENE

OLLIE BROWN JENKINS

PHILLIP FANT

ROSE THOMAS

SHERRI WIGGLETON

ACKNOWLEDGEMENTS

IT TOOK A VILLAGE to create *North of Main*. First of all, we thank the inspiring and steadfast efforts of the remarkable staff of the Kennedy Room at the downtown branch of the Spartanburg Public Libraries without whom *North of Main* would not be possible. Project partner and Assistant Director of Local History Brad Steinecke has been especially heroic, chasing down photographs, checking facts and pointing out numerous areas for deeper research. The library's fortuitous—and not inexpensive—decision to purchase Newsbank digital archives to the *Spartanburg Journal* and *Herald* in 2022 opened up a world of lost history to us. Everyone involved in this project would like to express their heartfelt gratitude for the library staff's efforts.

A big round of thanks goes to the Spartanburg African American Heritage and Culture Committee, whose members continue to explore and present our community's Black history. They have rounded up many of the photos that appear in this book. Additionally, Luther Norman shared his Whitmire family photo collection with us, as well as his extremely rare copy of Louvenia Barksdale's Back of the College book, and for that we are extremely grateful. Spartanburg City Councilwoman Janey Salley and her husband, Roland, graciously opened doors for us at Silver Hill Memorial United Methodist Church. A large meeting with congregants at Silver Hill kicked off this project several years ago.

Dr. Andrew Myers, professor of American Studies at the University of South Carolina Upstate, had a big hand in ensuring this history was presented factually. He continues to be the most important source of research about the Reconstruction era in the Upstate. We are grateful for his participation. At Wofford College, archivist Dr. Phillip Stone and Dr. Dwain Pruitt, the college's chief equity officer, closely reviewed the manuscript and made multiple helpful suggestions.

We are deeply indebted to the newspaper staff of the *Spartanburg Herald-Journal*, especially Linda Conley, who over the years have brought stories of

Black history to life and chronicled the dissolution of the neighborhoods north of Main. This book would not be possible without their fine reporting.

We would like to acknowledge the wonderful women and men interviewed for the North of Main Project. They gave their time and told their stories freely. We are deeply grateful to Russell Barrett, Darnese Bell, the late Doyle Boggs, Eddie Bowman, Woodrow Brown, Freda Byrd, James Cheek, Loetus Davis, Linda Dogan, Joe Dominic, Philip Fant, Joan Frazier, Norma Greene, Donald W. Gibson, Keith Harris, Michael Hill, Vicky (Coleman) Hogan, Judy Hutchinson, Ollie Brown Jenkins, Bertha Johnson, Ken Kolb, Tim Kuether, Joe Lesesne, Bernice Lewis, Horace Littlejohn, Cynthia (Harris) Logan, Willamae Mackey, Charles Mann, Mildred Means, Luther Norman, Norma Pitts, Donna Potruch, the Rev. Eugene Rivers III, Doris Posey, Dr. Glenda P. Sims, Gwen Steen, James Talley, Rose Thomas, Tony Thomas, Lisa Thornton, Monica Thornton, Deno Trakas, Will Wesly, Sherry Wiggleton and Winston Wingo.

The Wofford College students who worked on the project were instrumental in many ways, including helping to research and develop the residential data we present in the book and on the website (backofthecollege.org) and conducting the interviews of former residents and Cumming Street School alumni. Many thanks to Calin Wharton, Catherine Todd, Jara Dogan, Alex Rizzo-Banks, Matilda Redfern, Lucy Person, Carolyn Payne, Scotdaija Jenkins, Grace Sorrell, Ella Jarrett, Claire Minter, Jordan Holmes, Mary Beecy, Coleman Bryant, Elliott Campbell, Noah Chidester, Kobe Craig, Chad Gardner, Thomas Griffin, Dawson Henis, Aryk Hennings, Jurnee Jones, Zach Kurz, Austin Lufkin, Margaret Simon, Ryan Titus, Cameron Bloodworth, Kate Brown, Lamar Buchanan, Calhoun Cheek, Ethan Cornelius, John Dempsey, Brennen Dorighi, Rachel Evatt, Hayes Heinecke, Nolan Hester, Sophia Lamm, Natalie Lopez, SJ Vaughan, McCallee Watson, Deandre Yarbough, Tahir Anoor, Logan Barnes, John Beecy, Carlisle Benson, Jonathan Burns, Riley DeLavan, Hannah Dudley, Sara Faucett, Coltin Hallman, Matyah Jackson, Woods Wooten, Emory Wyatt, and Ben Baird. Dr. Kimberly Hall's expertise in digital media studies proved crucial in helping to get the website off the ground, and her ongoing insight and advice are deeply appreciated.

Mitch Kennedy, project partner and assistant city manager of Spartanburg, was invaluable in educating Wofford students involved in the project and organizing meetings at the city's recreation and community centers, including the C.C. Woodson Community Center and the Rev. James D. Thornton Activity Center. Monier Abusaft, project partner, attorney at law and Spartanburg County councilmember, has provided much needed insight and perspective and helped Wofford students understand the implications of their actions regarding their work on this project. Mayor Jerome Rice helped us promote the release of this book during his "Miles with the Mayor" walks.

Wade Dorsey and the staff at the South Carolina Department of Archives and History helped us find our way through early documents about Black education in Spartanburg. Michael Wilke at the Concordia Historical Institute in St. Louis provided photos and vital research about St. Luke's Lutheran Church.

Thanks, as always, to the remarkable staff at Hub City Press: Meg Reid, Kate McMullen, Julie Jarema and Mia Kilpatrick, who are continuing Hub City Writers Project's 30-year effort to document local history. We also salute the many donors who provided invaluable financial support toward the production of *North of Main*, especially our major donors: the Spartanburg County Public Libraries, Wofford College, the City of Spartanburg, the Featherston family, Lindsay Lavine Webster, and Mt. Moriah Baptist Church (in honor of Brenda Lee Pryce).

This book builds on the outstanding research and writing done by Ph.D. historians Bruce Eelman, Dwain Pruitt, Diane Vecchio, Melissa Walker, Philip Racine and Andrew Myers. For deeper information about this era in Spartanburg's history, we thoroughly recommend *Eelman's Entrepreneurs in the Southern Upcountry: The Case of Spartanburg, South Carolina 1815-1880* as well as the two-volume *Recovering the Piedmont Past* series, published by the University of South Carolina Press.

May this community project open many doors for further research to help Spartanburg and other communities across the South better understand their racial history.

NOTES & SOURCES

Birth dates, occupations, house locations, income, family information and literacy status of people mentioned in this book come from census information or city directories unless otherwise noted. All deed book references come from the Spartanburg County Register of Mesne Conveyance Office.

CHAPTER 1: FREEDOM

5 **Ned Kirby and Nelly Kirby:** The enslaved people at the home of the Kirby family appear on the "Colored Sunday School" roster of Central Methodist Church in both 1865 and 1866. The Central Methodist rosters from this era are located in the archives of Wofford College. Augustus Hilliard Kirby (1829-1917), a Spartanburg merchant, lived on Kirby Hill at what is now the intersection of South Church and West Henry. His mother, Patsey, lived adjacent. Both were enslavers, according to the 1860 U.S. Slave Schedule. There were extensive pastures for cattle on Kirby Hill (anygreenplace.com/kirbydurant.html).

5 **Jimmy Johnson:** *Spartanburg Herald*, Feb. 13, 1927.

5 **Lot Farrow:** Barred and Disallowed Case Files of the Southern Claims Commission, 1871-1880; Publication M1407, 4829 fiche; NAID: 562207 and 562208; Records of the U.S. House of Representatives, 1789-2015, Record Group 233; The National Archives in Washington, D.C., also available at Ancestry.com.

5 **Hercules Huggins:** During slavery, Huggins was called Hercules Dupre, and his enslaver was Warren DuPré, Wofford College professor of natural sciences. He appears on the Central Methodist rolls with the last name Dupre and took a new name after emancipation. The 1870 and 1880 U.S. censuses describe him as a blacksmith, originally from Virginia.

5 **Tobe Hartwell:** He appears as Toby Shipp in the 1865 rolls of Central Methodist. In 1866 the name Hartwell is written on top of the word Shipp.

6 **Roughly 2,200:** Estimates of total population in Spartanburg are roughly calculated from the results of the Spartanburg censuses in 1860 and 1870s. These numbers are not exact for 1865, as exact numbers are unavailable. The *Charleston Daily Courier* reported April 9, 1857, that population in the village of Spartanburg was 2,500. *The Carolina Spartan* pegged village population that same month as 2,000.

6 **800 enslaved:** This is an estimate based on various pieces of data. Three years after the end of the Civil War, 254 Black men registered to vote in Spartanburg; this number does not account for Black women and children. Additionally, the 1860 Spartanburg city slave census counts 884 enslaved men, women and children owned by people living in central Spartanburg. For large slaveholding families in the town (of which there are

about 20 who owned more than 12 slaves), an undisclosed number of these slaves could have been working farms elsewhere in the county or outside the state. There were a small number of enslaved people living at white homesteads in the area of South Church Street who are counted among the census of the Southern Division of Spartanburg County.

6 **Free people of color:** The 1860 census lists 30 free people of color in the village of Spartanburg. Nineteen were adults, and 11 were children. Among the adults: Clifton Johnson, 22, a barber; Nancy Eubanks, a mother of three small children; and David Hardy, 26, a laborer. It is possible that Nancy Eubanks is the same as "the girl Free Nancy" banned from the town by Spartanburg town council in 1863.

6 **Slave sales:** *Carolina Spartan*, July 10, 1856; *Charleston Daily Courier*, July 10, 1855; *Asheville News*, Nov. 29, 1855, quoting the *Spartanburg Express*. The second account describes the sale of a 70-year-old woman for $70, "a girl, just grown, sold for $1,150; a man (common field hand) for $1,250; a small plough boy for $850, and a child (held up in the arms of the auctioneer for inspection by bidders) brought $550."

6 **Simple cabins:** This is an estimate. The 1860 slave census of Spartanburg indicates there were 175 slave dwellings owned by white residents of the city. For large slave-holding families, some of these cabins could have been on farms outside the town.

7 **Slaves in the countryside, slave patrols:** Diane Vecchio, "From Slavery to Freedom: African American Life in Post–Civil War Spartanburg," *Recovering the Piedmont Past.* (University of South Carolina Press, 2013), 108-109.

7 **Spartanburg slave laws:** Town council minutes, 1850-1871, 233, 270, 277, 295.

8 **John B. Cleveland resignation:** Town minutes, 1850-1871, 299.

8 **Capt. Hutson Wigg:** Town minutes, 297. The assailant is not the William Walker known as "Singin' Billy" Walker.

8 **"carpetbagger":** *The State*, Sept. 29, 1927.

9 **Federal cavalry:** Joshua Beau Blackwell. *The 1865 Stoneman's Raid Ends.* (Charleston: The History Press, 2011), 67-68; Charles H. Kirk. *History of the Fifteenth Pennsylvania Volunteer Cavalry.* (Philadelphia: Society of the Fifteen the Pennsylvania Cavalry, 1906), 510; *Spartanburg Herald*, Dec. 19, 1926.

9 **Capt. Norris Crossman:** Information provided by Dr. Andrew Myers from Crossman's diaries, South Carolina Historical Society Manuscript (233.01 D).

9 **"Brother John":** First Baptist Church minutes, Book 1: 1839-1867, 53-54.

10 **"church secretary":** Central United Methodist Church roster, Wofford College archives, note on 1865 "Colored Sunday School Rolls."

10 **Wofford slaveholders:** U.S. Slave Census, 1860. From First Baptist Church Minutes: Gracy, Teletha and John were among those enslaved by Professor David Duncan. From Central Methodist Church rolls: George, Susan, Catie, Sarah and Tobe were among those enslaved by A.W. Shipp; Sam, Hercules, Hannah, Nancy Ann and Caroline were among those enslaved by Warren DuPré. Some of Warren DuPré's slaves worked a farm in the Lowcountry of South Carolina. Three of Whitefoord Smith's slaves worked in the Greenville (SC) District, and two others also were also outside the Spartanburg District, according to Wofford College archivist Phillip Stone.

11 **Brick cabins:** Linda Bilanchone (ed). *The Lives They Lived: A Look at Women in the History of Spartanburg County.* (Spartanburg: Altman Printing, 1981). Philip N. Racine, "Slave Women."

11 **Freedpeople on Main Street:** 1860 U.S. Slave Schedule, Spartanburg.

11 **Hattie Bell Penland:** Oral history (1995), Wofford College Digital Commons. https://digitalcommons.wofford.edu/oralhistory/1.

13 **"faced starvation":** Spartanburg Unit of the Writers' Program of the Works Projects Administration, *A History of Spartanburg County.* (Columbia SC: Band & White, 1940), 166.

14 **Fowler, Robison & Co:** The 1880 Spartanburg City Directory lists the following Black men as employees there: Monroe Burnett, John Campbell, Nat Chapman, George Clements, Henry Clements, Oscar Cooper, James Franklin, Alex Golightly, George Jones, Jake Kirby, James Logan, Berry Sloan and James Young.

14 **David Golightly Harris:** Philip N. Racine, ed. *Piedmont Farmer: The Journals of David Golightly Harris, 1855-1870.* (Knoxville: University of Tennessee Press, 1990), 396, 401.

15 **Freedmen's Bureau:** Susan Thoms. *Freedmen's Bureau: Spartanburg and Union Counties, 1865-1868.* (Spartanburg: Kennedy Free Press), 214.

15 **Troop drawdown:** Myers, 56.

15 **Delegates and Black Codes:** Bruce Eelman. *Entrepreneurs in the Southern Upcountry: Commercial Culture in Spartanburg, South Carolina 1845-1880.* (Athens: UGA Press, 2008), 213.

16 **Dawkins:** Eelman, 216.

16 **Road duty:** This was not just used for punishment, nor was it performed exclusively by Black people. It was a technique that was commonly used to maintain local roads. Able-bodied males of both races per required to perform a set number of days working on the roads or pay a fee so that an alternate laborer could be hired.

16 **Alley Brothers:** The story of the Burnett shootings is compiled from Spartanburg town council minutes 1850-1871, pages 305, 317, 326, 328, 336; and from the following newspapers: *The Carolina Spartan* as reported by *The Charleston Daily News*, Sept. 18 and Sept. 25, 1869; *The* (Anderson) *Intelligencer*, Sept. 23, 1869; *The Charleston Daily Courier*, Sept. 25, 1869; *The Yorkville Enquirer*, Sept. 23, 1869; *The Daily Phoenix*, Sept. 26, 1869.

16 **Recollections of Henry Alley:** *Spartanburg Herald*, Dec. 7, 1930 from Dr. Ed Bomar; Alley obituary, *Charleston News and Courier*, Jan. 15, 1896.

16 **Henry Alley's war injury:** *Charleston News and Courier*, Jan. 15, 1896; Confederate war record, Examining Board, January 1863, Fold3.

16 **"old Mr. Alley":** *Spartanburg Journal*, Dec. 9, 1916, recalled by A.H. Kirby.

16 **Henry Alley as police chief:** *Charleston News and Courier*, Nov. 17, 1887; *Spartanburg Herald*, Oct. 30, 1938.

16 **"yankee garrison":** The garrison mentioned in the town minutes during November 1865 likely refers to soldiers of Company E, 15th Maine Infantry. Whether the soldiers of this company stayed at the courthouse is unknown.

17 **"Negro boy Dennis":** Town minutes 1850-1871, 332.

18 **Henry Jones and Moses Young:** Disposition of these cases from Spartanburg County Court of General Sessions Criminal Journal G, 1869/1870, available at the Spartanburg County Public Libraries. Moses Young is inaccurately named Moses Littlejohn in early newspaper reports of the crime.

19 **Wingo and Foster:** *Charleston Mercury*, Feb. 17, 1868.

20 **Constitutional Club members:** Writers' Program, 144-145.

20 **White militias:** Members of the Black community in Spartanburg also joined and participated in state militia companies authorized by the governor and the legislature. According to Dr. Andrew Myers, USC Upstate, they demonstrated a willingness to use organized military force but were overmatched by whites who had far greater combat experience.

Spotlight: Lot Farrow and the Federal Cavalry

22 **Lot Farrow Testimony:** Barred and Disallowed Case Files of the Southern Claims Commission, 1871-1880; Publication M1407, 4829 fiche; NAID: 562207 and 562208; Records of the U.S. House of Representatives, 1789-2015, Record Group 233; The National Archives in Washington, D.C, also available at Ancestry.com.

Spotlight: Post-Slavery Labor Contracts

24 **Contracts:** Records for the Field Offices for the State of South Carolina, Bureau of Refugees, Freedmen, and Abandoned Lands, M-1910, Labor Contracts for Spartanburg, South Carolina, Series I, A-Z, Dec. 1865-June 1866. Available in alphabetical order by contractor on microfilm at the Spartanburg County Public Libraries.

24 **"control of blacks":** John Hope Franklin. *From Slavery to Freedom: A History of Nego Americans.* (New York: Alfred A. Knopf, 1947), 241.

CHAPTER 2: BIRTH OF THE NORTH DEAN STREET NEIGHBORHOOD

27 **Early history of Silver Hill:** WPA, Survey of State and Local Historical Records, Church Records Form, 1937, housed in the University of South Carolina Library Digital Collection https://digital.tcl.sc.edu/digital/collection/hrs/id/5500/rec/4.

27 **"assistant provost judge":** *Charleston Daily Courier*, Aug. 4, 1866.

27 **Legg bankruptcy:** *Yorkville Enquirer*, Feb. 18, 1869.

28 **Silver Hill land purchase:** Deed book II-222. The purchasers who signed the deed are Tobe Hartwell, Hercules Huggins, Ranse McKinney, E. Daniel, F. Mills, J. Moultrie.

28 **Founders of Silver Hill:** MacArthur Goodwin. *Silver Hill United Methodist Church, Spartanburg, South Carolina: 1869-1981.* (Silver Hill United Methodist Church, 1981), 12. The Goodwin history of the church also indicates that congregants met for a time in a brush arbor. Founders also are listed in the *Spartanburg Herald*, Jan. 28, 1940.

28 **John Pickenpack:** He arrived in Charleston from Hannover, Germany, about 1806. There he was a shopkeeper, a bank porter, and he built a home off Charleston's Logan Street about 1819, according to census records, newspaper accounts and the Historic Charleston Foundation. He arrived in Spartanburg in the 1820s and had at least a dozen slaves to farm his property, located near the northwest corner of what is now Main Street and Oakland Avenue. An 1882 map of Spartanburg shows a Pickenpack Street there. A relative, George Pickenpack, apparently joined him in Spartanburg—George is buried at Magnolia Cemetery.

28 **Land in trust to Thomas Pickenpack:** Deed book FF-82. Thomson also left contiguous property in trust to a second enslaved man, named Richard Pickenpack. According to census records, after the war Richard worked for Spartanburg physician Dr. Thomas K. Cureton, moved with the Cureton family to Charlotte and never returned. He likely sold or turned his lot over to Thomas Pickenpack. There are two other Black men named Pickenpack in the upstate after the war: Joe Pickenpack, who lived near members of the Thomson family in Beech Springs (Wellford), and Kelly Pickenpack, who lived in Union.

28 **"became a barber":** Citizen militia enrollment list for men aged 30-35, scdah.gov S192021, 73.

28 **Richard Rivers:** With Rivers as his last name, it is possible he came from one of the five plantations owned by the wealthy Rivers family on James Island. Richard Rivers was the third Black man elected to Spartanburg Town Council, after C.C. Bomar and John P. Boyden. He purchased his lot and home for $75 from I.H. Cantrell, owner of a local wagon factory. The

Rivers home was located behind present-day New Method Dry Cleaners.

29 **Thornton Williams land purchase:** Deed book RR-20. Abram Smalls purchase, Deed book TT-95.

29 **George Hardy land purchase:** Deed book MM-275, MM-687.

29 **Brother to Lot Farrow:** *Herald-Journal*, Aug. 9, 1999.

29 **Anthony Johnson:** *Charleston Daily News*, Jan. 9, 1871; Anderson *Intelligencer* and *Yorkville Enquirer*, Jan. 12, 1871.

29 **Peace resolution:** *Charleston Daily News*, Jan. 9, 1871.

30 **Other Hardy freedpeople:** Petitions of Guardianship of Free Persons of Color, 1823-1863, Spartanburg County Court of Common Pleas, housed at the Spartanburg County Public Libraries.

30 **Free Bill Hardy:** Deed book T-409, dated Jan. 27, 1824. This land was located along Harris Creek. Hardy ultimately encountered trouble with white authorities and lost possession of his land. *The Carolina Spartan* reported Aug. 6, 1857, that Hardy was accused of stealing corn, was tried and found guilty by Magistrate Hiram White. He was sentenced to two weeks imprisonment, "then to receive two hundred lashes, or leave the State, at his option." His land was later sold in a sheriff's sale, according to *The Carolina Spartan* of Sept. 13, 1866.

30 **Shooting of Peter Grant:** *The Carolina Spartan*, Jan. 2, 1878.

30 **Hardy fined:** Spartanburg town council minutes 1871-1879, 536.

31 **Other land purchases:** Willis Clawson, Deed book MM-612; Simpson Wiggins, PP-664.

31 **Brick Silver Hill Church:** WPA, Survey of State and Local Historical Records, Church Records Form, 1937, housed in the University of South Carolina Libraries Digital Collection https://digital.tcl.sc.edu/digital/collection/hrs/id/5500/rec/4.

31 **David Montague:** *Spartanburg Journal*, June 16, 1921. Article relates that Montague died at age 78. "He was the main dependence of the street superintendent in putting in brick and rock work" and died the day after working on a new sewer line for Evins Street. City Council placed an order for a funeral wreath to be placed over his grave.

31 **Montague lodging:** *Asheville Citizen-Times*, Nov. 14, 1899.

31 **Alderman John P. Boyden:** *Yorkville Enquirer*, quoting *Spartanburg Herald*, July 9, 1890, and *Charleston Post & Courier*, Sept. 11, 1889.

32 **Rosemond:** Goodwin, 9; A. V. Huff Jr. "A History of South Carolina United Methodism," *United Methodist Ministers in South Carolina.* (Columbia: South Carolina Conference of the United Methodist Church, 1984); South Carolina Historic Properties Record, S10817723014.

34 **Rosemond's reports of KKK:** *Minutes of the Seventh Session of the South Carolina Annual Conference of the Methodist Episcopal Church.* (Columbia SC: SC Methodist Conference, 1872), 22.

34 **Lewis Thompson's death:** Ibid., 23; *Yorkville Enquirer*, Aug. 3, 1871.

34 **Description of Silver Hill:** WPA, Survey of State and Local Historical Records, Church Records Form, 1937 https://digital.tcl.sc.edu/digital/collection/hrs/id/5500/rec/4.

35 **Lydia Hardy's cowbell:** *Spartanburg Herald*, Nov. 4, 1913. The 1809 map of Spartanburg's public square originally was drawn by a member of the Thomson family, which owned most of the public square at one time. The drawing pictured was copied from that map by merchant Jesse Cleveland.

36 **Hardy land:** Master's sale, *Spartanburg Herald*, April 13, 1911; Spartanburg County plat book 3, page 28.

36 **Southside growth:** Beatrice Hill and Brenda Lee. *South of Main.* (Spartanburg: Hub City

Press, 2005).

38 **Registering to vote:** Secretary of State, Abstract of Voter Registrations Reported to the Military Government, 1868, Spartanburg County, housed at the Spartanburg County Public Libraries, 48-67.

39 **Thomas M. Bomar as mason:** *Charleston News and Courier*, July 28, 1890. The article called Bomar "a well qualified mason and this is shown in his handiwork on the mills."

39 **"one of the biggest contractors":** *The Charlotte Star of Zion* as quoted in *The Idaho Statesman*, Feb. 6, 1898. This short article appeared in newspapers all over the U.S. and Canada.

40 **C.C. Bomar's stores:** *Spartanburg Herald*, August 5, 1910.

40 **Henry Lewis:** *Spartanburg Journal*, April 12 and 18, 1913.

41 **Jesse Carter:** *Spartanburg Herald*, March 11, 1911.

42 **"Trakas's backyard":** Deno Trakas. *Because Memory Isn't Eternal.* (Spartanburg: Hub City Press, 2010), 38.

42 **Colored Industrial Training School:** Hill and Lee, 105-106.

42 **Phyllis Goins:** *Spartanburg Journal*, June 17, 1945.

42 **Dr. G.W. Harry:** Grady and Walker, 123.

42 **Drs. White and Adams:** Dwain C. Pruitt. *Things Hidden: An Introduction to the History of Blacks in Spartanburg.* (Spartanburg: Community Relations Office, 1995), 38.

43 **John-Nina Hospital:** Linda Bilanchone (ed). *The Lives They Lived: A Look at Women in the History of Spartanburg.* (Spartanburg: The Spartanburg County Foundation, 1981), 40. Doris Gibbs, Harriet Dawkins and Cooper Smith. "Nina Littlejohn."

43 **Fire:** *Spartanburg Journal*, Aug. 26, 27; *Spartanburg Herald*, Aug. 31, 1920.

43 **People's Hospital and Training School for Nurses:** Initially located on Howard Street in 1909, this was the first Black Hospital in Spartanburg. It was forced to move to a house on South Liberty Street in 1910 after white neighbors complained to City Council. The 8-room, unlicensed hospital operated until 1915. Its supporters sought to borrow money from the City's Colored Cemetery Fund to pay off construction debt but were denied by the city attorney. It closed for financial reasons.

44 **Rosenwald:** *Spartanburg Herald*, March 9, 1930. The gift from Julius Rosenwald was the first time in U.S. history that Rosenwald funds had been used for a purpose other than education. The Negro Hospital was not without controversy. William N. Porter, proprietor of Our Drug Store, sued Spartanburg County to prevent construction in May 1928, seeking to have the hospital built in a Black neighborhood instead of at the General Hospital campus. (*Spartanburg Herald*, May 20, 1928). The suit delayed construction for about two years, but it ultimately proceeded.

44 **J.W. Alexander:** *Spartanburg Herald*, Dec. 5, 1927. Alexander would later assemble and embark on Spartanburg's first mega-suburb—the massive 600-lot Park Hills neighborhood—before dying suddenly in 1927, shortly after plans were announced.

46 **Chasander Hill:** *Spartanburg Herald*, Aug. 16, 1908 and April 10, 1910; Plat Book 002, 75, Spartanburg County RMC.

46 **Lizzie Judd:** *Spartanburg Journal* Feb. 5, 1918. Lizzie Judd went on to donate as much as $75,000 to the Spartanburg YMCA, Converse College and Presbyterian College, where buildings were named in her honor, as well as the Textile Industrial Institute and Wofford College. She died in 1918.

46 **Converse Heights:** *Spartanburg Herald*, Sept. 15, 1905. *Spartanburg Journal*, Sept. 6, 1906.

Spotlight: Mary H. Wright's Early Years

48 **Birthplace & Wilson family:** Hattie Mobley, "Mary H. Wright, Slave Born Educator, Spartanburg S.C.," Project 935, S-260-264-N, WPA Writers' Project on African American Life in South Carolina, 1936-37, housed in the University of South Carolina Libraries Digital Collection, 1.
48 **$130 purchase:** *Spartanburg Journal*, April 18, 1968.
48 **Mary Farrow's first school:** *Spartanburg Herald*, June 11, 1944.
49 **Farrow Bell Foster:** Ibid., Feb. 24, 1991, interview with Linda Conley.
49 **Lot Farrow:** *Carolina Spartan*, April 1, 1885.

Spotlight: The First Black Church

51 **St. John AME Zion:** WPA, Survey of State and Local Historical Records, Church Records Form, 1937, housed in the University of South Carolina Libraries Digital Collection. https://digital.tcl.sc.edu/digital/collection/hrs/id/5332/rec/13
51 **Metropolitan A.M.E:** Ibid.
51 **"community walking preacher":** *Herald-Journal*, Aug. 14, 1993.

CHAPTER 3: BIRTH OF BACK OF THE COLLEGE

53 **Back of the College:** Some residents of the neighborhood refer to the area as "Behind the College."
53 **Rev. Martin Luther King Jr.:** Art Sears Jr. "Negro who attended U. of So. Carolina," *Jet* magazine, Feb. 28, 1963, 23.
54 **Anson Cummings' life:** F.W. Beers. *History of Allegany County.* (New York, F.W. Beers & Co., 1879), 364-366; Rossiter Johnson. *The Twentieth Century Biographical Dictionary of Notable Americans.* (Boston: The Biographical Society, 1904), 4; and Richard Nye Price. *Holston Methodism: From its Origin to its Present Time, Vol. IV, 1844-1870.* (Charlottesville VA: University of Virginia, 1912), 428-430. Of Cummings, Price wrote: "It was his fate to always be in trouble." Also: Jesse Kass, "The professors of the Radical University: Anson W. Cummings, Part 1," https://blindmanwithmathdegree.blogspot.com/2021/11.
54 ***Asheville News*:** *Wilmington Daily Dispatch*, April 13, 1866.
55 **Named president:** *Carolina Spartan*, May 10, 1866.
55 **Trustees Spartanburg Female College:** *Charleston Daily News*, Sept. 18, 1867.
55 **"loved money too well":** Price, 430.
55 **"defraud the trustees":** Ibid., 428.
55 **"great success":** *Charleston Daily News*, Oct. 2, 1867.
56 **Cummings' Spartanburg home:** Deed book LL-189.
56 **Orphanage:** *Daily Phoenix*, Aug. 30, 1872.
56 **Cummings' voting records:** Cummings' testimony, United States Congress. *Joint Select Committee on the Condition of Affairs in the Late Insurrectionary States, Vol. 4.* (Washington DC: Government Printing Office, 1872), 917-936.
56 ***Carolina New Era*:** *Greenville Enterprise*, Jan. 27, 1871; *Daily Phoenix*, Dec. 27, 1871 and March 31, 1872; *Yorkville Enquirer*, Jan. 4, 1872; *Green Bay Weekly Gazette*, Oct. 5, 1872; *Spartanburg Journal* Feb. 16, 1967. John Christopher Winsmith, who was a militia brigadier general and whose father was attacked by the KKK, became editor of the *Carolina New Era* in 1872. Samuel Poinier, a Union Army veteran and Republican who was later city postmaster,

edited a predecessor newspaper called the *Spartanburg Republican.*

56 **"folded":** *Yorkville Enquirer*, Sept. 17, 1874.

57 **$34,000:** U.S. Census, 1870.

57 **Location of Cummings' property:** Cummings' testimony, Joint Select Committee, 918.

57 **Cummings' Spartanburg land purchase:** Deed book KK-51.

57 **Peter Quinn Camp:** Cummings' testimony, United States Congress, Joint Select Committee.

57 **List of 227 victims:** Ibid., 919-922. Cummings listed two other Black men murdered, Aaron Hughs and Robert Holcomb. Holcomb was found hanging from a tree in November 1865 near Hobbysville. No information is available about Hughs. At least one other local Black man was murdered by whites in this era: Wallace Fowler, 75, was killed in May 1871 at his home in Glenn Springs, according to the *Charleston Daily Courier* of May 11, 1871. The perpetrators allegedly shoveled hot coals on his chest as he died.

58 **Loyal League:** Ibid., 927-928.

58 **"strangely blamed":** Ibid., 936.

58 **"work of a spy":** *The State*, Feb. 5, 1905.

59 **$800 contract:** Eelman, 196-197.

59 **New England:** *Boston Evening Transcript*, Feb. 13, 1872.

59 **"2,810 Klansmen":** *Daily Phoenix*, March 22, 1872.

60 **True Whittier:** Deed book MM-70; Simpson Bobo, Deed book MMM-429.

60 **Joins USC:** *Intelligencer*, June 27, 1872.

60 **Riverside Seminary:** Beers, 365.

60 **Cummings book:** A.W. Cummings, *The Early Schools of Methodism.* (New York: Phillips & Hunt, 1886).

61 **Lot sales:** Cummings to George Sanders, Spartanburg RMC deed book SS-570; to Harriet Black, FFF-553; to Henry Jones, NN-247; to James Brown, AAA-603; to Lewis Thompson, BBB-634; and FFF-66; to George Nichols, DD-608; to G.T. Thompson, LL-697; to Thomas Thomson, NNN-83; to Asa Thompson, NNN-523; to Frank Thompson, YYY-1901.

61 **Cummings sale to C.C. Scott et al:** Ibid., deed book DDD-342.

62 **Early life of C.C. Scott:** A.B. Caldwell. *History of the American Negro, South Carolina Edition.* (Atlanta: A.B. Caldwell Publishing Co., 1919), 729-734; *Jet*, 23-27; obituary written by Rev. I. E. Lowery, *The Columbia Record*, Nov. 20, 1922.

62 **"born mathematician":** *The State*, May 8, 1911.

64 **Renovation of Silver Hill:** I.E. Lowery. *Life on the old plantation in the antebellum days or A Story Based on Facts.* (Columbia: The State Publishing Co., 1911).

64 **International Sunday School Conference:** *Hartford Courant*, "Negro Abroad," Sept. 5, 1889.

65 **Scott at town council:** Town Council minutes, 1888-1895, 136.

66 **Murder of William Atkins:** *The State*, July 17-18, 1892.

66 **Jeffries' near-lynching:** *Yorkville Enquirer*, July 20, 1892; *Pickens Sentinel*, July 28, 1892; *Charleston News and Courier*, July 23, 1892. Beyond the Jeffries incident, there is one documented lynching inside the city limits of Spartanburg. In late April 1886 a mob broke through an outer door of the Spartanburg jail, stole the keys and grabbed Obidiah Thomson, who had been accused of an assault on a Glenn Springs woman. They dragged him through a crowd of 2,000 people gathered in the public square for sales day, up East Main Street and into Dean's Grove, a wooded area across from the present-day First Presbyterian Church. There they hung him from a tree. (*Abbeville Messenger*, March 1, 1886; *Carolina Spartan* March 3, 1886). Mary O. Dean, who owned the property, later dug the tree up by the roots because she didn't want

a tree standing on the property where a Black man had been lynched. (*Spartanburg Journal*, March 10, 1935). Some sources mistakenly refer to the deceased as Abe Thomson.

66 **Meeting at courthouse:** *Carolina Spartan*, July 27, 1892.

66 **Jeffries' hanging:** *The State*, Sept. 9-10, 1892.

66 **Hanging of John Williams:** *Pickens Sentinel*, Oct. 20, 1892.

66 **Hanging of Milbry Brown:** *Union Times*, Oct. 14, 1892; Corinne T. Field and LaKisha Michelle Simmons. *The Global History of Black Girlhood.* (Urbana: University of Illinois Press, 2022), 151-164. Cynthia R. Greenlee. "The Girl Who is to Die at the Rope's End: The 1892 Execution of Milbry Brown and Definitions of Childhood in South Carolina Courts." This account and others argue that Milbry Brown may be the youngest female ever executed in the United States. The crime that Brown was convicted of occurred in Gaffney, but she was tried, jailed and hanged in Spartanburg.

67 **"Here I spent":** Goodwin, 16. Scott's son, Willie Tobias Scott, who died at age 1 in 1891, is buried at the Old City Cemetery in Spartanburg. His remains would have been moved from the original Black cemetery off West Main Street. The child's gravestone remains standing.

67 **"52 new lots":** Plat Book 2, page 52, Spartanburg RMC.

67 **Land sales by Scott:** C.H. Barber, Deed book VVV-379; Walter Kellett, 4-M-168; Fred Talley, 4-O-26; Ella Whitmire, 4-O-356; James Wiggins, 4-M-214.

67 **"negro clause":** *Spartanburg Herald*, May 10, 1910.

67 **Scott's death:** *Columbia Record*, Nov. 20, 1922.

69 **"tidy profit":** Caldwell, 734.

70 **$25,000:** *Columbia Record*, Nov. 23, 1922.

Spotlight: The Barksdale Book

72 **The book:** Louvenia Barksdale. *Historically and Statistically Yours: Back of the College 1887-1981.* (Spartanburg: self-published, 1981). Note: In addition to the early families mentioned in the Barksdale book, the 1880 U.S. census adds the following families: Adams, Bryce, Brown, Burnett, Copeland, Davis, Dyna, Hartwell, Jennings, Jones, McKinney, McLansen, Mintz (or Mentz), Mitchell, Montgomery, Moor, Roberson, Sams, Sanders, Smith, Stephen, Turner, Twitty, and Vandiver, Walker, Williams, White.

Spotlight: The Other Northside

74 **Trinity A.M.E Church:** WPA, Survey of State and Local Historical Records, Church Records Form, 1937, housed in the University of South Carolina Libraries Digital Collection https://digital.tcl.sc.edu/digital/collection/hrs/id/5192/rec/11; *Spartanburg Herald*, Jan. 1, 1922.

74 **Provident Hospital:** *Spartanburg Herald*, Jan. 9, 1921. Records sometimes refer to this as Providence Hospital.

75 **Arthur Herndon:** *The Afro-American*, Aug. 27 and Sept. 10, 1927.

CHAPTER 4: TOBE HARTWELL'S STORY

77 **Death of Catherine Hartwell:** *Carolina Spartan* via the *Daily Phoenix*, Dec. 3, 1874.

77 **Enslaved by John Wesley Carr:** *Spartanburg Journal*, Aug. 4, 1932; *Spartanburg Herald*, Jan. 16, 1940.

77 **Julius Shakespeare Carr:** Mena Webb. *Jule Carr: General without an Army.* (Chapel Hill NC: UNC Press, 1987). Julius Carr is notorious for the speech he gave in Chapel Hill at the dedication of the "Silent Sam" memorial to the Confederacy.

78 **Enslaved by Albert Shipp:** *Spartanburg Journal*, June 15, 1925 and Aug. 4, 1932.

78 **Chapel Hill Methodist Church:** Fletcher M. Green, ed. *The Chapel Hill United Methodist Church Centennial History 1853-1953.* (Chapel Hill: The Church, 1954).

78 **"20 enslaved":** U.S. Slave Census, 1860.

78 **Slaves at Central Methodist:** Central United Church rosters 1860-1866, Wofford College Archives.

79 **Results of 1872 election:** *Charleston Daily News*, Oct. 21, 1872. The first Black Spartan to run for public office was the Southside's Joseph Young Sr. He ran unsuccessfully for the state legislature and the town council in 1870.

79 **Location of first Hartwell home:** Deed book LL-741.

80 **Mitchell land purchase:** Deed book LL-739. The buyer was Kittie Mitchell.

80 **McKinney land purchase:** Deed book MM-66.

80 **Dr. Cleveland's paternity:** Lawrence P. Jackson. *Chester Himes.* (New York: W.W. Norton & Co., 2017), 3, from "Estelle's Notes," transcribed by Joseph Himes Jr., Michael Fabre Papers, Emory University, box 8, folder 26.; James Sallis. *Chester Himes: A Life.* (New York: Walker & Co., 2000), 11; Edward Margolies and Michael Fabre. *The Several Lives of Chester Himes.* (Jackson MS: University Press of Mississippi, 1997), 11.

80 **Alexander Jones:** *Spartanburg Journal*, June 15, 1925. "Squire" Alex Jones, a Black Republican politician, held the office of Spartanburg magistrate and trial justice for about a year. South Carolina Gov. Daniel Chamberlain stripped him of his office at the end of Reconstruction in November 1876. When Jones died in Spartanburg in 1899, the *Charleston News and Courier* reported that he had been a prominent figure in local public meetings. In his last years, however, Alexander was reduced to selling chicken and produce on the streets of Spartanburg. (May 31, 1899).

80 **Contract police officers:** *Spartanburg Herald*, Oct. 20, 1938.

82 **"the morning alarm":** *Spartanburg Journal*, Aug. 4, 1932.

82 **"night watchman":** *Spartanburg Herald*, Feb. 19 & 23. Description of lamp lighting from a framed document at Spartanburg Housing Authority, which accompanies Hartwell's portrait there.

82 **School at Silver Hill:** Hill and Lee, 105.

82 **Lincoln School:** Grady and Walker, 127.

83 **Dean Street School:** Pruitt, 40; Hill and Lee, 124.

83 **Northview Street:** Deed book 4Q-288. Sale was to Sallie Hartwell, two lots.

83 **Jesse Carter house:** *Spartanburg Herald*, May 10, 1909.

84 **"words of raillery":** *Spartanburg Journal*, May 9, 1925.

84 **"made and regretted":** *Jet*, 23.

85 **Sallie Hartwell death:** *Spartanburg Herald*, Aug. 14, 1932.

85 **"plea for charity":** *Spartanburg Journal*, Aug. 5, 1932.

85 **Nina Scott:** Ibid., Dec. 21, 1938.

85 **City Council meeting:** *Spartanburg Herald*, Jan. 16, 1940.

85 **"broke ground":** Ibid., Sept. 10, 1940.

85 **"widespread white conviction":** Marko Maunula. *Guten Tag, Y'all: Globalization and the South Carolina Piedmont 1950-2000.* (Athens: University of Georgia Press, 2009.), 27.

85 **"Nineteen Black homes":** *Spartanburg Herald*, Aug. 29, 1940.

86 **"large portrait":** Ibid,: Oct. 31, 1942. This portrait disappeared for years and was returned

in 2020 from a housing authority in Rome, GA. It now hangs in the Spartanburg Housing Authority on Arch Street.

86 **Campus of Learners:** *Herald-Journal*, Feb. 27, 1999.

Spotlight: The Black Poet Laureate

88 **"poet laureate":** Louvenia Barksdale. *Historically and Statistically Yours: Back of the College 1887-1981.* (Spartanburg: self-published, 1981).

88 **Johnson's life:** *Spartanburg Herald*, Feb. 13, 1927, July 30, 1927 and Jan. 23, 1939. These articles include more selections from Johnson's poetry.

88 **"taught music":** F.S. Dupre, interviewer. *A Folk History in the United States from Interviews with Former Slaves, Vol XIV, Part 3.* (Washington DC: WPA, 1941), 53-55.

89 **"nickname Kennedy":** Barksdale, 4.

Spotlight: The Muckenfuss Broom Factory

90 **"15 to 20 jobs":** *The Greenville News*, July 15, 1924.

90 **Factory employees:** U.S. Census, 1900.

90 **"75 dozen brooms a week":** *The Atlanta Constitution*, Oct. 26, 1902.

91 **Factory fire:** *Spartanburg Herald*, Nov. 18, 1909.

91 **"must be rebuilt":** *Greenwood Evening Index*, Dec. 16, 1909.

91 **"three times the previous volume":** *Spartanburg Herald*, Dec. 10, 1922.

91 **Muckenfuss obituary:** Ibid., Feb. 22, 1914.

91 **Rida Muckenfuss:** Ibid., Dec. 10, 1922.

91 **Hughes Green:** U.S. Census, 1940.

CHAPTER 5: EARLY EDUCATION

93 **Edward J. Snetter:** Eelman, 190. A Freedmen's Bureau correspondence addressed to Major Edward Deane on July 24, 1867, mentions a school for freed children in Spartanburg located in a house in the village owned by Mrs. McAlpin that had been rented for $10 a month. This is apparently Maria McAlpin, an Irish immigrant who ran a boardinghouse for Wofford College students before the war. McAlpin served as a nurse for the Confederate army, then moved to Brooklyn, New York and never returned to Spartanburg. Whether this is the same school Rev. Snetter served is not clear.

93 **"six-shooter":** Minutes of the Annual Conferences of the Methodist Episcopal Church (New York: Hunt & Eaton, 1892).

95 **"unable to read and write":** It was illegal in the Deep South to teach an enslaved person to read and write.

95 **"not carpetbaggers":** Hattie Mobley, "Mary H. Wright, Slave Born Educator, Spartanburg S.C.," Project 935, S-260-264-N, WPA Writers' Project on African American Life in South Carolina, 1936-37, housed in the University of South Carolina Libraries Digital Collection, 2.

95 **"a place I do not admire":** Eva Poole to Justus K. Jillson, Nov. 6, 1869, Correspondence of Justus K. Jillson, Department of Education files, SCDAH.

95 **Louis Poole:** Ronald E. Burchart. *Schooling the Freed People: Teaching, Learning and the Struggle for Black Freedom, 1861-1876.* (Chapel Hill: UNC Press, 2010), 66; Henry Lee Swint. *The Northern Teacher in the South, 1862-1870.* (Nashville: Vanderbilt University Press, 1941),

103.

95 **Roster of students at the Poole school:** "Teachers Reports for Salary and Expense Reimbursement Submitted by County School Commissioners (5152027), 1868-1870." Microfilm available at Spartanburg County Public Libraries.

95 **Hamilton School:** Reports of Free Schools in Spartanburg County, Eva Poole, 1869-1870, Department of Education Files, SCDAH. It is possible that Eva Poole's school was named for John T. Hamilton, the wealthiest Black man in town in the late 1860s. Hamilton was involved with plans for a different school for Black children by 1870. Eva Poole began calling her school "Spartanburg Colored School" in its last months in documents filed with the Department of Education, possibly because of a split with Mr. Hamilton.

95 **"Hostile":** Ibid.

96 **Coroner:** *Charleston Daily Courier*, Sept. 20, 1872.

96 **Letter to the Freedmen's Bureau:** South Carolina Assistant Commissioner, Registered Letters Received, Register 8, A-W, Jan. 1869-Feb.1870, Part 2, Freedmen's Bureau files, Smithsonian Institution.

96 **John T. Hamilton:** Deed book II-223. Hamilton was living in the village of Spartanburg in 1870 with a 50-year-old woman named Sella Price. Both of them disappear from the Spartanburg census records by 1880.

96 **Trustees:** Deed book II-223. There is no record of this lot changing hands again after it was bought by Joseph Young and others. Whether this lot ultimately became the site of Dean Street School is unclear. The Spartanburg School District bought its lot on North Dean Street in 1890 from Berry Thomson, who bought it from George Moose in 1875.

96 **"ran away":** *Spartanburg Herald*, March 17, 1907.

96 **Trinity AME School:** Deed book II-228 and 681. The trustee-landowners of this school were: Rev. Barnett Burton, Elias Daniels, Bassett Weaver, Alfred White, Samuel Norris, H.M. McIntyre and Nathaniel Aden. (Aden's name is spelled Eddin on the deed.) At the time this school was open, the name of the church was Methodist Episcopal Zion Church. By 1872, when the church built its first home at the intersection of College and Howard streets, it had changed its name to Trinity AME.

98 **Conflict with Cummings and railway:** Eelman, 196-197.

98 **"rancorous":** Eelman, 191.

98 **Rev. R.H. Reid:** Ibid., 194.

98 **John Evins:** Ibid., 192.

99 **"100,000 new Black students":** Ibid., 193.

100 **Silver Hill school:** *School Trustees Record*, School District No. 15, known by the local name of Spartanburg Township No. 1, 1873-1881. Department of Education files, SCDAH.

100 **"solicitation letter":** Margaret Newlin. *Memoir of Mary Anna Longstreth.* (Philadelphia: J.B. Lippincott Co, 1886), 192.

101 **1877 community meeting:** Eelman, 203-205.

102 **Walter I. Lewis:** Daniel Wallace Culp. *Twentieth Century Negro.* (Napierville, IL: J.L. Nichols & Co., 1902), 272. Lewis was a native of Chester, S.C.

102 **"ahead of the curve":** *Speight's Spartanburg Daily*, Oct. 30, 1878, in the collection of the SCPL.

102 **John L. Dart:** Descriptive Summary, John L. Dart Family Papers, 1844-1947, Avery Research Center for African American History and Culture, College of Charleston.

102 **Kenneth Young:** *The State*, May 8, 1911. Also attending the state university in Columbia with Kenneth Young and J.L. Dart in the mid-1870s was Cornelius C. Scott, who later served

Silver Hill Church.

102 **"seven other schools":** School Trustees Record, 1873-1881, SCDAH. In addition to Silver Hill, the following schools were certified by the state to teach Black students in the town of Spartanburg in 1880: Friendship School, led by Malinda Moore and Thomas J. Floyd; Daniel Academy, led by N.E. Farrow; Bureau School, led by M.A. Jones; Mount Moriah Baptist Church School, led by Sarah D. Steele; Howard Gap school, led by Emma J. Cockman; Allen's Chapel school, led by W.B. West; and Powell's Chapel School, led by Frank Moore. No additional information about these schools is available in this report.

102 **"four teachers":** Hill and Lee, 104.

103 **Grant Academy:** J. Frank Thompson, "The Grant Academy," *Herald and Presbyter*, June 26, 1901, 27; Annual reports of the Board of Missions for Freedmen of the Presbyterian Church, 1894 and 1895; Inez Moore Parker, *The Rise and Decline of the Program of Education for the Black Presbyterians of the United Presbyterian Church U.S.A., 1865-1970.* (San Antonio, Trinity University Press, 1977), 175-186.

103 **Westminster Presbyterian:** This church is described as "a single-story, gable-roofed building just north of the courthouse square" in Lawrence P. Jackson's book *Chester B. Himes*.

103 **Hammett's death:** *Lancaster News*, Nov. 12, 1898.

103 **Fire:** *Spartanburg Journal*, Nov. 17, 1933.

104 **Dean Street School:** Pruitt, 40; Hill and Lee, 124; *Charleston News and Courier*, Sept. 2, 1891.

104 **William Nesbitt Jones:** Hayward Farrar. *The Baltimore Afro-American 1892-1950* (Westport, CT: Greenwood Press: 1998), 71-72, 150-151; The Baltimore *Afro-American*, Oct. 7, 1933 and May 18 & May 25, 1940. Jones was the son of Janie and Julius Jones, who owned a home on South Church Street in Spartanburg in 1900. At age 17 William N. Jones was an apprentice printer in Spartanburg. He received a medical degree from the University of West Tennessee but never practiced. He helped raise his much-younger sister, Lula, who moved to Baltimore with him. She served as society editor of the *Afro-American* from 1929 to 1972, often publishing Spartanburg news in the pages of the Baltimore newspaper. Her column was called "Gadabouting in the USA."

104 **Baltimore *Afro-American:*** Additional Spartanburg correspondents for this newspaper included pharmacist William M. Porter (1950s and 1960s) and Lucinda Burgess (1960s and 1970s).

105 **C.C. Scott:** *Charleston News and Courier,* Jan. 29, 1894.

105 **Robert Milton Alexander:** Caldwell, 741-743; *Spartanburg Journal*, Feb. 28, 1930 and March 1, 1930.

106 **Benjamin Banneker:** *The State*, March 3, 1930. Alexander was the author of three books: *The Life of Benjamin Banneker, A Letter to Young Men,* and *A Letter to Farmers.*

106 **Bomar sisters:** Lawrence, 5-8. Hattie Bomar later taught presidential advisor Mary McLeod Bethune at Scotia Seminary. Estelle Bomar attended Scotia as well.

107 **"remarkable rapidity":** *Spartanburg Herald*, Aug. 11, 1916.

107 **Description of school:** *Herald-Journal*, Feb. 10, 2007, Linda Conley interview with Rosalind Patton Brown.

108 **Booker T. Washington:** Ibid., Jan. 26, 1907.

108 **Cane-bottom chairs:** *Spartanburg Herald*, Dec. 11, 1909.

109 **Elvira Alexander as principal:** Ibid., Dec. 16, 1966.

109 **Schools closed for funeral:** Ibid., Jan. 13, 1931.

109 **Frank Evans' tribute:** Ibid., March 2, 1930.

109 **Renaming of Dean Street School:** Ibid., Sept. 9, 1939.

Spotlight: St. Luke's Lutheran Day School

110 **St. Luke's Lutheran Day School**: Spartanburg City Directories; WPA, Survey of State and Local Historical Records, Church Records Form, 1937, housed in the University of South Carolina Libraries Digital Collection. https://digital.tcl.sc.edu/digital/collection/hrs/id/5379/rec/3; *Spartanburg Herald*, Oct. 29, 1966.

110 **School description and attendance:** Record of Congregation provided by Concordia Historical Institute, Department of Archives of the Lutheran Church, Missouri Synod, St. Louis. Mo.

Spotlight: Spartanburg's First Black Attorney

112 **Platt's life:** *Spartanburg Herald*, Nov. 10, 1922 and May 9, 1944; Oral accounts of family members, Findagrave.com.

112 **Piedmont Building and Loan:** *Spartanburg Journal*, Jan. 25, 1923. The bank was dissolved in 1929 by its president, W.M. Kirkland.

112 **"co-counsel":** W. Lewis Burke and Belinda F. Gergel. *Matthew J. Perry: The Man, His Times and His Legacy.* (U.S.C. Press: Columbia, 2004), 17-18.

113 **Nurses:** Damon Fordham. *Voices of Black South Carolina.* (Charleston: The History Press, 2009), 143-144, quoting the *Spartanburg News* column in the *Columbia Palmetto Leader.*

113 **Ice cream cone:** *Pittsburgh Courier*, Aug. 22, 1942.

CHAPTER 6: THE NEWSMEN AND THE NEIGHBORHOOD

115 **Laban Morgan's home and print shop:** Spartanburg City Directory, 1899-1900.

115 **"more subscribers":** *Remington Brothers Newspaper Manual.* (Pittsburgh: Remington Brothers, 1900.) One other Black-owned newspaper was larger, but it was affiliated with the Baptist Church. In comparison, *The Carolina Spartan* had 1,420 subscribers in 1900. There were five other Black-owned newspapers in the state that year.

115 **Shadrack Morgan:** Eric Foner. *Freedom's Lawmakers: A Directory of Black Lawmakers During Reconstruction.* (England: Oxford University Press, 1993), 154; *Orangeburg Times and Democrat*, Feb. 12, 2002. Shadrack Morgan appears in the 1880 census as the father of 11-year-old Laban Morgan. The name "Laban" appears in the Hebrew Bible in Genesis 24:29-60. In the Bible, Laban was the brother of Rebekah, who gave birth to Jacob.

115 **Laban Morgan's 1897 home purchase:** Deed book PPP-137.

115 **North Church Street businesses:** Spartanburg City Directory, 1899-1900.

116 **"no copies known to survive":** John Hammond Moore. *South Carolina Newspapers.* (Columbia SC: University of South Carolina Press, 1988).

116 **"master of ceremonies":** *Newberry Herald*, Jan. 10, 1899, quoting the *Spartanburg Herald.*

116 **Evins Street:** Barksdale, 2.

117 **Jack Thompson:** There is a freedman named Jack Thomson—no p—listed among Spartanburg's 1869 militia enrollments, which would indicate this man was formerly enslaved by the Thomson family, Spartanburg's largest slaveholders. There also is a slave named Jack on an 1845 list of Thomson slaves that were to be inherited by Henry H. Thomson, an antebellum mayor of Spartanburg and a resident of Main Street. Both the white Thomsons and the freedmen once owned by this family used the names Thomson and Thompson interchangeably.

While this is not proof that Jack Thompson had been owned by the Thomson family, it creates a possibility.

118 **Ben Thompson:** *Spartanburg Journal*, Nov. 5, 1927.

118 **Asa Thompson:** Ibid., Sept. 30, 1935.

118 **Joseph Thompson:** *Spartanburg Herald*, Dec. 30, 1937.

118 **Clifford Thompson:** Ibid., April 2, 1931.

118 **Frank Thompson:** *The State*, April 22, 1898. Free mail delivery began in Spartanburg in April 1898, and Thompson was one of four men hired to deliver. Kenneth Young was named as a substitute.

118 **Description of the Indicator:** *American Newspaper Annual.* (Philadelphia: N.W. Ayer & Son, 1898).

118 **"Black-owned cotton mill":** U.S. Department of the Interior. National Registration of Historic Places Registration Form, Coleman-Franklin-Cannon Mill, 2015.

118 **"put the negro in the mills":** *Union Times*, May 8, 1896, quoting *The Piedmont Indicator.*

118 **Asa Thompson, Spartanburg editor:** *The State*, Dec. 11, 1896.

119 **Rev. James A. Brown:** Caldwell, 107-110; Spartanburg City Directory, 1899-1900.

119 **Dr. Javan Bryant:** *History of Benton, Washington, Carroll, Madison, Crawford, Franklin and Sebastian Counties, Arkansas.* (Chicago: The Goodspeed Publishing Co., 1889), 919.

119 **A.B. Dean:** Spartanburg Town Council Minutes, 1895-1905, Chief of Police Annual Report, 345.

121 **Martin Hardy:** *The State*, May 7, 1903; *Abbeville Press and Banner*, May 12, 1903. Hardy lived on Howard Street with his wife, Kiziah, and children.

121 **George Blanchard:** *Lancaster News*, Feb. 10. 1904.

121 **Spartanburg streetcar boycott:** *The State*, Aug. 17, 1903, quoting *The Carolina Spartan.*

121 **Streetcar boycotts:** Blair M.L. Kelley. *Right to Ride: Streetcar Boycotts and African American Citizenship in the era of Plessy vs. Ferguson.* (Chapel Hill NC: UNC Press, 2010), 204; and Kidada E. Williams. "Walk! The Streetcar Protests," *Seizing Freedom* podcast, episode 5.

122 **Purchase of land for cemetery:** Deed book 4-H 352.

122 **Joseph Young:** *Spartanburg Herald*, June 26, 1906.

123 **Asa Thompson letter to the editor:** *Spartanburg Herald*, June 29, 1906. Other people signing this letter included Andy Young, S.F. Wiggins, William Foreman, William Mass, George Clement, David Montague, Tobe Hartwell and A.H. Floyd. Headstones for two members of Asa Thompson's family can be found at the Old City Cemetery; because they died prior to 1900, their remains would have been relocated from West Main Street.

124 **Sold for $5,500:** Ibid., Sept. 14, 1906.

124 **"obliterating":** Ibid., Nov. 15, 1912.

124 **"successful lawsuit":** Ibid., Feb. 21 and July 11, 1920. The lawsuit was brought by Dr. H.C. Hardy and businessmen Arthur Martin and W.M. Freeman. The Black plaintiffs argued that the railroad's replacement cemetery was badly neglected, washed out, "crowded with bodies," and had no roads leading to it. They asked for additional property and that streets and driveways be built. The lawsuit was filed in 1916, but because their white attorney had gone into the army, it took four years to come to trial. Judge T.S. Sease ordered City Council to spend as much as necessary to remedy the situation. By that time, the trust had grown to $7,644. In 1921 Council purchased 10 acres in Stephens Grove, near modern-day Hearon Circle and outside city limits, for a larger cemetery, spending $2,650. In 1925 it turned over remaining funds to the Spartanburg Colored Cemetery Co. for maintenance of the property on Cemetery Street.

125 **Laban Morgan house sale:** Deed book RRR-568.

125 **C.C. Scott, editor:** *The Southern Indicator*, June 6, 1914.
125 **Republican delegate:** *The State*, Feb. 25, 1904.
125 **Summer Normal School teacher:** *Spartanburg Herald*, July 16, 1911.
125 **"Colored Hospital":** Ibid., March 12, 1909.
125 **"carried mail":** *Spartanburg Journal*, April 13, 1917.
125 **"colored Progressive Party":** *Times & Democrat*, Oct. 19, 1912; *Yorkville Enquirer*, Oct. 15, 1915.
125 **"shifted his office":** *Spartanburg Herald*, April 16, 1912.
125 **Death of Laban Morgan:** *Columbia Record*, October 12, 1915; Death certificate, Ancestry.com.
125 **"leaders of the colored race":** *Yorkville Enquirer*, Oct. 15, 1915.
126 **Dr. Sexton's tribute:** *The Southern Indicator*, July 31, 1921.
126 **Harbison College**: *Abbeville Press and Banner*, March 23, 1901; *Spartanburg Herald*, June 14, 1910; *Columbia Record*, Dec. 7, 1910; Presbyterian Church in the U.S.A. Board of National Missions. Unit of Work with Colored People Records, Series V: (Harbison Institute) publicity material, circular letters, 1932-1937 (Call number: RG 301.10, Box 1, Folder 35).
126 **$1,260:** *Spartanburg Herald*, June 28, 1910.
126 **Emancipation parades:** Ibid., Dec. 26, 1915, Dec. 18 and 26, 1922.
128 **"automatic hoe and plow":** Ibid., April 17, 1915.
129 **"suffered an untold loss":** Ibid., April 30, 1919.
129 **"cause of his education:"** Ibid., Sept. 24, 1919.
130 **"modern school for negroes":** *Spartanburg Journal*, Dec. 1, 1925.
130 **Thompson's response to school news:** Ibid., Dec. 21, 1925.

CHAPTER 7: NOXIOUS AIR

133 **Announcement of Cummings Street incinerator:** *Spartanburg Herald*, Dec. 14, 1925. This was 12 days after the announcement of the new Cumming Street School.
133 **Burning of stray dogs:** *Spartanburg Herald*, Oct. 11, 1928.
133 **Soil testing:** Results provided by Dr. Grace Schwartz, Wofford College.
134 **"environmental injustice":** Robert. D. Bullard. *Dumping in Dixie: Race, Class and Environmental Quality*. (Boulder CO: Westview Press, 2000).
134 **"first Spartanburg incinerator":** *Spartanburg Journal*, Oct. 16, 1913; *Spartanburg Herald*, April 18, 1914.
134 **"set in a valley":** *Spartanburg Herald*, July 16, 1914.
134 **"prominent white landowners":** *Spartanburg Journal*, Dec. 2, 1921.
135 **"sites south and west:"** Ibid., March 4, 1925.
135 **Purchase of school site:** Deed book 6-Y 332.
135 **Purchase of incinerator site:** City Council minutes 1919-1932, 318. Council members voting in favor of the purchase were Mayor J.F. Floyd, G.E. Claxon, B.R. Littlejohn, G.T. Gallman and L.K. Brice.
135 **Theo Thompson:** *Spartanburg Herald*, May 6, 1927.
135 **"addition in 1940":** Ibid., Sept. 10, 1940.
135 **Frank McKain:** Ibid., March 7, 1939.
135 **"26,230 loads":** *Spartanburg Journal*, Jan. 18, 1940.
135 **"white neighbors downwind":** *Spartanburg Herald*, Sept. 3, 1940.
135 **"at the breaking point":** *Spartanburg Journal*, Aug. 31, 1945.

136 **"dead rat":** *Spartanburg Herald-Journal,* Jan. 27, 1946.
136 **Smoldering trash pile:** *Spartanburg Journal,* Jan. 31, 1945.
137 **"health hazard":** *Spartanburg City Schools: A Survey Report.* Division of Surveys and Field Services. (George Peabody College for Teachers, Nashville TN: 1948), 116.
137 **"makeshift dog pound":** *Spartanburg Herald,* June 29, 1951.
138 **J.G. McCracken and city dump:** *Spartanburg Journal,* Jan. 20 and May 5, 1954.
138 **Demolition:** *Spartanburg Herald,* Sept. 10-11, 1957. The incinerator site was sold to a local physician, Paul Cook. It is now owned by American Tower Corp., a cell tower company.

CHAPTER 8: A COMMUNITY CENTER AND A HIGH SCHOOL

141 **Opening day:** The opening of Cumming Street School was not covered by either Spartanburg daily paper. As late as Aug. 7, 1926, the city was still running an advertisement for a bid notice to contractors, indicating the school was not open until at least the following winter, possibly early 1927.
141 **Description of school:** Interview with Leotis Davis.
141 **Early teachers:** Asa Thompson. Letter to the editor, *Spartanburg Journal,* May 31, 1928.
141 **J. Frank Collins:** Doyle Boggs with Brad Steinecke and Mark Olencki. *Historic Spartanburg County: 225 Years of History.* (San Antonio TX: HPN Books), 27-28.
142 **Best buildings in the South:** *Spartanburg Journal,* May 28, 1927.
143 **"another agenda":** Asa Thompson. Letter to the Editor, *Spartanburg Herald,* Oct. 17, 1928.
143 **Colored Civic League:** *The Hub City Observer,* July 13, 1929, 1. *The Hub City Observer* was a Black-owned Spartanburg newspaper.
143 **Cedar Hill Academy:** Hill and Lee, 109-110.
143 **Brewton death:** *Spartanburg Herald,* June 23, 1928.
143 **Dendy and teachers:** *Spartanburg Journal,* May 29, 1929.
143 ***The Spartanburg Times:*** The (Baltimore) *Afro-American,* Oct. 7, 1933. Employees of *The Spartanburg Times* were reported as: Howard L. Neale, managing editor; George W. Pickenpack, city editor; A.M. Simpson, advertising manager; Miss E.M. Bates, secretary; and reporters G.W. Simpson, J.D. Western, James Scruggs, John Sherry, and Professor W. P. Dendy. The editor, Howard Neale, worked for N.C. Mutual Insurance and lived at 267 Northview Street. The city editor, George Pickenpack, served as principal of Stephen's Grove School in the 1930s.
143 **W.P. Dendy:** Dendy's 35-year-old brother, Norris, was lynched by a mob of 100 white men in Clinton in July 1933. After driving a truckload of picnickers to Lake Murray, Norris Dendy had an altercation with a white man. He was jailed, then taken out of the jail by four white men, dragged with a rope around his neck and murdered. (Baltimore *Afro-American* Aug. 5, 1933).
145 **C.C. Woodson Sr.:** Hill and Lee, 108.
145 **C.C. Woodson Jr.:** Ibid., 113-115. Woodson was a grandson of the Southside's Joseph and Priscilla Young.
145 **College attendees:** *Spartanburg Journal,* Nov. 10, 1930.
146 **Football stadium:** *Spartanburg Herald,* April 28, 1934.
147 **Hattie Bell Penland:** Oral history (1995), Wofford College Digital Commons. https://digitalcommons.wofford.edu/oralhistory/1.
148 **Death of Asa Thompson:** *Spartanburg Journal,* Sept. 30-Oct. 1, 1935; *Spartanburg Herald,*

Oct. 1, 1935.

148 **T.K. Gregg:** Goodwin, 20-21.

150 **Business college:** *Spartanburg Journal,* Oct. 25, 1935.

151 **Lobbying in Washington:** *The Afro-American,* May 16, 1936.

151 **William M. Porter:** Born in 1884 near Jonesville, Porter moved with his family to Spartanburg about 1900. He was licensed as a pharmacist in 1906 and purchased Our Drug Co., which he operated on Church Street for many years. He served as county chairman of the Republican Party in the 1940s and co-founded the Negro Citizens Committee. He operated Economy Prescription Co. on South Liberty Street in the 1950s and 60s. Porter served as a correspondent for the Baltimore *Afro-American* newspaper into the 1950s. He lived at 917 Howard Street and died in 1966.

151 **Colored Civic League:** *Spartanburg Journal,* Aug. 17, 1935.

151 **Description of community center:** *Spartanburg Herald,* May 29, 1938.

151 **Photo of community center:** (Norfolk) *New Journal and Guide,* Dec. 3, 1938.

153 **Death of T.K. Gregg:** *Spartanburg Journal,* March 29, 1939.

153 **Infection of the heart:** Dr. Gregg's death certificate.

153 **"man of culture":** *Spartanburg Herald,* March 29, 1939.

153 **Gregg funeral:** (Norfolk) *New Journal and Guide,* April 8, 1939.

154 **Carver High:** Hill and Lee, 113-114.

155 **Eugene Majied (Rivers) Jr.:** Michael Tisserand. "The Cartoonist and the Champ." *The Comics Journal,* April 24, 2018. https://www.tcj.com/the-cartoonist-and-the-champ/. Hussein, Kurham. "Muhammad Speaks for Justice, Freedom, and Equality." Daily JSTOR.org, May 13, 2021. Interview with Rev. Eugene Rivers III, Jan. 12, 2024. Rivers III, an anti-violence activist in Boston, served as an advisor to President George W. Bush on urban affairs.

156 **Emerson Coleman:** *Spartanburg Herald,* July 12, 1952; *Herald-Journal,* June 5, 1989.

156 **"additional wing":** *Spartanburg Herald,* Aug. 18, 1957.

160 **Chuck Carree:** *Wilmington Star News,* Feb. 20, 2013.

160 **"historic register:"** *Herald-Journal,* May 19, 2022.

160 **Nayef Samhat:** Robert W. Dalton. "The Back of the College Neighborhood: A Story of People, Place and Change." *Wofford Today.* (Spartanburg: Wofford College, Fall 2020). https://www.wofford.edu/about/news/wofford-today/archive/2020/fall/the-back-of-the-college-neighborhood.

161 **Littlejohn family:** Five Littlejohn siblings attended Cumming Street School in the 1950s and 60s. Each of the three Littlejohn sons retired from the U.S. Air Force, Horace Littlejohn as a lieutenant colonel. One daughter, Val, became senior vice provost at North Carolina A&T University. Another, Gaynell, became a professor of English.

Spotlight: Camp Friendship

162 **The camp:** *Spartanburg Herald,* May 9, 1930; July 16, 1930; Aug. 30, 1930; Sept. 9, 1933; Sept. 29, 1933. July 3, 1934, July 31, 1934; April 30, 1935; July 8, 1935.

CHAPTER 9: HEYDAY

166 **20 percent of farms:** Cheryl Greenberg. *To Ask For An Equal Chance: African Americans in the Great Depression.* (Lanham MD: Rowan & Littlefield, 2009), 22.

166 **"skilled positions":** Ibid., 25.

166 **South Carolina Penitentiary:** United States, Department of Justice, National Institute of Justice, Bureau of Justice Statistics. "Historical Statistics on Prisoners in State and Federal Institutions, Yearend 1925-86," by Patrick A. Langan, John V. Fundis, Lawrence A. Greenfield, and Victoria W. Schneider. May 1988. https://www.ojp.gov/pdffiles1/Digitization/111098NCJRS.pdf

166 **Ladies Mutual Aid Society:** Jessica Gordon-Nembhard. *Collective Courage: A History of African American Cooperative Economic Thought and Practice.* (University Park PA: Penn State University Press, 2014), 129.

169 **Cummings Street Baptist:** WPA, Survey of State and Local Historical Records, Church Records Form, 1937, housed in the University of South Carolina Libraries Digital Collection. https://digital.tcl.sc.edu/digital/collection/hrs/id/5519/rec/1

169 **Walker Memorial Methodist Episcopal Church:** Ibid. https://digital.tcl.sc.edu/digital/collection/hrs/id/5366/rec/1. The Mintz family (Squire and Ann) is referred to in earlier documents as Mentz.

169 **Mt. Zion Baptist Church:** Oral history interviews.

171 **Greater Trinity AME:** *Spartanburg Herald*, Jan. 4, 1941 and March 18, 1949; *Spartanburg Journal*, Feb. 7, 1953.

171 **John "Bootsie" Wilson:** *Herald-Journal*, Sept. 24, 2009; https://www.thesilhouettes.org/profiles/john-wilson.htm

172 **Big Newt Whitmire:** Edwin Epps. *Duncan Park.* (Spartanburg: Hub City Press, 2023), 30-35.

172 **Little Newt Whitmire:** Ibid.

172 **Ella Whitmire's children:** Interviews with Luther Norman, April 2023.

173 **Stacey Whitmire:** Lesesne, Joe. Interview. Conducted by Jim Neighbors. Feb 27, 2020.

173 **Louvenia Barksdale:** Obituary, *Herald-Journal*, Sept. 25, 1990.

179 **Happy Saturdays:** *Herald-Journal*, March 22, 1970; May 14, 1970.

182 **Octavia Jones:** *Herald-Journal*, Feb. 28, 1991.

183 **Charles and Littlejohn stores:** Barksdale, 19.

183 **Littlejohn Family:** Valerie Giddings. *A Family Is ….* (Blacksburg VA: Self-published for the 1995 Littlejohn-Clifton Reunion, 1995), 5.

183 **Marshall Grocery and Jones Dry Cleaning:** Barksdale, 19.

Spotlight: Kiddie College

186 **Walter and Sophia Hart:** *Spartanburg Herald*, Oct. 3, 1943; Nov. 8, 1941; Nov. 25, 1982.

186 **Description of Kiddie Kollege:** Interview with Dr. Keith Harris, grandson of the Harts, January 2024.

Spotlight: The Saint of Swain Street

188 **Rachel Glover:** *Spartanburg Herald*, Feb. 15 & 24, 1952; June 7, 1957; Aug. 11 & 13, 1958.

CHAPTER 10: LUNCH COUNTERS

191 **People's Citizens Committee:** *Spartanburg Herald*, Jan. 20, 1950.

191 **Spartanburg Memorial Auditorium:** Ibid., Nov. 5, 1951.

191 **Spartanburg General Hospital:** Ibid., Jan. 22, 1952.
191 **"definite time":** *Spartanburg Journal*, July 25, 1955.
192 **Newman testimony:** *Spartanburg Herald*, April 17, 1959.
192 **Hampton Institute sit-ins:** Donnie L. Everett and Kennell A. Jackson. "The Hampton Sit-ins and the Southern Society," Hampton student paper provided by Zachary McKiernan, Department of History, UC Santa Barbara.
195 **Julius Eroshell Williams:** *Spartanburg Herald*, story by Michael Leonard, May 9, 1982.
195 1960 **Spartanburg sit-in:** *Spartanburg Journal* and *Spartanburg Herald*, July 27-30 and Aug. 11, 1960; *The State*, July 28, 1960.
198 **1962 Spartanburg sit-ins:** I. DeQuincey Newman. "Special Report." South Carolina University Libraries. https://digital.tcl.sc.edu/digital/collection/idn/id/502/rec/27; *Spartanburg Herald*, July 28, 1962.
199 **Pickets:** Ibid., "Special Report #3." https://digital.tcl.sc.edu/digital/collection/idn/id/632/rec/47.
200 **Spartanburg lunch counter desegregation:** Maxie Myron Cox, Jr. "1963 – The Year of Decision: Desegregation in South Carolina." Thesis, University of South Carolina, 1996.
201 **Myrtle Williams Bell:** Binghamton, NY *Press and Sun-Bulletin*, Nov. 25, 1973; Dignity Memorial obituary, https://www.dignitymemorial.com/obituaries/austin-tx/myrtle-bell-11248625.

Spotlight: Courageous Wynona Douglas

202 **Interviews with the Douglas family:** *Herald-Journal*, May 17, 1984 and Aug. 28, 1988.

CHAPTER 11: GAS BOTTOM AND URBAN RENEWAL

205 **History of steam plant:** *Spartanburg Journal*, April 12, 1967.
205 **15 miles of track:** *Spartanburg Herald*, Sept. 16, 1972.
205 **Fumes:** *Herald-Journal*, Jan. 1, 1989.
206 **Adolphe Vermont:** *Spartanburg Journal*, Dec. 9, 1925.
206 **Fowler's Row**: *Spartanburg Herald*, Nov.18, 1909.
206 **Jerry Zolton.** *Great God A'mighty: The Dixie Hummingbirds and the Rise of Soul Gospel Music.* (Oxford: Oxford University Press, 2003), 51.
206 **"Power House":** Barksdale, 11. This gas plant was later owned by Piedmont Natural Gas Co., which eventually tore it down. There is a fenced, empty lot there in 2024.
206 **"skin game":** *Spartanburg Herald*, Sept. 14, 1926.
207 **"stormed a house":** Ibid., Jan. 21, 1933.
207 **Willie Fowler shooting:** *Spartanburg Journal*, July 14-15, 1941.
207 **Hudson Barksdale:** Steve Jobe. *Hudson Barksdale: Educator, Legislator, and Civil Rights Leader.* (Spartanburg: Kennedy Free Press, 2019); Obituary, *Herald-Journal*, April 14-15, 1986.
209 **Alexander School:** Ibid., July 3, 1985.
209 **Metropolitan AME music:** *Spartanburg Herald*, Jan. 11 and June 19, 1928; *Spartanburg Journal*, Jan. 8, 1931.
209 **Ira Tucker:** Zolton, 53-56, 58-59, 61-62.
212 **Simmie Dooley:** Ibid., 56-57; and Bruce Bastian, *Red River Blues: The Blues Tradition in the Southeast.* (Urbana and Chicago: University of Illinois Press, 1986), 182-186.

213 **KKK in Spartanburg:** *Spartanburg Herald* and *Journal*, Oct. 25-26, 28, 30, 1940.
213 **KKK trial:** Ibid., June 19-22, 1941.
213 **KKK parade:** Ibid., June 24-25, 1941.
216 **Hot dog stand:** *Spartanburg Journal*, March 25, 1942.
216 **federal planning grant:** *Spartanburg Herald*, Jan. 26, 1957.
217 **"Grand Canyon":** Ibid., May 3, 1957.
217 **83 houses:** Ibid., Oct. 20, 1958.
217 **"in general agreeable":** *Spartanburg Journal*, June 25, 1959.
217 **"unscrupulous":** Ibid., April 7, 1959.
217 **Gas Bottom park:** Ibid., June 2, 1959
217 **$200 moving expenses:** Ibid., Nov. 8, 1979.
217 **"not enough houses":** *Spartanburg Herald*, Aug. 17, 1960.
217 **FHA loans:** Ibid., Aug. 18, 1960.
218 **"easily carry disease":** Ibid., Holcombe, April 19, 1959.
218 **"slums breed crime":** Ibid., Holcombe, Nov. 9, 1958.
218 **"attempt at crime control":** Amanda Rowe Tillotson. "Pathologizing Race and Place: The Rhetoric of Slum Clearance and Urban Renewal 1930-1965." (New York: *Agora: The Urban Planning Journal*, 2010), 13-20.
219 **Highland, Southside urban renewal:** Hill and Lee, 218-219.
219 **"among the highest in the country":** *Herald-Journal*, Aug. 28, 2020, quoting City Planner Natalia Rosario.
219 **Brotherhood playground:** *Spartanburg Journal*, June 19, 1952 and April 30, 1954.
219 **T.K. Gregg Center:** *Herald-Journal*, June 19, 1979.
221 **Closing of Northview Street:** *Herald-Journal*, Oct. 25, 1985; *Greenville News*, Oct. 22 and 29, 1985.
222 **Miller letter to the editor:** Ibid., Nov. 6, 1985.

Spotlight: Gospel Great Bob Beatty

224 **Bob Beatty:** *Herald-Journal*, Feb. 3, 1985, Oct. 3, 2008, Jan. 12, 2011; Tony Cummings, "The Heavenly Gospel Singers: The Precursors of Do-Wop." https://www.crossrhythms.co.uk/articles/music/The_Heavenly_Gospel_Singers_Precursors_of_doowop/40318/p1/.

CHAPTER 12: DEMOLITION BACK OF THE COLLEGE

227 **Tennis courts:** *Herald-Journal*, Oct. 16 and Nov. 19, 1991.
228 **"undesirable neighbors":** David Duncan Wallace. *History of Wofford College*, 1854-1949. (Spartanburg: Wofford College, 1954), 43.
229 **Roger Milliken:** Doyle Boggs, JoAnn Mitchell Brasington and Phillip Stone. *Wofford: Shining with Untarnished Honor.* (Spartanburg: Hub City Press, 2005), 162.
230 **17 lots:** *Spartanburg Journal*, Feb. 2, 1966.
230 **1969 Rezoning:** *Spartanburg Herald*, Aug. 30, 1969.
232 **Ed Greene on Planning Commission:** *Spartanburg Herald*, Nov. 9, 1972. Greene died in 2003.
232 **Universities and eminent domain:** Brandy Kellam and Louis Hansen, "Erasing the Black Spot: How a Virginia College Expanded by Uprooting a Black Neighborhood," Pro-Publica and the Virginia Center for Investigative Journalism, Sept. 5, 2023, https://www.propublica.

org/article/how-virginia-college-expanded-by-uprooting-black-neighborhood.

233 **Baehr's platform:** *Spartanburg Herald*, April 28, 1973.

233 **1973 mayoral vote totals:** Ibid., May 2, 1973. Baehr was voted out of office four years later. He died in 2020.

233 **Cable TV:** Ibid., Sept. 21, 1975. Note: Questions to this column were posed anonymously.

234 **1973 Urban Renewal Plan:** Project area map, Prather, Thomas & Campbell Associates, City of Spartanburg Collection, Spartanburg County Public Libraries.

235 **Tim Kuether:** Interview, Sept. 15, 2023.

235 **Ed Greene's letter:** "Letter to William H. Carstarphan, City Manager" in Papers of President Joab M. Lesesne, Official Files, Ed Greene Highlights file, Box #6, Archives, Wofford College.

236 **"loss of community cohesiveness":** Mindy Fullilove. *Root Shock: How Tearing Up City Neighborhoods Hurts America and What We Can Do About It.* (New York: New Village Press, 2016).

236 **Cheryl Harleston meeting:** Ed Greene Highlights file, Box #6, Archives, Wofford College.

236 **Letter from Ed Greene to city:** Ibid.

237 **"A Plan for the 70s":** in Papers of President Joab M. Lesesne, Official Files, Buildings and Grounds Task Force file. Box #6, Archives, Wofford College.

237 **Milliken Fund:** Minutes of the Meeting of the Board of Trustees, in Papers of President Joab M. Lesesne, Official Files, Buildings and Grounds Task Force file. Box #6, Archives, Wofford College.

237 **Conversion to playing fields:** Task Force Implementation, in Papers of President Joab M. Lesesne, Official Files, Buildings and Grounds Task Force file. Box #8, Archives, Wofford College.

238 **Depreciation fund:** Task Force Implementation, Box #6, Archives, Wofford College.

238 **Letter to Carstarphen:** Ibid., "Letter to William H. Carstarphan, City Manager."

238 **1986-87 strategic plan:** Ibid., Task Force Implementation.

239 **Arthur Griffin:** *Herald-Journal*, Aug. 7, 1987.

239 **Charlevoix Street resident charged:** Jan. 18, 1989.

240 **Boston Boys:** Ibid., April 23, 1989 and Dec. 4, 1989.

240 **Mildred Littlejohn:** Ibid., Nov. 19, 1991.

241 **"like a prison":** Ibid., Oct. 16, 1991.

241 **Phone call to Richardson:** *Charlotte Observer*, Oct. 26, 1993.

242 **One-third of houses disappeared by 1980s:** *Herald-Journal*, Feb. 22, 1998.

244 **Street closures:** Ibid., April 27, 1994.

244 **City Council vote:** Ibid. Sept. 17 and Sept. 20, 1994.

244 **Honeycutt, Woodward, Miller sales:** Ibid., May 22, July 3, and July 31, 1994.

244 **Appalachian Council of Government grant:** Ibid., Feb, 23, March 5, Sept. 9, 1995.

245 **Icie Hamilton:** Ibid., Feb. 9, 1997.

246 **Stacey Whitmire sale:** Ibid., Nov. 28, 1998.

247 **Jeanette Wiggins:** Ibid., May 16, 1996.

247 **"Red-letter day":** Ibid., June 5, 1996.

248 **Where residents moved:** Interviews with James Cheek and Linda Dogan.

249 **"common border":** *Herald-Journal*, Oct. 3, 1999.

250 **275 parcels:** Robert Dalton, "The Back of the College Neighborhood," *Wofford Today*, Fall 2020.

250 **Richardson philanthropy:** https://www.wofford.edu/about/news/news-archives/2021/richardson-gift.

Spotlight: Loss of a Landmark

252 **Cummings Street Baptist Church:** Oral histories, Lisa and Monica Thornton.

CHAPTER 13: THE RENAISSANCE PROJECT

More than 100 newspaper stories appeared in the Herald-Journal *about the Renaissance Project between 1996 and 2007. This chapter is written from those stories.*

257 **Renaissance Project unveiling:** *Herald-Journal*, Dec. 15, 1996.
258 **Linda Dogan and meeting at T.K. Gregg:** Ibid., Jan. 15, 1997.
258 **"our say in the matter":** Ibid., March 18, 1997.
258 **Goodwin letter:** Ibid., March 3, 1997.
259 **Duncan-DuPre mansion:** Ibid., Nov. 4, 7-9, 1999.
260 **Renaissance home sales:** Jerome Davis, Deed book 69-V-97; Bennie Johnson, Deed book 69-V-73; Donna McJimpsey, Deed Book 67-J-139 & 142; Genevieve Fuller Robinson, Deed Book 67-B-165; Raymond Floyd, Deed Book 72-T-939; Knuckles family, Deed Book 70-F-672.
261 **Phyllis Goins:** *Herald-Journal*, June 9, 1999.
261 **Gilmore-Perry house swap:** Ibid., June 9, 1999.
261 **Dorothy and Curtis Boyd:** Ibid., Jan. 15, 1997.
263 **Silver Hill church offer:** Interview with Bernice Lewis.
263 **UMC grant and leave taking service:** *Herald-Journal*, Aug. 9-10, 1998.
264 **Leonard Hicks:** Ibid., Oct. 5, 1998.
264 **Mounds of debris:** Ibid., Jan. 14, 2000.
264 **Barnet Park:** Ibid., March 31, July 28, 1998.
265 **Vagrants:** Ibid., Aug. 18, 1999.
266 **Opening of Marriott:** Ibid., Jan. 16, 2004.
266 **BB&T foreclosure:** Ibid., April 23, 2004.
266 **Missed deadline:** Ibid., April 28, June 13, 2004.
266 **Hotel sale:** Ibid., Oct. 3-5, 2007.
267 **Terranova Group:** Ibid., July 24-25, July 9, 2018.
267 **Silver Hill and Rudasil home prices:** Zillow listings.

EPILOGUE

270 **Greenville gentrification:** "The Cost of Unity," *Greenville News*, Jan. 11, 2023.
271 **Spartanburg City Council resolution:** City Council minutes, Sept. 28, 2020.
271 **Median incomes:** U.S. Census 2020.
271 **Subsidized housing waiting list:** Information provided Nov. 7, 2023 by Teresa Moultrie, Spartanburg Housing.

INTERVIEWS

Barrett, Russell. By Brenda Lee Pryce. July 16, 2022.
Boggs, Doyle. By Jim Neighbors. June 26, 2019.
Bowman, Eddie. By Wofford students. October 2018.
Brown, Woodrow. By Wofford students. October 2018.
Byrd, Freda. By Wofford students. October 2019.
Cheek, James. By Wofford students. October 2019.
Davis, Loetus. By Wofford students. October 2018.
Dogan, Linda. By Wofford students. October 2018.
Dominic, Joe. By Wofford students. October 2019.
Fant, Philip. By Wofford students. October 2017.
Frazier, Joan. By Wofford students. October 2018.
Gibson, Donald W. By Brenda Lee Pryce. July 16, 2022.
Greene, Norma (Foster). By Wofford students. October 2017.
Hill, Michael. By Wofford students. October 2018.
Hogan, Vicki (Coleman). By Wofford students. October 2017.
Hutchinson, Judy. By Wofford students. October 2019.
Jenkins, Ollie Brown. By Wofford students. October 2018.
Johnson, Bertha. By Wofford students. October 2017.
Kolb, Ken. By Betsy Teter. October 2023.
Lesesne, Joe. By Jim Neighbors. Feb. 27, 2020.
Lewis, Bernice. By Betsy Teter. March 2023.
Littlejohn, Horace. By Wofford students. October 2019.
Logan, Cynthia (Harris). By Wofford students. October 2017.
Mackey, Willamae. By Betsy Teter. March 2023.
Means, Mildred. By Wofford students. October 2019.
Norman, Luther. By Wofford students. October 2019.
Pitts, Norma. By Wofford students. October 2017.
Posey, Doris. By Jim Neighbors. May 2019.
Potruch, Donna. By Betsy Teter. January 2024.
Rivers, Rev. Eugene III. By Betsy Teter. January 2024.
Sims, Glenda P. By Brenda Lee Pryce. July 16, 2022.
Steen, Gwen. By Wofford students. October 2018.
Thomas, Rose. By Wofford students. October 2017.
Thomas, Tony. By Betsy Teter. August 2023.
Thornton, Lisa. By Wofford students. October 2019.
Thornton, Monica. By Wofford students. October 2019.
Trakas, Deno. By Jim Neighbors. September 2021.
Wingo, Winston. By Betsy Teter. August 2023.

PHOTO CREDITS

Bell, Darnese: 193, 194A
Campbell, Charlie Mae: 39A, 84,
Cannon, Margaret: 6A
City of Spartanburg Collection, SCPL: 77, 131, 170, 207, 216, 218, 220B, 221, 234, 236
Concordia Historical Institute: 52, 92, 111A-B, 128
Cumming Street School Yearbook: 161B
Family of Dr. T.K. Gregg, 150B
George Peabody College, Spartanburg survey: 159
Gray, O.W. & Son map: 124
Greene, Norma: 164, 182A-B, 183A-B, 184
Harris, Keith: 144A, 167, 181A-B, 187, 231
Hill, Michael: 180
History of the American Negro, SC Edition (1919): 43, 63, 107, 120, 127, 149
Hogan, Vickie: 185B
Hub City Observer: 45B
Jackson, Jeffrey: 75, 106, 147
Jeffers, Cynthia: 200
Johnson, Bertha: 232
Lane, John: 211
Lewis, Bernice: 44
Littlejohn, Horace: 161A
Miller, Harold, 39B
New York City Municipal Index (1929): 136
Norman, Luther: 69, 144B, 145, 146, 163, 168, 175A-D,
Olencki, Mark: 268, 273, 274-27
Silver Hill United Methodist Church: 150A
Smithsonian National Museum of Afri-
can-American History: 210
Spartanburg County Comprehensive Develop-
ment Plan: 1
Spartanburg County Historical Association Collection, SCPL: 6B, 26, 33, 35, 37, 45, 49C, 55, 68B, 82, 91, 117, 133, 204, 259
South of Main: 38A, 141
Spartanburg City Directory (1899): 40
Spartanburg County Plat Books: 68A
Spartanburg County Public Libraries: 32, 170B, 177, 179, 190, 196B, 214, 229
Spartanburg Herald-Journal Collection, SCPL 12, 45A, 49A-B, 51, 157, 176, 194B, 203, 208, 223A-B, 224, 227, 223B, 243, 245, 247, 249, 250, 252, 255A-B, 256, 262, 263
Spartanburg High School Saga: 84
Spartanburg Housing Authority: 87
Twentieth Century Negro Literature (1902): 101
Wheeler, Richard: 264
Willis Collection, SCPL: 21, 45C, 104, 108, 142
Wofford College: 10A-B, 58, 79 , 226, 241, 248, 251

BIBLIOGRAPHY

Louvenia Barksdale. *Historically and Statistically Yours: Back of the College 1887-1981.* (Spartanburg: self-published, 1981).

Bruce Bastian. *Red River Blues: The Blues Tradition in the Southeast.* (Urbana and Chicago: University of Illinois Press, 1986).

F.W. Beers. *History of Allegany County.* (New York, F.W. Beers & Co., 1879).

Linda Bilanchone (ed). *The Lives They Lived: A Look at Women in the History of Spartanburg.* (Spartanburg: The Spartanburg County Foundation, 1981).

Doyle Boggs with Brad Steinecke and Mark Olencki. *Historic Spartanburg County: 225 Years of History.* (San Antonio TX: HPN Books, 2012).

Doyle Boggs, JoAnn Mitchell Brasington and Phillip Stone. *Wofford: Shining with Untarnished Honor* (Spartanburg: Hub City Press, 2005).

Joshua Beau Blackwell. *The 1865 Stoneman's Raid Ends* (Charleston: The History Press, 2011).

Robert. D. Bullard. *Dumping in Dixie: Race, Class and Environmental Quality*, (Boulder CO: Westview Press, 2000).

Ronald E. Burchart. *Schooling the Freed People: Teaching, Learning and the Struggle for Black Freedom, 1861-1876.* (Chapel Hill: UNC Press, 2010).

W. Lewis Burke and Belinda F. Gergel. *Matthew J. Perry: The Man, His Times and His Legacy* (U.S.C. Press: Columbia, 2004).

A.B. Caldwell. *History of the American Negro, South Carolina Edition.* (Atlanta: A.B. Caldwell Publishing Co., 1919).

Maxie Myron Cox, Jr. "1963 – The Year of Decision: Desegregation in South Carolina." Masters thesis. (Columbia: University of South Carolina, 1996).

Daniel Wallace Culp. *Twentieth Century Negro Literature.* (Napierville, IL: J.L. Nichols & Co., 1902).

F.S. Dupre, interviewer. *A Folk History in the United States from Interviews with Former Slaves, Vol XIV, Part 3*, 53-55 (Washington DC: WPA, 1941).

Bruce Eelman. *Entrepreneurs in the Southern Upcountry: Commercial Culture in Spartanburg, South Carolina 1845-1880.* (Athens: UGA Press, 2008).

Edwin Epps. *Duncan Park.* (Spartanburg: Hub City Press, 2023).

Hayward Farrar. *The Baltimore Afro-American 1892-1950* (Westport, CT: Greenwood Press: 1998).

Eric Foner. *Freedom's Lawmakers: A Directory of Black Lawmakers During Reconstruction.* (England: Oxford University Press, 1993).

John Hope Franklin. *From Slavery to Freedom: A History of Nego Americans* (New York: Alfred A. Knopf, 1947).

Mindy Fullilove. *"Root Shock: How Tearing Up City Neighborhoods Hurts America and What We Can Do About It."* (New York: New Village Press, 2016).

Valerie Giddings. *A Family Is …* (Blacksburg VA: Self-published for the 1995 Little-john-Clifton Reunion, 1995).

Cheryl Greenberg. *To Ask For An Equal Chance: African Americans in the Great Depression.* (Lanham MD: Rowan & Littlefield, 2009).

Cynthia R. Greenlee. "The Girl Who is to Die at the Rope's End: The 1892 Execution of Milbry Brown and Definitions of Childhood in South Carolina Courts," *The Global History of Black Girlhood* (Urbana: University of Illinois Press, 2022).

MacArthur Goodwin, *Silver Hill United Methodist Church, Spartanburg, South Carolina: 1869-1981* (Silver Hill United Methodist Church, 1981).

Fletcher M. Green, ed. *The Chapel Hill United Methodist Church Centennial History 1853-1953* (Chapel Hill: The Church, 1954).

Beatrice Hill and Brenda Lee. *South of Main* (Spartanburg: Hub City Press, 2005).

A. V. Huff Jr. "A History of South Carolina United Methodism," *United Methodist Ministers in South Carolina.* (Columbia: South Carolina Conference of the United Methodist Church, 1984.

Lawrence P. Jackson. *Chester Himes* (New York: W.W. Norton & Co., 2017).

Steve Jobe. *Hudson Barksdale: Educator, Legislator, and Civil Rights Leader* (Spartanburg: Kennedy Free Press, 2019).

Rossiter Johnson. *The Twentieth Century Biographical Dictionary of Notable Americans.* (Boston: The Biographical Society, 1904).

Blair M.L. Kelley. *Right to Ride: Streetcar Boycotts and African American Citizenship in the era of Plessy vs. Ferguson.* (Chapel Hill NC: UNC Press, 2010).

Charles H. Kirk. *History of the Fifteenth Pennsylvania Volunteer Cavalry* (Philadelphia: Society of the Fifteen the Pennsylvania Cavalry, 1906).

I.E. Lowery. *Life on the old plantation in the antebellum days or A Story Based on Facts,* (Columbia: The State Publishing Co., 1911).

Edward Margolies and Michael Fabre. *The Several Lives of Chester Himes* (Jackson MS: University Press of Mississippi, 1997).

Marko Maunula. *Guten Tag, Y'all: Globalization and the South Carolina Piedmont 1950-2000.* (Athens: University of Georgia Press, 2009).

John Hammond Moore. *South Carolina Newspapers* (Columbia SC: University of South

Carolina Press, 1988).

Margaret Newlin. *Memoir of Mary Anna Longstreth.* (Philadelphia: J.B. Lippincott Co, 1886).

Inez Moore Parker, *The Rise and Decline of the Program of Education for the Black Presbyterians of the United Presbyterian Church U.S.A., 1865-1970* (San Antonio, Trinity University Press, 1977).

Richard Nye Price. *Holston Methodism: From its Origin to its Present Time, Vol. IV, 1844-1870* (Charlottesville VA: University of Virginia, 1912).

Dwain C. Pruitt. *Things Hidden: An Introduction to the History of Blacks in Spartanburg.* (Spartanburg: Community Relations Office, 1995).

Philip N. Racine (ed). *Piedmont Farmer: The Journals of David Golightly Harris, 1855-1870.* (Knoxville: University of Tennessee Press, 1990).

James Sallis. *Chester Himes: A Life* (New York: Walker & Co., 2000).

Spartanburg Unit of the Writers' Program of the Works Projects Administration, *A History of Spartanburg County* (Columbia SC: Band & White, 1940).

Henry Lee Swint. *The Northern Teacher in the South,* 1862-1870. (Nashville: Vanderbilt University Press, 1941).

Susan Thoms. *Freedmen's Bureau: Spartanburg and Union Counties, 1865-1868.* (Spartanburg: Kennedy Free Press).

Deno Trakas. *Because Memory Isn't Eternal.* (Spartanburg: Hub City Press, 2010).

Timothy P. Grady and Melissa Walker (ed). *Recovering the Piedmont Past* (University of South Carolina Press, 2013).

David Duncan Wallace. *History of Wofford College, 1854-1949.* (Spartanburg: Wofford College, 1954).

Mena Webb. *Jule Carr: General without an Army.* (Chapel Hill NC: UNC Press, 1987).

Jerry Zolton. *Great God A'mighty: The Dixie Hummingbirds and the Rise of Soul Gospel Mus*ic. (Oxford: Oxford University Press, 2003).

INDEX

PUBLISHING
New & Extraordinary
VOICES FROM THE
AMERICAN SOUTH

FOUNDED IN Spartanburg, South Carolina in 1995, Hub City Press has emerged as the South's premier independent literary press. Hub City is interested in books with a strong sense of place and is committed to finding and spotlighting extraordinary new and unsung writers from the American South. Our curated list champions diverse authors and books that don't fit into the commercial or academic publishing landscape.

Funded by the National Endowment for the Arts, Hub City Press books have been widely praised and featured in the *New York Times,* the *Los Angeles Times, NPR,* the *San Francisco Chronicle,* the *Wall Street Journal, Entertainment Weekly,* the *Los Angeles Review of Books*, and many other outlets.

HUB CITY PRESS books are made possible through the generous support of grants and donations from corporations, state and federal grant programs, family foundations, and the many individuals who support our mission of building a more inclusive literary arts culture in the South, in particular: Byron Morris and Deborah McAbee, Charles and Katherine Frazier, and Michel and Eliot Stone. Hub City Press gratefully acknowledges support from the National Endowment for the Arts, the Amazon Literary Partnership, the South Carolina Arts Commission, the Chapman Cultural Center, Spartanburg County Public Library, and the City of Spartanburg.